Shakespeare our Contemporary

JAN KOTT

Shakespeare
our Contemporary

TRANSLATED BY BOLESLAW TABORSKI

PREFACE BY PETER BROOK

METHUEN & CO LTD

11 NEW FETTER LANE · LONDON EC4

First published in Great Britain February 18, 1965
Reprinted 1965
Second edition, revised, 1967
First published in University Paperbacks 1967
Copyright © 1964 by Państwowe Wydawnictwo Naukowe
Copyright © 1965, 1966 by Doubleday & Company Inc
Printed and bound in Great Britain by Cox & Wyman Ltd,
Fakenham, Norfolk

To Lidia

Contents

Preface

I first met Jan Kott in a night club in Warsaw: it was midnight: he was squashed between a wildly excited group of students: we became friends at once: a beautiful girl was arrested by mistake under our eyes: Jan Kott leaped to her defence and an evening of high adventure followed which ended at about four o'clock in the morning with Kott and myself in the supreme headquarters of the Polish police trying to secure her release. It was only at this point when the tempo of events was slowing down that I suddenly noticed that the police were calling my new friend 'Professor'. I had guessed that this quick-witted and combative man was an intellectual, a writer, a journalist, perhaps a Party member. The title 'Professor' sat ill on him. 'Professor of what?' I asked as we walked home through the silent town. 'Of drama,' he replied.

I tell this story to point to a quality of the author of this work which is to my mind unique. Here we have a man writing about Shakespeare's attitude to life from direct experience. Kott is undoubtedly the only writer on Elizabethan matters who assumes without question that every one of his readers will at some point or other have been woken by the police in the middle of the night. I am sure that in the many million words already written about Shakespeare – almost precluding anything new ever being said by anyone any more – it is still unique for the author discussing the theory of political assassination to assume that a producer's explanation of his actors could begin: 'A secret organization is preparing an action . . . You will go to Z and bring a case with grenades to the house No. 12.'

His writing is learned, it is informed, his study is serious and precise, it is scholarly without what we associate with scholar-

ship. The existence of Kott makes one suddenly aware how
rare it is for a pedant or a commentator to have any experience
of what he is describing. It is a disquieting thought that the
major part of the commentaries on Shakespeare's passions and
his politics are hatched far from life by sheltered figures behind
ivy-covered walls.

In contrast, Kott is an Elizabethan. Like Shakespeare, like
Shakespeare's contemporaries, the world of the flesh and the
world of the spirit are indivisible: they coexist painfully in the
same frame: the poet has a foot in the mud, an eye on the stars,
and a dagger in his hand. The contradictions of any living process cannot be denied: there is an omnipresent paradox that
cannot be argued, but must be lived: poetry is a rough magic
that fuses opposites.

Shakespeare is a contemporary of Kott, Kott is a contemporary of Shakespeare – he talks about him simply, first-hand,
and his book has the freshness of the writing by an eyewitness
at the Globe or the immediacy of a page of criticism of a current
film. To the world of scholarship this is a valuable contribution
– to the world of the theatre an invaluable one. Our greatest
problem in England where we have the best possibility in the
world for presenting our greatest author is just this – the relating of these works to our lives. Our actors are skilled and
sensitive, but they shy away from overlarge questions. Those
young actors who are aware of the deadly issues at this moment
at stake in the world tend to shy away from Shakespeare. It is
not an accident that at rehearsals our actors find plottings, fights
and violent ends 'easy' – they have clichés ready to deal with
these situations which they do not question – but are deeply
vexed by problems of speech and style which though essential
can only take their true place if the impulse to use words and
images relates to experience of life. England in becoming
Victorian lost almost all its Elizabethan characteristics – today,
it has become a strange mixture of Elizabethan and Victorian
worlds: this gives us a new possibility of understanding Shakespeare side by side with an old tendency to blur and romanticize
him. It is Poland that in our time has come closest to the tumult,

the danger, the intensity, the imaginativeness and the daily involvement with the social process that made life so horrible, subtle and ecstatic to an Elizabethan. So it is quite naturally up to a Pole to point us the way.

PETER BROOK

FOR HE IS BUT A BASTARD TO THE TIME,
THAT DOTH NOT SMACK OF OBSERVATION . . .

(King John, I, 1)

PART I: TRAGEDIES

The Kings

> What, do you tremble? are you all afraid?
> Alas, I blame you not; for you are mortal...
> *(Richard III,* I, 2)

I

A careful reading of the list of characters in *Richard III* is
enough to show what sort of historical material Shakespeare
used in order to illustrate facts relating to his own period and to
fill the stage with his real contemporaries. Here, in one of his
earliest plays – or rather in its historical raw material – one can
already see the outline of all the later great tragedies: of *Hamlet,
Macbeth* and *King Lear.* If one wishes to interpret Shakespeare's
world as the real world, one should start the reading of the plays
with the Histories, and in particular, with *Richard II* and
Richard III.

Let us begin with the list of *dramatis personae:*

King Edward IV – deposed the last Lancastrian king, Henry
VI, and imprisoned him in the Tower, where he was murdered
by Edward's brothers, Gloster and Clarence. A few months
earlier, at Tewkesbury, the only son of Henry VI had been
stabbed to death by Richard.

Edward, Prince of Wales, son to Edward IV, afterwards
King Edward V – murdered in the Tower, on Richard's order,
at the age of twelve.

Richard, Duke of York, Edward IV's other son – murdered
in the Tower, on Richard's order, at the age of ten.

George, Duke of Clarence, brother to Edward IV – murdered
in the same gloomy Tower, on Richard's order.

A son of Clarence – imprisoned by Richard immediately after
his coronation.

A daughter of Clarence – forced, when still a child, to

marry a commoner so that she could not become the mother of kings.

The Duchess of York, mother of two kings, grandmother of a king and a queen – her husband and youngest son killed, or murdered in the War of the Roses; another of her sons stabbed to death in the Tower by hired assassins; her third son, Richard, was responsible for the murder of both her grandsons. Of all her offspring, only one son and one granddaughter died a natural death.

Margaret, Henry VI's widow – her husband was murdered in the Tower, her son was killed in battle.

Lady Anne, the wife of Richard III, who had killed her father at the battle of Barnet and her first husband at Tewkesbury and had even earlier let her father-in-law be murdered in the Tower – imprisoned by Richard immediately after their wedding.

The Duke of Buckingham, Richard's confidant and right-hand man in the struggle for power – beheaded on Richard's orders within a year of the coronation.

Earl Rivers, brother to Queen Elizabeth, Lord Grey, son of Queen Elizabeth, Sir Thomas Vaughan – all executed on Richard's orders at Pomfret, even before the coronation.

Sir Richard Ratcliff, who organized the Pomfret executions and the *coup d'état* – killed at Bosworth two years later.

Lord Hastings, a nobleman and follower of the House of Lancaster – arrested, released, then arrested again and beheaded by Richard on the charge of plotting against him.

Sir James Tyrrel, murderer of Edward IV's children at the Tower – later executed.

We are nearing the end of the list of characters, or rather – victims. There is Sir William Catesby, executed after the battle of Bosworth, and the Duke of Norfolk, who died in the battle. There are one or two other lords and barons who saved their heads by fleeing abroad. And in the last few lines of the list: characters without names of their own. It is enough to quote those at the end: 'Lords, and other Attendants; a Pursuivant, Scrivener, Citizens, Murderers, Messengers, Soldiers, etc. Scene – England.'

Shakespeare is like the world, or life itself. Every historical period finds in him what it is looking for and what it wants to see. A reader or spectator in the mid-twentieth century interprets *Richard III* through his own experiences. He cannot do otherwise. And that is why he is not terrified – or rather, not amazed – at Shakespeare's cruelty. He views the struggle for power and the mutual slaughter of the characters far more calmly than did many generations of spectators and critics in the nineteenth century. More calmly, or, at any rate, more rationally. Cruel death, suffered by most *dramatis personae*, is not regarded today as an aesthetic necessity, or as an essential rule in tragedy in order to produce *catharsis*, or even as a specific characteristic of Shakespeare's genius. The violent deaths of the principal characters are now regarded rather as an historical necessity, or as something altogether natural. Even in *Titus Andronicus*, written, or rewritten, by Shakespeare probably in the same year as *King Richard III*, modern audiences see much more than the ludicrous and grotesque accumulation of needless horrors which nineteenth-century critics found in it. And when *Titus Andronicus* received a production like that of Peter Brook, today's audiences were ready to applaud the general slaughter in Act Five no less enthusiastically than Elizabethan coppersmiths, tailors, butchers and soldiers had done. In those days the play was one of the greatest theatrical successes. By discovering in Shakespeare's plays problems that are relevant to our own time, modern audiences often, unexpectedly, find themselves near to the Elizabethans; or at least are in the position to understand them well. This is particularly true of the Histories.

Shakespeare's History plays take their titles from the names of kings: *King John, King Richard II, Henry IV, Henry V, Henry VI, Richard III* (*King Henry VIII*, a work partly written by Shakespeare towards the close of his literary activities, belongs to the History plays solely in a formal sense). Apart from *King John*, which deals with events at the turn of the thirteenth century, Shakespeare's Histories deal with the struggle for the English crown that went on from the close of the fourteenth to the end of the fifteenth century. They constitute an historical epic covering over a hundred years and divided into long chapters corresponding to reigns. But when we read these chapters chronologically, following the sequence of reigns, we are struck by the thought that for Shakespeare history stands still. Every chapter opens and closes at the same point. In every one of these plays history turns full circle, returning to the point of departure. These recurring and unchanging circles described by history are the successive kings' reigns.

Each of these great historical tragedies begins with a struggle for the throne, or for its consolidation. Each ends with the monarch's death and a new coronation. In each of the Histories the legitimate ruler drags behind him a long chain of crimes. He has rejected the feudal lords who helped him to reach for the crown; he murders, first, his enemies, then his former allies; he executes possible successors and pretenders to the crown. But he has not been able to execute them all. From banishment a young prince returns – the son, grandson, or brother of those murdered – to defend the violated law. The rejected lords gather round him, he personifies the hope for a new order and justice. But every step to power continues to be marked by murder, violence, treachery. And so, when the new prince finds himself near the throne, he drags behind him a chain of crimes as long as that of the until now legitimate ruler. When he assumes the crown, he will be just as hated as his predecessor. He has killed enemies, now he will kill former allies. And a new pretender appears in the name of violated justice. The wheel has turned full circle. A new chapter opens. A new historical tragedy:

> Then thus: –
> Edward the Third, my lords, had seven sons:
> The first, Edward the Black Prince, Prince of Wales;
> The second, William of Hatfield; and the third,
> Lionel duke of Clarence; next to whom
> Was John of Gaunt, the duke of Lancaster;
> The fifth was Edmund Langley, duke of York;
> The sixth was Thomas of Woodstock, duke of Gloster;

William of Windsor was the seventh and last.
Edward the Black Prince died before his father;
And left behind him Richard, his only son,
Who, after Edward the Third's death, reign'd as king;
Till Henry Bolingbroke, duke of Lancaster,
The eldest son and heir of John of Gaunt,
Crown'd by the name of Henry the Fourth,
Seiz'd on the realm, depos'd the rightful king,
Sent his poor queen to France, from whence she came,
And him to Pomfret, – where, as all you know,
Harmless Richard was murder'd traitorously.

(Henry VI, p. II, II, 2)

This scheme of things is not, of course, marked with an equally clear-cut outline in all Shakespeare's Histories. It is clearest in *King John* and in two masterpieces of historical tragedy, *Richard II* and *Richard III*. It is least clear in *Henry V*, an idealized and patriotic play which depicts a struggle with an enemy from without. But in Shakespeare's plays the struggle for power is always stripped of all mythology, shown in its 'pure state'. It is a struggle for the crown, between people who have a name, a title and power.

In the Middle Ages the clearest image of wealth was a bag full of gold pieces. Each of them could be weighed in the hand. For many centuries wealth meant fields, meadows and woods, flocks of sheep, a castle and villages. Later it was a ship loaded with pepper, or cloves, or big granaries filled with sacks of wheat, cellars full of wines, warehouses along the Thames emitting a sour smell of leather and the choking dust of cotton. Riches could be seen, handled and smelt. It was only later that they dematerialized, became a symbol, something abstract. Wealth ceased to be a concrete thing and became a slip of paper with writing on it. Those changes were described by Karl Marx in *Das Kapital*.

In a similar fashion power was dematerialized, or rather, disembodied. It ceased to have a name. It became something abstract and mythological, almost a pure idea. But for Shakespeare power has names, eyes, mouth and hands. It is a relentless struggle of living people who sit together at one table.

> For God's sake, let us sit upon the ground
> And tell sad stories of the death of kings: –
> How some have been depos'd; some slain in war;
> Some haunted by the ghosts they have depos'd;
> Some poison'd by their wives; some sleeping kill'd;
> All murder'd.   (*Richard II*, III, 2)

For Shakespeare the crown is the image of power. It is heavy.
It can be handled, torn off a dying king's head, and put on one's
own. Then one becomes a king. Only then. But one must wait
till the King is dead, or else precipitate his death.

> He cannot live, I hope; and must not die
> Till George be pack'd with post-horse up to heaven. –
> I'll in, to urge his hatred more to Clarence,
> With lies well steel'd with weighty arguments.
>
> . . . .
>
> Which done, God take King Edward to his mercy,
> And leave the world for me to bustle in!
>   (*Richard III*, I, 1)

In each of the Histories there are four or five men who look into
the eyes of the dying monarch, watch his trembling hands.
They have already laid a plot, brought their loyal troops to the
capital, communicated with their vassals. They have given
orders to hired assassins; the stony Tower awaits new prisoners.
There are four or five men, but only one of them may remain
alive. Each of them has a different name and title. Each has a
different face. One is cunning, another brave; the third is cruel,
the fourth – a cynic. They are living people, for Shakespeare
was a great writer. We remember their faces. But when we
finish reading one chapter and begin to read the next one, when
we read the Histories in their entirety, the faces of kings and
usurpers become blurred, one after the other.

Even their names are the same. There is always a Richard, an
Edward and a Henry. They have the same titles. There is a
Duke of York, a Prince of Wales, a Duke of Clarence. In the
different plays different people are brave, or cruel, or cunning.
But the drama that is being played out between them is always

the same. And in every tragedy the same cry, uttered by mothers of the murdered kings, is repeated:

> *Queen Margaret.* I had an Edward, till a Richard kill'd him;
> I had a Harry, till a Richard kill'd him;
> Thou hadst an Edward, till a Richard kill'd him;
> Thou hadst a Richard, till a Richard kill'd him.
> *Duchess of York.* I had a Richard too, and thou didst kill him;
> I had a Rutland too, thou help'st to kill him.
>
> . . . .
>
> *Queen Margaret.* Thy Edward he is dead, that kill'd my Edward;
> Thy other Edward dead, to quit my Edward;
> Young York he is but boot, because both they
> Match not the high perfection of my loss:
> Thy Clarence he is dead that stabb'd my Edward;
> And the beholders of this tragic play,
> Th'adulterate Hastings, Rivers, Vaughan, Grey,
> Untimely smother'd in their dusky graves.
>
> *(Richard III, IV, 4)*

Emanating from the features of individual kings and usurpers in Shakespeare's History plays, there gradually emerges the image of history itself. The image of the Grand Mechanism. Every successive chapter, every great Shakespearian act is merely a repetition:

> The flattering index of a direful pageant;
> One heav'd a-high, to be hurl'd down below.
>
> *(Richard III, IV, 4)*

It is this image of history, repeated many times by Shakespeare, that forces itself on us in a most powerful manner. Feudal history is like a great staircase on which there treads a constant procession of kings. Every step upwards is marked by murder, perfidy, treachery. Every step brings the throne nearer. Another step and the crown will fall. One will soon be able to snatch it.

> . . . that is a step
> On which I must fall down, or else o'erleap.
>
> *(Macbeth, I, 4)*

From the highest step there is only a leap into the abyss. The monarchs change. But all of them – good and bad, brave and cowardly, vile and noble, naïve and cynical – tread on the steps that are always the same.

Was this how Shakespeare conceived the tragedy of history in his first, youthful period that has light-heartedly been called 'optimistic'? Or was he, perhaps, an adherent of absolute monarchy and used the bloody stuff of fifteenth-century history to shock the audience by his spectacle of feudal struggles and England's internal disruption? Or did he write about his own times? Perhaps *Hamlet* is not so far removed from the two *Richard* plays? On what experiences did he draw? Was he a moralist, or did he describe the world he knew or foresaw, without illusions, without contempt, but also without indignation? Let us try to interpret *Richard II* and *Richard III* as best we can.

II

Let us begin by tracing the working of the Grand Mechanism as Shakespeare shows it in his theatre. On the forestage two armies fight each other. The tiny inner stage is turned into the House of Commons, or the King's chamber. On the balcony the King appears, surrounded by bishops. Trumpets are blown: the forestage is now the Tower courtyard where the imprisoned princes are being led under guard. The inner stage has been turned into a cell. The successor to the throne cannot sleep, tormented by thoughts of violence. Now the door opens, and hired assassins enter with daggers in their hands. A moment later the forestage is a London street at night: frightened townsmen hurry past talking politics. Trumpets again: the new monarch has made his appearance on the balcony.

Let us begin with the great abdication scene in *Richard II*, the scene omitted in all editions published in Queen Elizabeth's lifetime. It revealed the working of the Grand Mechanism too brutally: the very moment when power was changing hands. Authority comes either from God, or from the people. A flash of the sword, the tramping of the guards; applause of intimidated noblemen; a shout from the forcibly gathered crowd; and behold: the new authority, too, comes from God, or from the will of the people.

Henry Bolingbroke, later king Henry IV, has returned from exile, landed with an army and captured Richard II, deserted by his vassals. The *coup d'état* has been accomplished. It has yet to be legalized. The former king still lives.

> Fetch hither Richard, that in common view
> He may surrender; so we shall proceed
> Without suspicion.

Richard enters under guard, deprived of his royal robes. Following him are noblemen carrying royal insignia. The scene takes place in the House of Lords. The forestage represents Westminster Hall, which has been reconstructed by Richard and given its famous oak roof. He has been brought beneath it only once, in order to abdicate.

Says the King, deprived of his crown:

> Alack, why am I sent for to a king,
> Before I have shook off the regal thoughts
> Wherewith I reign'd? I hardly yet have learn'd
> To insinuate, flatter, bow, and bend my knee:
> Give sorrow leave awhile to tutor me
> To this submission. Yet I well remember
> The favours of these men: were they not mine?
> Did they not sometime cry, 'All hail!' to me?

But he is not allowed to speak for long. He is handed the crown to hold it for a moment and give it to Henry. Give it of his own free will. He has already renounced his power, rents and revenues. He has cancelled his decrees and statutes. What else can they want of him? 'What more remains?' Shakespeare knew:

> No more, but that you read
> These accusations, and these grievous crimes
> Committed by your person and your followers
> Against the state and profit of this land;
> That, by confessing them, the souls of men
> May deem that you are worthily depos'd.

Says the King, deprived of his crown:

> Must I do so? and must I ravel out
> My weav'd-up follies? Gentle Northumberland,
> If thy offences were upon record,
> Would it not shame thee in so fair a troop
> To read a lecture of them?

But again he is not allowed to speak for long. The act of dethronement has to be completed quickly and absolutely. The King's royal majesty must be extinguished. The new King is waiting. If the former King is not a traitor, then the new one is a usurper. One can well understand Queen Elizabeth's censors:

> *Northumberland.* My lord, dispatch; read o'er these articles.
> *King Richard.* Mine eyes are full of tears, I cannot see:
> And yet salt water blinds them not so much
> But they can see a sort of traitors here.
> Nay, if I turn mine eyes upon myself,
> I find myself a traitor with the rest;
> For I have given here my soul's consent
> T'undeck the pompous body of a king . . .

When dramatizing history, Shakespeare first and foremost condenses it. For history itself is more dramatic than the particular dramas of John, the Henrys and the Richards. The greatest drama consists in the working of the Grand Mechanism. Shakespeare can contain years in a month, months in a day, in one great scene, in three or four speeches which comprise the very essence of history.

Here is the grand finale of any dethronement:

> *King Richard.* Then give me leave to go.
> *Bolingbroke.* Whither?
> *King Richard.* Whither you will, so I were from your sights.
> *Bolingbroke.* Go, some of you, convey him to the Tower.
> . . . .
> On Wednesday next we solemnly set down
> Our coronation: lords, prepare yourselves.
>
> (*Richard II*, IV, 1)

It is nearly the end. There is just one more act to come. The last one. But this act will at the same time be the first act of a new tragedy. It will have a new title, of course: *Henry IV*. In *Richard II* Bolingbroke was a 'positive hero'; an avenger. He defended violated law and justice. But in his own tragedy he can only play the part of Richard II. The cycle has been completed. The cycle is beginning again. Bolingbroke has mounted half-way up the grand staircase of history. He has been crowned; he is reigning. Dressed in the royal robes, he is awaiting the dignitaries of the realm at Windsor Castle. They duly arrive.

> *Northumberland.* First, to thy sacred state wish I all happiness.
> The next news is, I have to London sent
> The heads of Salisbury, Spencer, Blunt, and Kent:
> . . . .
> *Bolingbroke.* We thank thee, gentle Percy, for thy pains;
> And to thy worth will add right worthy gains.
> (*Enter Fitzwater*)
> *Fitzwater.* My lord, I have from Oxford sent to London
> The heads of Brocas and Sir Bennet Seely,
> Two of the dangerous consorted traitors
> That sought at Oxford thy dire overthrow.
> *Bolingbroke.* Thy pains, Fitzwater, shall not be forgot;
> Right noble is thy merit, well I wot.   (*Richard II*, V. 6)

The most terrifying thing about this scene is its natural matter-of-factness. As if nothing had happened. As if everything went according to the natural order of things. A new reign has begun: six heads are being sent to the capital for the new King. But Shakespeare cannot end a tragedy in this way. A shock is needed. The working of the Grand Mechanism has to be highlighted by a flash of awareness. Just one; but it is a flash of genius. The new King is waiting for one more head; the most important one. He has commanded his most trusted follower to commit the murder. Commanded – this is too simple a word. Kings do not order assassination; they only allow it, in such a way that they shall not know about it themselves. But let us go back to Shakespeare's own words. For this is one of those great scenes that history will repeat; scenes that have been written once and for all. There is everything in them: the mechanism of the human heart, and the mechanism of power; there is fear, flattery, and 'the system'. In this scene the King does not take part, and no name is mentioned. There are only the King's words, and their double echo. This is one of the scenes in which Shakespeare is truer to life than life itself.

> *Exton.* Didst thou not mark the king, what words he spake, –
>   'Have I no friend will rid me of this living fear?'
>   Was it not so?
> *Servant.* Those were his very words.
> *Exton.* 'Have I no friend?' quoth he: he spake it twice,
>   And urg'd it twice together, – did he not?
> *Servant.* He did.   (*Richard II,* V, 4)

And now, in the very last scene of *Richard II*, this most faithful of loyal subjects enters, with servants carrying a coffin:

> Great king, within this coffin I present
> Thy buried fear: herein all breathless lies
> The mightiest of thy greatest enemies,
> Richard of Bordeaux, by me hither brought.
>   (*Richard II,* V, 6)

It is now that a flash of genius manifests itself. Let us omit the King's reply: it is pedestrian. He will banish Exton, order a state funeral for Richard with himself as the chief mourner. All this is still within the bounds of the Grand Mechanism, described dryly, as in a medieval chronicle. But the King lets slip a sentence that foreshadows the problems of *Hamlet*. And, indeed, *Hamlet* must only be interpreted in the light of the two *Richard* plays. This sentence expresses a sudden fear of the world and its cruel mechanism, from which there is no escape, but which one cannot accept. For there are no bad kings, or good kings; kings are only kings. Or let us put it in modern terms: there is only the king's situation, and the system. This situation leaves no room for freedom of choice. At the end of the tragedy the King speaks a sentence that might have been spoken by Hamlet:

> They love not poison that do poison need.
>   (*Richard II,* V, 6)

In Shakespeare's world there is a contradiction between the order of action and the moral order. This contradiction is human fate. One cannot get away from it.

III

The tragic character of Shakespeare's world is thus gradually revealed. But before we return to *Hamlet*'s great questions, we have to describe the world once again, and see that it was a real world. The world we live in. Once again we have to trace the working of the Grand Mechanism: from the foot of the throne to the streets of London; from the royal chamber to the Tower prison.

Henry VI and the Duke of Clarence have been murdered, Edward IV has died. In the first two acts of *Richard III* Shakespeare compressed eleven long years of history, as if they were a week. There is only Richard and the steps he has yet to climb on his way to the throne. Each of these steps is a living man. Finally, only two sons of the dead king are left. They, too, have to die. It is part of Shakespeare's genius that in writing about history he has cleared it of all descriptive elements, of anecdote, almost of the story. It is history distilled of irrelevancies.

Historical names, or the literal accuracy of historic events are of no importance. The situations are true; I would say: super-true. In this long unending Shakespearian week there may be morning, evening, or night. Time does not exist. Only history is present; its working, felt by us almost physically. There is night; one of those dramatic nights when the fate of the whole kingdom may depend on one council held at the castle, perhaps even on one thrust of a dagger. One of those historic nights when the air is heavier than usual and the hours longer. When one is waiting for news. Shakespeare not only dramatizes history; he dramatizes psychology, gives us large slices of it; and in them we find ourselves.

Richard has already assumed power as Lord Protector. In the royal palace there are two frightened women: the Queen Mother and the Queen Dowager. Beside them a ten-year-old

boy is playing: their son and grandson. The Archbishop has
arrived. They are all waiting and concerned only about one
thing: what will Richard do? The boy, too, knows the history
of his family, of the country, the names of those who have
been murdered. In a few days' time, in a few hours, he will
be the brother of the King. Or . . . The boy says something
careless, teasing his powerful uncle. The Queen reproaches
him.

> *Archbishop of York.* Good madam, be not angry with the child.
> *Queen Elizabeth.* Pitchers have ears.

This palace, in which every member of the royal family is
named after someone murdered, is very much like Elsinore.
Not only Denmark is a prison. At last comes the messenger.

> *Archbishop of York.* Here comes a messenger.
>   What news?
> *Messenger.* Such news, my lord, as grieves me to report.
> *Queen Elizabeth.* How doth the prince?
> *Messenger.* Well, madam, and in health.
> *Duchess of York.* What is thy news, then?
> *Messenger.* Lord Rivers and Lord Grey are sent to Pomfret,
>   With them Sir Thomas Vaughan, prisoners.
> *Duchess of York.* Who hath committed them?
> *Messenger.* The mighty dukes
>   Gloster and Buckingham.
> *Queen Elizabeth.* For what offence?
> *Messenger.* The sum of all I can I have disclosed;
>   Why or for what these nobles were committed
>   Is all unknown to me, my gracious lady. (*Richard III*, II, 4)

The same long week continues, as does the night when power
is changing hands. Earlier on Shakespeare compressed eleven
years of history into a few violent scenes; now he shows us one
hour after another. We are in a London street. Townsmen
hurry by in frightened groups of two or three. They have just
heard something, they know something. But they are not a
chorus from an ancient tragedy to comment on the events or
proclaim the will of the gods. There are no gods in Shakespeare.

There are only kings, every one of whom is an executioner, and a victim, in turn. There are also living, frightened people. They can only gaze upon the grand staircase of history. But their own fate depends on who will reach the highest step, or leap into the abyss. That is why they are frightened. Shakespearian tragedy, unlike ancient tragedies, is not a drama of moral attitudes in the face of immortal gods; there is no fate which decides the hero's destiny. The greatness of Shakespeare's realism consists in his awareness of the extent to which people are involved in history. Some make history and fall victims to it. Others only think they make it, but they, too, fall victims to it. The former are kings; the latter – the kings' confidants who execute their orders and are cog-wheels in the Grand Mechanism. There is also a third category of people: the common citizens of the kingdom. Grand historical events are performed on the fields of battle, in the royal palace, and the Tower prison. But the Tower, the royal palace, and the battlefields are actually situated in England. That was one of the discoveries of Shakespeare's genius which helped to create modern historical tragedy. Let us, then, listen to the voices in the street:

Third Citizen. Doth the news hold of good King Edward's death?
Second Citizen. Ay, sir, it is too true; God help the while!
Third Citizen. Then, masters, look to see a troublous world.
First Citizen. No, no; by God's good grace his son shall reign.
. . . .
Third Citizen. . . . For emulation who shall now be nearest,
   Will touch us all too near, if God prevent not.
   O, full of danger is the Duke of Gloster,
   And the queen's sons and brothers haught and proud!
   And were they to be rul'd, and not to rule,
   This sickly land might solace as before.
First Citizen. Come, come, we fear the worst; all will be well.
Third Citizen. When clouds are seen, wise men put on their cloaks.
                                             (*Richard III*, II, 3)

Still the same long week, and the same London street. Only one day has passed. Richard has sent his confidants to fetch the Prince of Wales. Trumpets are blown. The child successor to the throne is entering London. But he is not greeted by his brother, or his mother. The Duke of York and the Queen Dowager have, for fear of Richard, sought refuge in the white gothic cathedral of St Paul's, as if they had been common criminals, whose right of sanctuary was protected by law. They have to be got out of there. The Archbishop of Canterbury has objections. But the Duke of Buckingham knows how to produce convincing arguments:

> You are too senseless-obstinate, my lord,
> Too ceremonious and traditional:
> Weigh it but with the grossness of this age . . .

And the Cardinal replies:

> My lord, you shall o'er-rule my mind for once. –
>   (*Richard III,* III, 1)

The long week does not seem to end. Both successors to the throne – the Prince of Wales and the Duke of York – have been placed in the Tower; the executioner is on his way to Pomfret castle to cut off the heads of the Queen's closest relatives and friends. Richard is making long strides towards the throne. But the *coup d'état* is yet to be accomplished. The House of Lords and the Privy Council have yet to be cowed, the City intimidated. It is only now that we shall see how those who think they are the makers of history are actually enmeshed in the Grand Mechanism. We shall see the image of political practice in its pure form, free from all mythology, and sketched in broad outlines. We shall see a dramatized version of a chapter from Machiavelli's *Prince*, the great scene of the *coup d'état*. But this scene will be played by living people, and it is in this fact that Shakespeare's superiority over Machiavelli's treatise is revealed. It will be played by people who know they are mortal, and try to save their skin, or bargain with history for a little self-respect, a semblance of courage, of decency. They will not succeed. History will first of all disgrace them, and then will cut off their heads.

IV

It is 4 a.m. For the first time in tragedy, Shakespeare gives the exact time. It is significant that this should be 4 a.m. It is the hour between night and dawn; the hour when decisions in high places have been taken, when what had to be done has been done. But it is also the hour when one can still save oneself by leaving one's home. The last hour in which freedom of choice is still possible. The sound of a knocker is heard: someone knocks hastily on the door.

> *Messenger.* My lord! my lord! –
> *Hastings (within).* Who knocks?
> *Messenger.* One from the Lord Stanley.
> *Hastings (within).* What is't o'clock?
> *Messenger.* Upon the stroke of four.
> *Enter Hastings.* Cannot thy master sleep these tedious nights?
> *Messenger.* So it appears by that I have to say.
>   First, he commends him to your noble self.
> *Hastings.* What then?
>
> . . . .
>
> *Messenger.* Besides, he says there are two councils held.

I greatly admire in Shakespeare those brief moments when tragedy is suddenly projected on to an everyday level; when the characters, before a decisive battle, or having woven a plot on which the fate of a kingdom will depend, go to supper, or to bed. ('Come, let us sup betimes, that afterwards We may digest our complots in some form.') They sleep, or cannot sleep, they drink their wine, they call their servants, do all sorts of things. They are only men. Like Homer's heroes they eat, sleep and fidget about on their uncomfortable beds. Shakespeare's genius shows itself also in the way he depicts the events occurring at 4 a.m. Who has not been awakened in this way at 4 a.m., at least once in his life?

> Therefore he sends to know your lordship's pleasure,
> If presently you will take horse with him,
> And with all speed post with him towards the north,
> To shun the danger that his soul divines.

Lord Hastings was awakened at 4 a.m. He has been warned by his friends. But he cannot bring himself to flee. He waits.

> Go, fellow, go, return unto thy lord;
> Bid him not fear the separated councils:
> His honour and myself are at the one,
> And at the other is my good friend Catesby.
> . . . .
> Tell him his fears are shallow, wanting instance:
> And for his dreams, I wonder he's so simple
> To trust the mockery of unquiet slumbers:
> To fly the boar before the boar pursues,
> Where to incense the boar to follow us,
> And make pursuit where he did mean no chase.
> Go, bid thy master rise and come to me;
> And we will both together to the Tower,
> Where he shall see the boar will use us kindly.
> (*Richard III*, III, 2)

The hour of decision is over. All are assembled in the Tower: Lord Stanley, who had given the warning; Hastings, who ignored the warning; the Bishop of Ely; and Ratcliff, who has just carried out the executions at Pomfret. All of them are assembled at one table: the Council of the Crown, the most powerful lords of the realm, temporal and spiritual; the men who wield power over Church, Treasury, Army, and Prisons. These are the ones before whom others tremble. They are all there, except Number One: Richard, the Lord Protector. He has not come. And in the meantime they have to speak, vote, express their opinions. They are to do so before the Lord Protector will express his. No one knows what Richard thinks. No one, except his confidants. But they have no wish to speak. They are waiting. And the Council, the men before whom all England trembles, are silent.

> *Buckingham.* Who knows the lord Protector's mind herein?
> Who is most inward with the noble duke?
> *Bishop of Ely.* Your Grace, we think, should soonest know his mind.
> *Buckingham.* Who? I, my lord? We know each other's faces,
> But for our hearts, he knows no more of mine

> Than I of yours; nor I no more of his
> Than you of mine.
> Lord Hastings, you and he are near in love.
> *Hastings*. I thank his Grace, I know he loves me well;
> But, for his purpose in the coronation,
> I have not sounded him, nor he deliver'd
> His gracious pleasure any way therein:
> But you, my noble lords, may name the time . . .

At this point Richard enters. The noble lords will hear his voice at last. They will learn what is going on. And they do hear him speak:

> My Lord of Ely, when I was last in Holborn,
> I saw good strawberries in your garden there:
> I do beseech you send for some of them.

Where and when did Shakespeare hear the tyrant's cruel laugh? And if he did not hear it, how did he have a presentiment of it?

Let us look again at the men before whom England trembles. They sit in silence; they avoid looking in each other's eyes; they try to penetrate into the minds of others. Above all, they want to know what he, the Lord Protector, is thinking. But he has left again, without another word.

> *Stanley*. What of his heart perceive you in his face
> By any likelihood he shew'd to-day?
> *Hastings*. Marry, that with no man here he is offended;
> For, were he, he had shewn it in his looks.
> *Stanley*. I pray God he be not, I say.

Richard enters again. He has made his decision. He knows already who has doubts. He has chosen his victim. In this great Council scene, Shakespeare maintains a tremendous tension and does not let the audience relax for a moment. It is so still that one hears people breathing. This is indeed the essence of history.

Richard speaks. We know these words by heart:

> I pray you all, tell me what they deserve
> That do conspire my death with devilish plots
> Of damned witchcraft, and that have prevailed
> Upon my body with their hellish charms?

Lord Hastings did not want to provoke the boar. Lord Hastings had friends on the Council. He believed in legality. He was not against a *coup d'état*, but wanted it to be backed by the majesty of law. Only three hours ago he had defended the rule of law. He refused to take part in what was clear outrage. He wanted to preserve the last vestiges of shame and honour. He was a brave man. He *was*. It is possible that Shakespeare never saw the sea or, as other learned commentators maintain, a battlefield. He did not know geography. He gives Bohemia a seashore. Proteus boards a ship in order to go from Verona to Milan, waiting moreover for the tide. Florence, too, is for Shakespeare a port. Shakespeare did not know history either. In his plays Ulysses quotes Aristotle, and Timon of Athens makes references to Seneca and Galen. Shakespeare did not know philosophy, had no knowledge of warfare, confused customs of different periods. In *Julius Caesar* a clock strikes the hour. A serving maid takes off Cleopatra's corset. In King John's time gunpowder is used in cannons. Shakespeare had not seen the sea, or a battle, or mountains; he did not know history, geography, or philosophy. But Shakespeare knew that at the Council meeting the noble Hastings will have spoken first, after Richard, and pronounced a death sentence on himself. I can still hear his voice:

> *Hastings.* The tender love I bear your Grace, my lord,
>   Makes me most forward in this noble presence
>   To doom th'offenders: whosoe'er they be,
>   I say, my lord, they have deserved death.

It is too late to save one's head, but not too late to disgrace oneself: to bring oneself to believe in witchcraft and the devil, in anything; to accept anything, even in the last hour before one is due to die:

> *Gloster.* Then be your eyes the witness of their evil:
>   Look how I am bewitch'd; behold mine arm
>   Is, like a blasted sapling, wither'd up:
>   And this is Edward's wife, that monstrous witch,
>   Consorted with that harlot-strumpet Shore,
>   That by their witchcraft thus have marked me.

Hastings. If they have done this thing, my gracious lord, –
Gloster. If! Thou protector of this damned strumpet,
    Talk'st thou to me of 'ifs'? Thou art a traitor: –
    Off with his head! – now, by Saint Paul, I swear
    I will not dine until I see the same. –
    Lovel and Ratcliff, look that it be done: – (*Richard III*, I, 4)

I see this scene in Olivier's film. They have all dropped their eyes.
Nobody looks at Hastings. One by one all those sitting next to
him at the big table move away from him. Richard pushes aside
his chair and takes his leave. The others, too, push aside their
chairs and one by one leave the chamber. The Bishop of Ely,
as well as the faithful friend, Lord Stanley. No one has turned
his head to look behind. The chamber is empty except for Lord
Hastings and the two grand executioners of the realm: Lord
Lovel and Sir Richard Ratcliff. They have drawn their swords.

The crime must now be legalized. There has not been time
for a trial. But the trial must and will take place, with all the
appropriate ceremony. Except that the accused cannot be
brought to court. Shakespeare knew the working of the Grand
Mechanism. What are the Lord Mayor of London, and the
judges, for? They have only to be persuaded. Richard and the
Duke of Buckingham call for the Lord Mayor. He comes at
once. No, he does not have to be persuaded. He is persuaded
already. He is always persuaded.

Mayor of London. Now, fair befall you! he deserv'd his death;
    And your good Graces both have well proceeded,
    To warn false traitors from the like attempts.

  . . . .

Buckingham. Yet had we not determin'd he should die,
    Until your lordship came to see his end;
    Which now the loving haste of these our friends,
    Somewhat against our meaning, have prevented;
    Because, my lord, we would have had you heard
    The traitor speak, and timorously confess
    The manner and the purpose of his treason;
    That you might well have signified the same
    Unto the citizens, who haply may
    Misconster us in him, and wail his death.

Mayor of London. But, my good lord, your Grace's word shall
      serve,
As well as I had seen, and heard him speak;
And do not doubt, right noble princes both,
But I'll acquaint our duteous citizens
With all your just proceedings in this case.

                            (*Richard III*, III, 5)

This scene has a really fine ending. The Mayor rushes to the
Guildhall. Gloster and Buckingham go to dinner. The forestage is empty. It is still the same long week. Morning has
come. A Scrivener enters, with a paper in his hand:

Here is th'indictment of the good Lord Hastings;
Which in a set hand fairly is engross'd,
That it may be to-day read o'er in Paul's.
And mark how well the sequel hangs together:
Eleven hours I have spent to write it over,
For yesternight by Catesby was it sent me;
The precedent was full as long a-doing:
And yet within these five hours Hastings liv'd,
Untainted, unexamined, free at liberty.
Here's a good world the while! Why, who's so gross
That cannot see this palpable device?
Yet who so bold but says he sees it not?
Bad is the world; and all will come to naught
When such ill dealing must be seen in thought

                            (*Richard III,* III, 6)

'Here's a good world the while!' . . . It is remarkable how
closely this court clerk, with his cruel irony, resembles the fools
of later Shakespearian comedies and tragedies. Would the
clown, who philosophizes, for such is his job at court, and the
scrivener, who knows everything but is not allowed to speak,
be the only ones to know the truth about the world? 'Here's a
good world . . .'. But what world? What sort of world is it that
Shakespeare writes about?

    What did Shakespeare want to say in *Richard III*? He took the
historical substance of the play from Hall's and Holinshed's
chronicles, based on notes made by Sir Thomas More. He did
not change its character, or the order of events. Even the out-

rageous scene with the strawberries had been described in almost the same words by More. Was Shakespeare merely reshaping, and putting new life into old historical dramas, popular in the London theatre, such as *Richardus Tertius* by Thomas Legge, or the anonymous *True History of Richard III*? Was *Richard III* intended to be just a page from history, a cruel chapter in the old annals of England?

'Here's a good world the while!' . . . But what world? Richard III's? Shakespeare's? What world did Shakespeare write about, what times did he want to depict? Was it the world of feudal barons, slaughtering one another in the middle of the fifteenth century, or perhaps the world of the reign of the good, wise and devout Queen Elizabeth? That same Elizabeth, who cut off Mary Stuart's head when Shakespeare was twenty three-years old, and sent to the scaffold some fifteen hundred Englishmen, among them her own lovers, ministers of the realm, doctors of theology and doctors of law, generals, bishops, great judges. 'Here's a good world . . .' Or did Shakespeare consider history to be one continuous chain of violence, an unending stormy week, with the sun only very infrequently breaking through the thick clouds at noon with an occasional quiet, peaceful morning, or a calm evening when lovers embrace and go to sleep under the trees of a Forest of Arden?

> Go, hie thee, hie thee from this slaughter-house,
> Lest thou increase the number of the dead.
>
> (*Richard III*, IV, 1)

'Here's a good world . . .' But what did in fact the Grand Mechanism mean for Shakespeare? A succession of kings climbing and pushing one another off the grand staircase of history, or a wave of hot blood rising up to one's head and blinding the eyes? A natural order that has been violated, so that evil produces evil, every injury calls for revenge, every crime causes another? Or a cruel social order in which the vassals and superiors are in conflict with each other, the kingdom is ruled like a farm, and falls prey to the strongest? A naked struggle for power, or a violent beat of the human heart that reason cannot accelerate or stop, but a dead piece of sharp iron breaks once and for all? A dense and impenetrable night of history where dawn does not break, or a darkness that fills the human soul?

V

Richard III contains answers to only some of those great questions. In this tragedy, which abounds in violence, equalling, if not surpassing that of *Titus Andronicus*, only one character has some scruples, and experiences a brief moment of doubt. It is a hired assassin, one of the two sent by Richard to murder the Duke of Clarence in the Tower.

> *First Murderer.* What, art thou afraid?
> *Second Murderer.* Not to kill him, having a warrant for it; but to be damn'd for killing him, from the which no warrant can defend me.

In this world of kings, bishops, judges, chancellors, lords and generals, the only man, who, for a brief moment, shrinks from committing murder, is the one whose profession it is to murder for money. He is not afraid of violating the laws of the kingdom, or the social order. He knows he occupies in it a definite place; not a very honourable one, but none the less generally tolerated and necessary. He has a warrant for this murder from the King himself. The hired assassin fears the Last Judgement, damnation and hell. He is the only believer in this play. He hears the voice of conscience but at the same time realizes that conscience cannot be reconciled with the laws and order of the world he lives in, that it is something superfluous, ridiculous and a nuisance.

> *Second Murderer.* I'll not meddle with it: it is a dangerous thing: it makes a man a coward: a man cannot steal, but it accuseth him; he cannot swear, but it checks him; he cannot lie with his neighbour's wife, but it detects him: it is a blushing shame-faced spirit that mutinies in a man's bosom; it fills one full of obstacles: it made me once restore a purse of gold, that by chance I found; it

beggars any man that keeps it: it is turn'd out of all towns and
cities for a dangerous thing; and every man that means to live
well endeavours to trust to himself and to live without it.

Only two people in this tragedy reflect on the order of the
world: King Richard III, and a hired assassin. The one who is
at the top of the feudal ladder, and one placed at its very
bottom. Richard III has no scruples or doubts; the hired
assassin experiences a moment of doubt. But they both see the
Grand Mechanism equally clearly, although from opposite
angles. Neither of them has any illusions: they are the only ones
who can afford not to have them. They accept the world as it
really is. Moreover, the King and the hired assassin represent
the world's order in its 'pure form'. Shakespeare wanted to say
just this. There are sudden flashes of genius in this early, youthful play. One of them is the equation of a hired assassin with the
King's brother:

> *Clarence.* In God's name, what art thou?
> *First Murderer.* A man, as you are.
> *Clarence.* But not, as I am, royal.
> *First Murderer.* Nor you, as we are, loyal.

This fragment of dialogue already foreshadows *Hamlet*. For
what are hired assassins if not history's gravediggers? In the
Elsinore churchyard, too, gravediggers talk to a king's son.
They too look at great historical events and human dramas
from the same point of view: of those who dig graves and put
up gallows. Viewed from this angle there is no difference
between a king's son and a beggar. They are both mortal. They
were born to die. A hired assassin and the King's son have been
made doubly equal. In the order of history they are both just
cog-wheels of the Grand Mechanism. From the perspective of
a cemetery and the gallows they are both only human beings.
Shakespeare excels in unexpected confrontations in which – as if
illumined by lightning – the entire immense landscape of history
suddenly comes into view. Thus *Richard III* already points the
way to the interpretation of *Hamlet* as a political drama, and,
conversely, *Richard*, interpreted through *Hamlet*, becomes a

philosophical drama about discrepancy between the moral order and the order of practical behaviour.

Two assassins come to the prison cell in order to murder Richard's own brother at his request. Both the Duke of Clarence and the assassins kill by the order of the King and in his name. Only yesterday Clarence could, on the King's behalf, order them to commit any murder. Today he is in prison himself, and must die by the order, and in the name, of the same King. The Duke and the hired assassins are only men, and cog-wheels in the same mechanism.

Let us consider this scene once more. The King's brother used to command assassins to kill for the sake of political order. He has been put in prison and meets the same assassins. He defends himself. He speaks to them of conscience. Their reply is that he himself had mocked conscience. He tells them that he is a minister of the crown. Their reply is that in prison there are no ministers. He speaks to them of lofty ideas. They reply that the very same ideas now demand his death.

> *Clarence.* . . . Wherein, my friends, have I offended you?
> *First Murderer.* Offended us you have not, but the King.
> *Clarence.* I shall be reconcil'd to him again.
> *Second Murderer.* Never, my lord; therefore prepare to die.
>
> . . . .
> *First Murderer.* What we will do, we do upon command.
> *Second Murderer.* And he that hath commanded is the king.
>
> (*Richard III*, I, 4)

And so the two hired assassins drown the Duke of Clarence in a barrel of malmsey.

Thus has the long week begun. It will end with the great coronation scene. Richard has by now eliminated all those who had stood in his way to the throne. He has terrorized the Council, the House of Lords, and the City. It is night. The forestage represents a courtyard of the royal palace. The terrified nobles, assembled here, watch in silence. Gloster's agents walk about everywhere. In a corner of the courtyard there is a crowd of townspeople dragged from their houses. It is they who are to proclaim Richard king, for he has agreed to reign only by the will of the people. At last he shows himself on the balcony, with a prayer-book in his hand. He is praying. After all, he is to be king by the will of God.

> *Mayor of London.* See, where his Grace stands 'tween two
> clergymen!
> *Buckingham.* Two props of virtue for a Christian prince,
> To stay him from the fall of vanity.

On this little wooden circle, the 'O' to which Shakespeare has several times compared the Globe stage, one of history's great scenes is now being performed. Richard lets himself be implored to accept the crown.

> *Mayor of London.* Do, good my lord; your citizens entreat you.
> *Buckingham.* Refuse not, mighty lord, this proffer'd love.
> *Catesby.* O, make them joyful, grant their lawful suit!
> (*Richard III,* III, 7)

Both the nobles and the townspeople are silent. They will only say: 'Amen.' This is enough. Richard has agreed to accept the crown. He has put away his prayer-book. He turns to the bishops still standing at his side, and says:

> Come, let us to our holy work again.

VI

History in the theatre is mostly just a grand setting, a background against which the characters love, suffer, hate, and experience their personal dramas. Sometimes they are involved in history, which complicates their lives, but even then does not cease to be a more or less uncomfortable costume: a wig, a farthingale, a sword knocking about their feet. Of course, such plays are only superficially historical. But there are plays in which history is not just a background or a setting in which it is played, or rather repeated on the stage, by actors disguised as historical personalities. They know history, have learned it by heart, and do not often go wrong. Schiller was a classic author of this kind of historical drama. Marx used to call his characters speaking trumpets of modern ideas. They interpret history because they know the solutions it offers. They can sometimes express real trends and conflicts of social forces. But even this does not mean that the dramatization of history has been effected. It is only an historical textbook that has been dramatized. The textbook can be idealistic, as in Schiller and Romain Rolland, or materialistic, as in some dramas of Büchner and Brecht; but it does not cease to be a textbook.

Shakespeare's concept of history is of a different kind than the two mentioned above. History unfolds on the stage, but is never merely enacted. It is not a background or a setting. It is iself the protagonist of tragedy. But what tragedy?

There are two fundamental types of historical tragedy. The first is based on the conviction that history has a meaning, fulfils its objective tasks and leads in a definite direction. It is rational, or at least can be made intelligible. Tragedy consists here in the price of history, the price of progress that has to be paid by humanity. A precursor, one who pushes forward the relentless roller of history, but must himself be crushed by it for the very reason of his coming ahead of his time, is also tragic. This is the concept of historical tragedy proclaimed by Hegel. It was near to the views of the young Marx, even though he substituted the objective development of ideas. He compared history to a mole which unceasingly digs in the earth

> Well said, old mole! canst work i'th'earth so fast?
> A worthy pioneer!   (*Hamlet*, I, 5)

A mole lacks awareness, but digs in a definite direction. It has its dreams but they just dimly express its feeling for the sun and sky. It is not the dreams that set the direction of its march, but the movement of its claws and snout, constantly digging up the earth. A mole will be tragic if it happens to be buried by the earth before it emerges to the surface.

There is another kind of historical tragedy, originating in the conviction that history has no meaning and stands still, or constantly repeats its cruel cycle; that it is an elemental force, like hail, storm, or hurricane, birth and death. A mole digs in the earth but will never come to the surface. New generations of

moles are being born all the time, scatter the earth in all directions, but are themselves constantly buried by the earth. A mole
has its dreams. For a long time it fancied itself the lord of creation, thinking that earth, sky and stars had been created for
moles, that there is a mole's God, who had made moles and promised them a mole-like immortality. But suddenly the mole has
realized that it is just a mole, that the earth, sky and stars had
not been created for it. A mole suffers, feels and thinks, but its
sufferings, feelings and thoughts cannot alter its mole's fate. It
will go on digging in the earth and the earth will go on burying
it. It is at this point that the mole has realized that it is a tragic
mole.

It seems to me that the latter concept of historical tragedy
was nearer to Shakespeare, not only in the period when he was
writing *Hamlet* and *King Lear*, but in all his writings, from the
early Histories up to the *Tempest*.

> ... for within the hollow crown
> That rounds the mortal temples of a king
> Keeps Death his court; and there the antick sits,
> Scoffing his state, and grinning at his pomp;
> Allowing him a breath, a little scene,
> To monarchize, be fear'd, and kill with looks;
>
> . . . .
> ... and humour'd thus,
> Comes at the last, and with a little pin
> Bores through his castle-wall, and – farewell king!
>
> (*Richard II*, III, 2)

We began our considerations with a metaphor of the grand
staircase of history. It was on such a staircase that Leopold
Jessner set *Richard III* in his famous production at the Berlin
Schauspielhaus. That metaphor has philosophical consequences
and is also dramatically fruitful. There are no good and bad
kings; there are only kings on different steps of the same stairs.
The names of the kings may change, but it is always a Henry
who pushed a Richard down, or the other way round. Shakespeare's Histories are *dramatis personae* of the Grand Mechanism,
but what is this Grand Mechanism which starts operating at the

foot of the throne and to which the whole kingdom is sub
jected? A mechanism whose cog-wheels are both great lord
and hired assassins; a mechanism which forces people to
violence, cruelty and treason; which constantly claims new
victims? A mechanism according to whose laws the road to
power is at the same time the way to death? This Grand
Mechanism is for Shakespeare the order of history, in which the
King is the Lord's Anointed.

> Not all the water in the rough rude sea
> Can wash the balm from an anointed king;
> The breath of worldly men cannot depose
> The deputy elected by the Lord.   (*Richard II,* III, 2

The sun circles round the earth, and with it the spheres, planet
and stars all arranged in a hierarchic order. There is in the
universe an order of the elements, an order of angelic choirs
and a corresponding order of rank on earth. There are superior
and vassals of the vassals. Royal power comes from God, and
all power on earth is merely a reflection of the power wielded by
the King.

> The heavens themselves, the planets, and this centre,
> Observe degree, priority, and place,
> Insisture, course, proportion, season, form,
> Office and custom, in all line of order:
> And therefore is the glorious planet Sol
> In noble eminence enthron'd and sphered
> Amidst the other; whose med'cinable eye
> Corrects the ill aspects of planets evil,
> And posts, like the commandment of a king,
> Sans check, to good and bad: but when the planets,
> In evil mixture, to disorder wander,
> What plagues, and what portents, what mutiny,
> What raging of the sea, shaking of earth,
> Commotion in the winds, frights, changes, horrors,
> Divert and crack, rend and deracinate
> The unity and married calm of states
> Quite from their fixture! O, when degree is shaked,
> Which is the ladder to all high designs,
> The enterprise is sick!   (*Troilus and Cressida,* I, 3

Richard II is a tragedy of dethronement. It is, however, not just Richard's dethronement, but that of the King. Dethronement, in fact, of the idea of regal power. We have seen how Shakespeare equalled a prince of royal blood – the King's brother – with a hired assassin. In *Richard II*, the Lord's Anointed, the King deprived of his crown, becomes a mere mortal. In the first acts of the tragedy the King was compared to the sun: others had to lower their eyes when faced with his dazzling Majesty. Now the sun has been hurled down from its orbit, and with it the entire order of the universe.

> . . . what can we bequeath,
> Save our deposed bodies to the ground?
> Our lands, our lives, and all are Bolingbroke's,
> And nothing can we call our own but death,
> And that small model of the barren earth
> Which serves as paste and cover to our bones.
>
> . . . .
> . . . throw away respect,
> Tradition, form, and ceremonious duty;
> For you have but mistook me all this while:
> I live with bread like you, feel want,
> Taste grief, need friends: – subjected thus,
> How can you say to me, I am a king? (*Richard II*, III, 2)

'*E pur si muove!*' These words can be read with different intonations. 'And still it moves . . .' There is also a bitter sort of laughter in those words. There is no heaven and hell, no order of spheres. The earth moves round the sun, and the history of the Renaissance is just a grand staircase, from the top of which ever new kings fall into the abyss. There exists only the Grand Mechanism. But the Grand Mechanism is not just cruel. There is another side to it: it is a tragic farce.

Richard III foreshadows *Hamlet*. *Richard II* is a tragedy of knowledge gained through experience. Just before being hurled into the abyss, the deposed King reaches the greatness of Lear. For *King Lear*, like *Hamlet*, is also a tragedy of man contemporary with Shakespeare, a political tragedy of Renaissance humanism, a tragedy of the world stripped of illusions. Slowly,

step by step, King Lear walks down the grand staircase, to learn
the whole cruelty of the world, over which he had once ruled
but which he did not know, and to drain the bitter cup to the
dregs. Richard II is brutally and suddenly pushed into the
abyss. But with him will founder the structure of the feudal
world. It is not only Richard who has been deposed. It is the
sun that has ceased to move round the earth.

> Give me the glass, and therein will I read.
> No deeper wrinkles yet? hath sorrow struck
> So many blows upon this face of mine,
> And made no deeper wounds! – O flattering glass,
> Like to my followers in prosperity,
> Thou dost beguile me! Was this face the face
> That every day under his household roof
> Did keep ten thousand men? was this the face
> That, like the sun, did make beholders wink?
> Was this the face that fac'd so many follies,
> And was at last out-fac'd by Bolingbroke?
> A brittle glory shineth in this face:
> As brittle as the glory is the face;
>   (*Dashes the glass against the ground.*)
> For there it is, crack'd in a hundred shivers. –
> Mark, silent king, the moral of this sport . . .
>   (*Richard II*, IV, 1

The tragedy of Richard II has been performed on the uppermost
step. The main scenes of *Richard III* are unfolded on the lower
steps, on the protagonist's way up. There is no tragedy of
history without awareness. Tragedy begins at the point where
the King becomes aware of the working of the Grand Mechanism. This can happen when he falls victim to it, or when he
acts as executioner. These are the points at which Shakespeare
carries out his great confrontations, contrasting the moral order
with the order of history.

Richard III compares himself to Machiavelli, and is a real
prince. He is, at any rate, a prince who has read *The Prince*.
Politics is to him a purely practical affair, an art, with the acquisi-
tion of power as its aim. Politics is amoral, like the art of
bridge construction, or the practice of fencing. Human passions

and men themselves, are clay that can be shaped at will. The whole world is a huge piece of clay which can be shaped by hand. Richard III is not just the name of one of the kings who have mounted the grand staircase. Nor is he a collective term for one of many royal situations depicted by Shakespeare in his historical chronicles. Richard III is the mastermind of the Grand Mechanism, its will and awareness. Here for the first time Shakespeare has shown the human face of the Grand Mechanism. A terrifying face, in its ugliness and the cruel grimace of its lips. But also a fascinating face.

VII

Richard III is the first of those great personalities that Shakespeare endowed with the full range of historical experience, in order to conclude his tragic reckoning with the real world. This reckoning starts with Richard's meeting with Lady Anne. It is one of the greatest scenes written by Shakespeare, and one of the greatest ever written.

Lady Anne follows an open coffin in which servants are carrying the body of her father-in-law, Henry VI. Richard has had him murdered in the Tower. He had earlier killed her husband, Edward, and her father, the Earl of Warwick. Was it the day before? A week, a month, a year ago? Time has no meaning here. It has been condensed to one long night, one long, oppressive week.

Richard interrupts the funeral procession. In the course of six minutes, counted by the tower clock, in the space of three pages of the Folio, in forty-three speeches, he will persuade the woman, whose husband, father, and father-in-law he has murdered, to enter his bedchamber of her own accord.

> Stay, you that bear the corse, and set it down.

These are Richard's first words in this scene. Lady Anne, like furies in ancient tragedies, is all suffering and hate. But Lady Anne knows well what times she is living in. From the outset Shakespeare places the scene in a country of terror and awe, where all are paralysed by fear, and no one is sure of his life. Halberdiers flee before Richard, servants throw down the coffin. Nothing surprises Lady Anne any more. She has seen everything:

> What, do you tremble? are you all afraid?
> Alas, I blame you not; for you are mortal . . .

She will be left alone with Richard. She has lost all her dear ones. She is now free from fear. She cries, implores, curses, mocks, sneers:

> No beast so fierce but knows some touch of pity.

And Richard replies:

> But I know none, and therefore am no beast.

Once again Shakespeare reminds us that the action takes place on earth, the cruellest of planets, and among men, who are more cruel than beasts. In order to conclude his reckoning he searches for ultimate, extreme forms of love and suffering, crime and hate. Lady Anne is as yet the superior in this duel. Richard is insipid, tries to deny his crime, tells lies. Lady Anne makes him admit them. And only now, in a world stripped of appearances, and in which violence has been openly revealed, in a world where the murderer stands face to face with his victim, does Richard become stronger than Anne. He admits he has killed the King.

> *Gloster.* Let him thank me, that holp to send him thither;
> For he was fitter for that place than earth.
> *Lady Anne.* And thou unfit for any place but hell.
> *Gloster.* Yes, one place else, if you will hear me name it.
> *Lady Anne.* Some dungeon.
> *Gloster.* Your bed-chamber.

This is the moment of Richard's first victory. As long as he lied, beat about the bush, denied his crime – he recognized the existence of moral order. Now he has annihilated it. They are alone on the stage; but not only there. They are alone in a world full of murder, violence, brute force and cruelty.

Lady Anne. I'll rest beside the chamber where thou liest!
Gloster. So will it, madam, till I lie with you.
Lady Anne. I hope so.

At this point Lady Anne is already lost. Richard has pulled the rug from under her feet. So the entire cruel mechanism, the death of her dear ones, the sufferings of great lords of the realm, the struggle for power and the crown – all this it seems was for her, and only for her. The world has been stripped of appearances, the moral order has been annihilated, now history ceases to exist. There is only a woman, a man, and a sea of spilt blood.

Gloster. Your beauty was the cause of that effect;
        Your beauty, that did haunt me in my sleep
        To undertake the death of all the world,
        So I might live one hour in your sweet bosom.
Lady Anne. If I thought that, I tell thee, homicide,
        These nails should rend that beauty from my cheeks.

Shakespeare has the gift of psychological clairvoyance. In this great scene he undertakes, in bold short-cuts of frantic dialogue, his own journey to the heart of darkness. He reduces the world to elemental forces of hate and lust. Lady Anne still hates Richard, but is already alone with her hate, in a world in which only lust exists. This scene should be interpreted through our own experiences. One must find in it the night of nazi occupation, concentration camps, mass-murders. One must see in it the cruel time when all moral standards are broken, when the victim becomes the executioner, and vice versa. Lady Anne will spit in Richard's face, but this is her last gesture, her last defence before surrender.

Lady Anne does not give herself to Richard out of fear. She will follow him to reach rock-bottom – to prove to herself that all the world's laws have ceased to exist. For when all has been lost, only memory remains, but it, too, must be stifled. One must kill oneself, or kill in oneself the last vestiges of shame. Lady Anne goes into Richard's bed to be destroyed.

If history is no more than a gigantic slaughter, what remains, except a leap into the darkness, a choice between death and pleasure? Shakespeare was great in the way he made Lady Anne take exactly this choice, the final and only choice left to her.

Richard gives her his sword.

> *Gloster*. Nay, do not pause; for I did kill King Henry,
>   But 'twas thy beauty that provoked me.
>   Nay, now dispatch; 'twas I that stabb'd young Edward,
>   But 'twas thy heavenly face that set me on . . .
> *Lady Anne* (*falls the sword*).
>   . . . though I wish thy death,
>   I will not be thy executioner.

Half a century later another play was written in which a man faces a woman whose father he has killed. Chimène's father had insulted Rodrigue's father, and Rodrigue avenged his father's shame. Chimène in turn has to avenge her father and demands Rodrigue's head. Throughout the whole tragedy there goes on a dialogue between love and duty conducted in smooth alexandrines, whose hard rhythm is not broken even for a moment. Corneille's world is cruel, too, but neither its moral order, nor its intellectual order have been violated. Honour, love and law have remained intact. In Shakespeare's royal Histories there is only hate, lust and violence: the Grand Mechanism, which transforms the executioner into a victim, and the victim into an executioner. Corneille's heroes are worthy of each other and self-confident. They do not experience doubt, and their features are never twisted by passion. They live in an unshaken world. This may be the reason why they seem to be people from another planet. In full view of the audience they try to outbid each other with their noble-mindedness, but this does not cost them much and does not inwardly change them. I cannot help preferring the wild snatches of Shakespearian dialogue to Corneille's grand rhetoric, in which passion is declined according to immutable rules of grammar.

> *Lady Anne*. I would I knew thy heart.
> *Gloster*. 'Tis figur'd in my tongue.
> *Lady Anne*. I fear me both are false.
> *Gloster*. Then never man was true.

Lady Anne. Well, well, put up your sword.
Gloster. Say, then, my peace is made.
Lady Anne. That shalt thou know hereafter.
Gloster. But shall I live in hope?
Lady Anne. All men, I hope, live so.   (*Richard III*, I, 2)

Corneille's heroes are stronger than the world, and there is no
darkness in their innermost souls. But Lady Anne, who spits in
the face of her husband's murderer and then goes to bed with
him, seems to me more human, or perhaps only more contemporary than the statue-like Chimène. In Shakespeare all human
values are brittle, and the world is stronger than men. The implacable roller of history crushes everybody and everything.
Man is determined by his situation, by the step of the grand
staircase on which he happens to find himself. It is that particular step that determines his freedom of choice.

In *Richard II* Shakespeare deposed not only the King, but the
idea of kingly power. In *Richard III* he showed the crumbling of
the entire moral order. After the great abdication scene Richard
II calls for a mirror, and when he finds his face unchanged,
breaks it. The King has become a man, the crown has been torn
off the head of the Lord's Anointed. But the world has not been
shaken to its foundations, and nothing has changed, not even
his own face. So the crown was no more than sham.

Having forced Lady Anne into his bedchamber, Richard III,
too, calls for a mirror. Everything has turned out to be sham:
loyalty, love, even hate. Crime goes unpunished; beauty has
chosen beast; human fate is clay that can be shaped in one's
hands. There is no God, no law.

> Having God, her conscience, and these bars against me,
> And I no friends to back my suit withal
> But the plain devil and dissembling looks,
> And yet to win her, – all the world to nothing!
>   (*Richard III*, I, 2)

Richard III calls for a mirror. But he is wiser than Richard II.
He calls for a mirror, but at the same time he calls for tailors to
cut him a new suit.

VIII

Shakespeare views the implacable mechanism without medieval awe, and without the illusions of the early Renaissance. The sun does not circle round the earth, there is no order of the spheres, or of nature. The King is no Lord's Anointed, and politics is only an art aiming at capturing and securing power. The world offers a spectacle similar to a storm or hurricane. Weak bushes are bowed down to the earth, while tall trees fall uprooted. The order of history and the order of nature are both cruel; terrifying are the passions that breed in the human heart.

Only in his comedies does Shakespeare recall the images of the Renaissance utopia. In the Forest of Arden lovers find each other, a son regains the property of which he had been deprived, free men hunt and sing, a just prince is restored to his throne. But even the utopia of Arden Forest and the hot dream of a midsummer night are split by inner contradictions. Harmony is only a brief and fleeting moment of stillness, The idyll is disturbed by Jaques's bitter mockery.

Of all the important works written by Shakespeare before 1600, i.e. in what nineteenth-century scholars called his optimistic period, only *Henry IV* can be called a cheerful play. In both the *Richard* plays, and in the other *Henrys*, history is the only *dramatis persona* of the tragedy. The protagonist of *Henry IV* is Falstaff.

The great feudal barons are still butchering one another. King Henry IV, who had recently deposed Richard II, and let him be murdered together with his followers, did not atone for his crimes by a journey to the Holy Land. The allies who have put him on the throne are rebelling. For them he is a new tyrant. Wales and Scotland rise. History will begin again from the beginning. But in *Henry IV* history is only one of many actors in the drama. It is being played out not only in the royal palace and in the courtyards of feudal castles; not only on battlefields, in dungeons of the Tower, and in the London street, where frightened townsmen are hurrying by. Near the royal palace there is a tavern called the Boar's Head. In it

Falstaff is king. Somehow, between the chapters of an austere historical chronicle there has been interpolated a rich Renaissance comedy about a fat knight, unable for many years to see his own knees under his huge belly.

I prefer *Richard II* and *Richard III* to *Henry IV*. They seem to me a far deeper and more austere kind of tragedy. Shakespeare exposes in them the mechanism of power directly, without resorting to subterfuge or fiction. He dethrones regal majesty, strips it of all illusion. He finds that the succession of reigns, the mere mechanism of history, is sufficient to achieve this. In *Henry IV* the position is different. The successor to the throne is a future national hero, the victor of Agincourt. *Henry IV* is already a patriotic epic.

Shakespeare never renounces his great confrontations. It is only that he poses them differently. Against the feudal barons butchering one another he sets the gargantuan figure of Falstaff. Sir John Falstaff not only personifies the Renaissance lust for life, its thunderous laughter at heaven and hell, at the crown and all other laws of the realm. The fat knight possesses a plebeian wisdom and experience. He will not let history take him in. He scoffs at it.

There are two excellent scenes in *Henry IV*. The first one shows Falstaff as a newly created captain of foot walking with his men to the place where the army has assembled. He has recruited only cripples and the poorest wretches in rags and tatters, because all those who had a little money could evade enlistment. The young prince looks aghast at this sorry army. But Falstaff, undisturbed, replies:

> Tut, tut; good enough to toss; food for powder, food for powder; they'll fill a pit as well as better: tush, man, mortal men, mortal men.   (*Henry IV*, p. I, IV, 2)

This entire scene might have been put, as it stands, into a play by Brecht. And only on reading it does one realize how much Brecht has taken from Shakespeare.

The other scene shows Falstaff on the battlefield. He soliloquizes while looking for the best place to hide himself:

What is honour? a word. What is that word honour? air. A trim
reckoning! – Who hath it? he that died o' Wednesday. Doth he
feel it? no. Doth he hear it? no. 'Tis insensible then? yea, to the
dead. But will it not live with the living? no. Why? detraction will
not suffer it. Therefore I'll none of it: honour is a mere scutcheon:
– and so ends my catechism.   (*Henry IV*, p. I, V, 1)

In *Henry IV* two notions of England are continuously set in
contrast to each other. The feudal barons slaughter one another.
The young prince robs merchants on the highways and has a
gay time in taverns with a band of rascals. *Henry IV* is one of
the few apologetic dramas written by Shakespeare. The young
prince grows up to become a wise and brave king. There is,
however, a sting in the moral. It appears that the company of
Falstaff and cutpurses is a far better school for royalty than the
feudal slaughter. After all, the two occupations are not so very
different. It is enough to recall *King John*:

> Cousin, away for England: haste before:
> And ere our coming, see thou shake the bags
> Of hoarding abbots; their imprison'd angels
> Set thou at liberty: the fat ribs of peace
> Must by the hungry now be fed upon. (*King John,* III, 3)

IX

We have now to return for the last time to Shakespeare's metaphor of the grand staircase. Richard II grows in the course of
his tragedy. On the lower steps he is just the name of a king;
only on the last step do we see him in a big tragic close-up. He
has regained his human face. The dramatic optics of Richard III
reverse this order. Here the King is, in the first half of the
tragedy, the mastermind of the Grand Mechanism, a demiurge
of history, the Machiavellian Prince. But Shakespeare is wiser
than the author of *The Prince*. As he walks up the grand stairs,
Richard becomes smaller and smaller. It is as if the Grand
Mechanism was absorbing him. Gradually he becomes just one
of its cogs. He has ceased to be the executioner, he is now a
victim, caught in the wheels.

Richard had been making history. The whole world was for him a piece of clay to shape in his hands. And now he himself is a piece of clay, shaped by someone else. In the Histories I have always admired Shakespeare's perception of the moment when history pushes the hitherto all-powerful prince into a blind alley; the moment when he who has been making history, or thinks he has been making it, becomes no more than its object. The moment when the Grand Mechanism turns out to be stronger than the man who has put it in motion.

In the last act of the tragedy, Richard III is only the name of a pursued king. The scene shifts from battlefield to battlefield. They are after him. He flees. He becomes weaker and weaker. They have caught up with him. Now he just tries to save his life.

> A horse! a horse! my kingdom for a horse!
>
> *(Richard III*, V, 4)

So, this is how much all his efforts have been worth. This is the real price of power, of history, of the crown adorning the Lord's Anointed. One good horse is worth more than the entire kingdom. This is the last sentence of the great cycle of Shakespeare's historical chronicles.

X

In 1958, Jacek Woszczerowicz with a group of young actors performed some scenes from *Richard III* in the Warsaw House of Culture. The room was full and the tiny platform was almost covered by the crowd. No special lighting and no props were used. Woszczerowicz took off his coat and remained dressed in a thick black pullover with a high collar. He rolled up his left sleeve exposing a withered hand. On the forefinger of his right hand there was a large ring. Lady Anne wore an ordinary dress. The man in the black pullover had murdered her father and husband. Now he asked her to sleep with him. The black pullover, with a collar covering the lower part of his chin, looked like armour. But does one need armour to commit murder? I had never before seen a Shakespeare performance so compact and consistent. Since then I waited for *Richard III* with Woszczerowicz. At last, early in the winter of 1960, Woszczerowicz produced *Richard III* at the Ateneum Theatre in Warsaw.

He walks briskly in, dragging one of his feet slightly. He stops and begins to laugh. He says that the war is over, that peace has come, and jagged swords can be laid aside. From above, rows of iron bars are lowered down to the stage, one after the other, forming the background. Richard talks to himself, not to us. He laughs again, not at himself, but at us. He has a broad face, untidy hair, and wears a soiled and torn tunic. 'Woszczer' might thus begin the part of Sganarelle: with the same make-up, the same tone, the same laughter. He stands there with legs wide apart, and his withered left arm hanging down.

Sir Laurence Olivier was fascinating from the outset. His deformity was only slightly sketched, he was overpowering and awesome, a brother of the King. Woszczerowicz speaks about peace – laughing. This misshapen dwarf begins with tomfoolery. This is the first revelation, and shock. He is smaller than all the other characters: he has to look up in order to look them in the face. He is a figure of fun. He knows it; he knows everything

In the nineteenth century the part of Richard was acted by tragedians, in a tragic fashion. He was represented as a pathological type of great criminal, or a 'superman'. Woszczerowicz is the first to build up Richard's part with all the means available to a comic actor. His Richard shows off, goes down on his knees, affects pity and anger, kindness, rage and lust, even cruelty. His Richard is above all situations; he does not identify himself with them, he just plays them. He is not, he only pretends he is. Woszczerowicz is a great actor, but his Richard is an even greater actor. An actor in the literal sense is the one who acts and plays his cards. In legal terminology an actor is the plaintiff, not the defendant. Similarly, one talks about the great actors of history. They both act and play their cards. They are not ashamed of tomfoolery. They are not ashamed of anything Just as the actor is not ashamed of any part he is to play, because he only enacts it. He is above the part. If he is the producer, he chooses the part and imposes situations. Then everything is a theatre to him. He has 'outplayed' everybody. When he remains alone on the empty earth, he can laugh. He can even afford to recognize himself for a clown; a super-clown.

Shakespeare was very fond of comparing life to the theatre. It is a comparison that goes back to ancient times, but it was Shakespeare who endowed it with depth and clarity. 'Teatrum Mundi' is neither tragic nor comic. It just employs tragic and comic actors. What is the tyrant's part in that theatre? Richard is impersonal like history itself. He is the consciousness and mastermind of the Grand Mechanism. He puts in motion the roller of history, and later is crushed by it. Richard is not even cruel. Psychology does not apply to him. He is just history, one of its ever-repeating chapters. He has no face.

But the actor who plays Richard must have a face. Woszcze-rowicz's Richard has a broad face and laughs. It is a frightening laughter. The most terrifying kind of tyrant is he who has recognized himself for a clown, and the world for a gigantic buffoonery. Of all actors in the part, Woszczerowicz has been the first thus to interpret Shakespeare. To my mind it is an interpretation with the mark of genius. He begins his performance with buffoonery, and buffoonery is the substance of his part. All his attitudes are those of a clown: the sly and cruel ones, as well as gestures of love and power. But buffoonery is not just a set of gestures. Buffoonery is a philosophy, and the highest form of contempt: absolute contempt.

Richard has become king. On his shoulders he wears the royal robe. It has been tailored in a couple of hours. Others may care about pretty clothes; he does not need them. He is always in a hurry. Others have time for trifles, not he. A throne has been carried on to the empty stage. It is a wooden structure looking rather like a gallows. The dwarf is now sitting high like a spider, holding the royal insignia. He despises them, too. He has put his sceptre under one of his thighs. What is a sceptre? A golden stick. Richard knows the price of that stick.

Richard ceases to be a clown only in the last act. Until then he affected outbursts of rage and fury, devotion, even fear. Now he is really afraid. Until now he had been the one to choose the part and stand above others. Now he is simply himself: a man whom they want to murder. Richard does not want to accept this part, but he must. He is not laughing any more. He is just a heavy, misshapen dwarf. Soon he will be butchered like a pig. From the head of the corpse the crown will be torn. A new, young king will now talk of peace. Rows of bars are lowered from above. Henry VII speaks of peace, forgiveness, justice. And suddenly he gives a crowing sound like Richard's, and, for a second, the same sort of grimace twists his face. The bars are being lowered. The face of the new King is radiant again.

Hamlet of the Mid-Century

I

he bibliography of dissertations and studies devoted to *Hamlet*
twice the size of Warsaw's telephone directory. No Dane of
esh and blood has been written about so extensively as Ham-
t. Shakespeare's prince is certainly the best known represen-
tive of his nation. Innumerable glossaries and commentaries
ave grown round Hamlet, and he is one of the few literary
eroes who live apart from the text, apart from the theatre. His
ame means something even to those who have never seen or
ad Shakespeare's play. In this respect he is rather like Leo-
ardo's Mona Lisa. We know she is smiling even before we
ave seen the picture. Mona Lisa's smile has been separated
om the picture, as it were. It contains not only what Leonardo
xpressed in it but also everything that has been written about
. Too many people – girls, women, poets, painters – have tried
> solve the mystery of that smile. It is not just Mona Lisa that
smiling at us now, but all those who have tried to analyse, or
nitate, that smile.

This is also the case with *Hamlet*, or rather – with *Hamlet* in
le theatre. For we have been separated from the text not only
y Hamlet's 'independent life' in our culture, but simply by the
ze of the play. *Hamlet* cannot be performed in its entirety,
ecause the performance would last nearly six hours. One has to
:lect, curtail and cut. One can only perform one of several
amlets potentially existing in this arch-play. It will always be a
oorer *Hamlet* than Shakespeare's *Hamlet* is; but it may also be a
amlet enriched by being of our time. It *may*, but I would
ther say – it *must* be so.

For *Hamlet* cannot be played simply. This may be the reason
hy it is so tempting to producers and actors. Many generations
ave seen their own reflection in this play. The genius of *Hamlet*

consists, perhaps, in the fact that the play can serve as a mirro
An ideal *Hamlet* would be one most true to Shakespeare, an
most modern at the same time. Is this possible? I do not know
But we can only appraise any Shakespearian production b
asking how much there is of Shakespeare in it, and how much c
us.

What I have in mind is not a forced topicality, a *Hamlet* th
would be set in a cellar of young existentialists. *Hamlet* has bee
performed, for that matter, in evening dress and in circus tights
in medieval armour and in Renaissance costume. Costumes d
not matter. What matters is that through Shakespeare's text w
ought to get at our modern experience, anxiety and sensibility

There are many subjects in *Hamlet*. There is politics, forc
opposed to morality; there is discussion of the divergenc
between theory and practice, on the ultimate purpose of life
there is the tragedy of love, as well as family drama; politica
eschatological and metaphysical problems are considered
There is everything you want, including deep psychologica
analysis, a bloody story, a duel, and general slaughter. One ca
select at will. But one must know what one selects, and why.

II

The *Hamlet* produced in Cracow a few weeks after the XXt.
Congress of the Soviet Communist Party lasted exactly thre
hours. It was light and clear, tense and sharp, modern and con
sistent, limited to one issue only. It was a political drama *pa
excellence*. 'Something is rotten in the state of Denmark' – wa
the first chord of *Hamlet*'s new meaning. And then the dea
sound of the words 'Denmark's a prison', three times repeated
Finally the magnificent churchyard scene, with the gravediggers
dialogue rid of metaphysics, brutal and unequivocal. Grave
diggers know for whom they dig graves. 'The gallows is buil
stronger than the church,' they say.

'Watch' and 'inquire' were the words most commonly hear
from the stage. In this performance everybody, without excep
tion, was being constantly watched. Polonius, minister to th

royal murderer, sends a man to France even after his own son.
Was Shakespeare not a genius for our time? Let us listen to the
minister:

> Inquire me first, what Danskers are in Paris;
> And how, and who, what means, and where they keep,
> What company, at what expense; and finding,
> By this encompassment and drift of question,
> That they do know my son, come you more nearer
> Than your particular demands will touch it. (II, 1)

At Elsinore castle someone is hidden behind every curtain. The
good minister does not even trust the Queen. Let us listen to
him again:

> 'Tis meet that some more audience than a mother,
> Since nature makes them partial, should o'erhear
> The speech, of vantage. (III, 3)

Everything at Elsinore has been corroded by fear: marriage,
love and friendship. Shakespeare, indeed, must have experienced terrible things at the time of Essex's plot and execution, since he came to learn so well the working of the Grand
Mechanism. Let us listen to the King talking to Hamlet's young
friends:

> . . . I entreat you both,
> That, being of so young days brought up with him,
> And sith so neighbour'd to his youth and haviour,
> That you vouchsafe your rest here in our court
> Some little time: so by your companies
> To draw him on to pleasures, and to gather,
> So much as from occasion you may glean,
> Whether aught, to us unknown, afflicts him thus,
> That, open'd, lies within our remedy. (II, 2)

The murderous uncle keeps a constant watchful eye on Hamlet.
Why does he not want him to leave Denmark? His presence at
court is inconvenient, reminding everybody of what they would
like to forget. Perhaps he suspects something? Would it not be
better not to issue him with a passport and keep him at hand?
Or does the King wish to get rid of Hamlet as soon as possible,

but has given way to the Queen, who wants to have her son near her? And the Queen? What does she think about it all? Does she feel guilty? What does the Queen know? She has been through passion, murder and silence. She had to suppress everything inside her. One can sense a volcano under her superficial poise.

Ophelia, too, has been drawn into the big game. They listen in to her conversations, ask questions, read her letters. It is true that she gives them up herself. She is at the same time part of the Mechanism, and its victim. Politics hangs here over every feeling, and there is no getting away from it. All the characters are poisoned by it. The only subject of their conversation is politics. It is a kind of madness.

Hamlet loves Ophelia. But he knows he is being watched; moreover – he has more important matters to attend to. Love is gradually fading away. There is no room for it in this world. Hamlet's dramatic cry: 'Ophelia, get thee to a nunnery!' is addressed not to Ophelia alone, but also to those who are over-hearing the two lovers. It is to confirm their impression of his alleged madness. But for Hamlet and for Ophelia it means that in the world, where murder holds sway, there is no room for love.

Hamlet was performed in Cracow, in 1956, unequivocally and with a terrifying clarity. Doubtless it was a simplified *Hamlet*. But it is equally certain that this interpretation was so sugges-tive that when I reached for the text after the performance, I saw in it only a drama of political crime. To the classic question whether Hamlet's madness is real or feigned, the Cracow pro-duction gave the following reply: Hamlet feigns madness, he puts on, in cold blood, a mask of madness in order to perform a *coup d'état*; Hamlet is mad, because politics is itself madness, when it destroys all feeling and affection.

I have nothing against such an interpretation. And I am not sorry for all the other Hamlets: for the moralist, unable to draw a clear-cut line between good and evil; for the intellectual, unable to find a sufficient reason for action; for the philosopher, to whom the world's existence is a matter of doubt.

I prefer the youth, deeply involved in politics, rid of illusions, sarcastic, passionate and brutal. A young rebel who has about him something of the charm of James Dean. His passion sometimes seems childish. No doubt he is more primitive than all previous Hamlets. Action, not reflection, is his forte. He is wild and drunk with indignation. The Polish Hamlet after the XXth Party Congress. One of many. He does not yet experience deep moral doubts, but he is not a simpleton. He wants to know if his father has really been murdered. He cannot fully trust the Ghost. or any ghosts for that matter. He looks for more convincing evidence, and that is why he arranges a psychological test by staging the crime that has been committed. He loathes the world and that is why he sacrifices Ophelia. But he does not flinch from a *coup d'état*. He knows, however, that a coup is a difficult affair. He considers all the pros and cons. He is a born conspirator. 'To be' means for him to revenge his father and to assassinate the King; while 'not to be' means – to give up the fight.

It is significant that very similar conclusions have been reached by Hans Reichenbach, who, in the last book published before his death, entitled *The Rise of Scientific Philosophy*, unexpectedly devotes two pages to Hamlet's soliloquy. Reichenbach was one of the most outstanding modern neo-positivists and concerned himself with the application of the theory of anticipation to particular branches of science. In Hamlet's soliloquy he sees an inner dialogue between logician and politician. It is the law of averages applied to the moral justification of an act. Without war and post-war experiences the learned neo-positivist would never have written those two pages.

But the *Hamlet* I saw in Cracow was modern not only because the problems of the play have been brought up to date. It was modern in its psychological and dramatic qualities. Action developed under great stress, similar to that experienced by us in real life. This production, deprived of the great soliloquies and of narrative quality, was marked by a violence typical of modern conflicts. Political, erotic and career motives intermingle, reactions are brutal, solutions are quickly effected. In this *Hamlet* there were even the 'black outs' of modern political cabaret, and great ironic humour. Let us quote Shakespeare:

King. Now, Hamlet, where's Polonius?
Hamlet. At supper.
King. At supper! where?
Hamlet. Not where he eats, but where he is eaten.   (IV, 3)

This joke might have been taken out of the Little Vocabulary of the Surrealists. It is in the same style, and has two meanings, one of which is derisive, the other cruel. This, too, is a new model of the theatre of cruelty and irony. Let us quote Shakespeare. By all means, let us quote Shakespeare.

III

Hamlet is like a sponge. Unless produced in a stylized or anti-quarian fashion, it immediately absorbs all the problems of our time. It is the strangest play ever written; by its very imper-fections. *Hamlet* is a great scenario, in which every character has a more or less tragic and cruel part to play, and has magnificent things to say. Every character has an irrevocable task to fulfil, a task imposed by the author. This scenario is independent from the characters; it has been devised earlier. It defines the situa-tions, as well as the mutual relations of the characters; it dictates their words and gestures. But it does not say who the characters are. It is something external in relation to them. And that is why the scenario of *Hamlet* can be played by different sorts of characters.

An actor always enters a ready part, written not only for him. In this respect *Hamlet* does not, of course, differ from other plays. At the first rehearsal the actors sit at a table. 'You will be the King' – says the producer – 'you will be Ophelia, and you will be Laertes. We shall now read the play.' So far so good. But in the play itself similar things happen. Hamlet, Laertes, Ophelia also have to play parts imposed on them, parts against which they revolt. They are actors in a drama they do not always wholly understand, in which they have become involved. The scenario dictates the actions of the *dramatis personae*, but does not dictate the motives underlying the actions, i.e. the psychology. This is true of life, as well as of the theatre.

A secret organization is preparing an action. The plan has been carefully worked out: Place, time-table, direction of retreat. Then the parts have to be distributed. You will stand on that corner and raise your handkerchief when you see the grey car. You will go to Z and bring a case with grenades to house No. 12. You will shoot in direction W and escape in direction M. The tasks have been allotted, the parts taught. Even gestures have been defined. But, the evening before, the boy, who is to shoot in direction N, could have read Rimbaud or drunk vodka, or both. He may be a young philosopher, or just a Teddy-boy. The girl, who is to bring grenades, may be having an unhappy love affair, or may be a good-time girl, or possibly both. The plan of action will not be altered because of that. The scenario remains unchanged.

Hamlet can be summarized in a number of ways: as an historical chronicle, as a thriller, or as a philosophical drama. They will probably be three different plays, though all three have been written by Shakespeare. But if the summary is fair, the scenarios of the three plays will be the same. Except that every time there will be a different Ophelia, or Hamlet, or Laertes. The parts are the same, but performed by different actors.

Let us have a look at the scenario. For, after all, Shakespeare had written, or rather rewritten, an old scenario, and the parts in it. But he did not distribute the parts. This has been done anew in every age. Every age has its own Poloniuses, Fortinbrases, Hamlets and Ophelias. Before they enter the stage, they have to go to dressing-rooms. But let them not stay there too long. They may put on huge wigs, shave off their moustaches, or stick on beards, put on medieval-looking tights, or throw byronic capes over their shoulders; they may play in armour or in tails. This does not really make much difference, on condition that their make-up is not overdone; for they must have modern faces. Otherwise they would perform a costume piece, instead of *Hamlet*.

Bertolt Brecht wrote in his *Little Organum for the Theatre*:

c

... The theatre should always be mindful of the needs of its time.
Let us take, as an example, the old play of *Hamlet*. I believe that in
view of the bloody and gloomy times in which I am writing this,
in view of the criminal ruling classes and general despair of
reason (. . .) the story of this play may be read thus: It is a time of
war. Hamlet's father, the king of Denmark, had, in a victorious
war of plunder, killed the king of Norway. While the latter's son,
Fortinbras, is preparing himself for a new war, the king of Denmark is also killed, by his brother. The brothers of the dead kings,
having become kings themselves, conclude peace with each other.
Norwegian troops, on their way to a war of plunder against
Poland, have been permitted to cross Danish territory. Just at this
time, the warlike father's ghost asks young Hamlet to revenge the
crime committed on himself. After some hesitation as to whether
he should add one bloody deed to another, Hamlet – willing even
to go into exile – meets at the sea shore young Fortinbras and his
troops on their way to Poland. Following his example he turns
back, and, in a scene of barbaric slaughter, kills his uncle, his
mother, and himself, leaving Denmark to the Norwegians. Thus
we observe how, in these circumstances, the young man, already
somewhat stout, badly misuses his new knowledge acquired at
Wittenberg university. This knowledge gets in the way when it
comes to resolving the conflicts of the feudal world. His reason is
impractical when faced with irrational reality. He falls a tragic
victim to the discrepancy between his reasoning and his action.

Brecht was writing his *Little Organum* in the years of the Second
World War. No wonder that in Shakespeare's tragedy he saw,
above all, armies devastating the country, wars of aggression,
the powerlessness of reason. Hamlet's personal drama, or
Ophelia's misfortunes, were made insignificant by the events of
history. Brecht was sensitive to the politics in *Hamlet*. He was
more interested in the sequences of historical conflict than in
the depths of the Prince of Denmark's soul. The point of departure of Polish productions of *Hamlet* in 1956 and 1959 was
very similar, however they might have differed from Brecht's
concepts. *Hamlet* was a political play in 1956, and remained such
in 1959, although the Prince of Denmark had by then become a
much more complex personality and had passed through new
experiences.

Let us have a look at the scenario in order to find out what parts it contains, knowing that they will be played by modern characters. *Hamlet*, envisaged as a scenario, is the story of three young boys and one girl. The boys are of the same age. They are called Hamlet, Laertes, Fortinbras. The girl is younger, and her name is Ophelia. They are all involved in a bloody political and family drama. As a result, three of them will die; the fourth will, more or less by chance, become the King of Denmark.

I have deliberately written that they are involved in a drama. For none of them has chosen his part; it is imposed on them from outside, having been conceived in the scenario. The scenario has to be played to the end, no matter who Hamlet, Ophelia, and the other characters are. I am not concerned at the moment with what the scenario itself is supposed to be. It may be the Mechanism of history, fate, or the human condition, depending on how we want to envisage *Hamlet*. *Hamlet* is a drama of imposed situations, and here lies the key to modern interpretations of the play.

The King, the Queen, Polonius, Rosenkrantz and Guildenstern have been clearly defined by their situations. It may be a tragic situation, as in the case of the Queen; or grotesque, as in the case of Polonius. But character and situation are closely connected. Claudius does not play the part of a murderer and a king. He *is* the murderer and the King. Polonius does not play the part of a despotic father and a king's councillor. He *is* the despotic father and the King's councillor.

It is different with Hamlet. He is more than the heir to the throne who tries to revenge himself for the murder of his father. The situation does not define Hamlet, or at any rate does not define him beyond doubt. The situation has been imposed on him. Hamlet accepts it, but at the same time revolts against it. He accepts the part, but is beyond and above it.

In his student days Hamlet had carefully studied Montaigne. It is with Montaigne's book in his hand that he chases the medieval ghost on the terraces of Elsinore castle. The ghost has hardly disappeared than Hamlet writes on the book's margin that 'one may smile, and smile, and be a villain'.

Shakespeare has thrust the most attentive of Montaigne's readers back into the feudal world. He has also set a mousetrap for him.

'Poor boy with a book in his hand . . .' Thus was Hamlet described in 1904 by Stanislaw Wyspiański, painter, dramatist, designer, whom Gordon Craig used to call the most universal artist of the theatre. Wyspiański made the Polish Hamlet walk round the renaissance galleries of Cracow's Royal Castle. The scenario of history imposed on the Polish Hamlet at the turn of the century a duty to struggle for the nation's liberation. That particular Hamlet used to read Polish romantic poets and Nietzsche. He experienced his powerlessness as a personal failure.

Every Hamlet has a book in his hand. What book does the modern Hamlet read? Hamlet in the Cracow production of late autumn, 1956, read only newspapers. He shouted that 'Denmark's a prison', and wanted to improve the world. He was a rebellious ideologist, and lived only for action. Hamlet in the Warsaw production of 1959 was full of doubts again; and again he was the 'sad boy with a book in his hand . . .' We can easily visualize him in black sweater and blue jeans. The book he is holding is not by Montaigne, but by Sartre, Camus or Kafka. He studied in Paris, or Brussels, or even – like the real Hamlet – in Wittenberg. He returned to Poland three or four years ago. He very much doubts if the world can be reduced to a few simple statements. Occasionally he is tormented by thoughts of the fundamental absurdity of existence.

This latest, the most modern of Hamlets, returned to the country at a moment of tension. His father's ghost demands revenge. His friends expect him to fight for succession to the throne. He wants to go away again. He cannot. Everybody involves him in politics. He has been trapped into finding himself in a compulsory situation; a situation he does not want but which has been thrust upon him. He is looking for inner freedom, and does not want to commit himself. At last he accepts the choice imposed on him; but only in the sphere of action. He is committed but only in what he does, not in what he thinks.

He knows that all action is clear-cut, but he refuses to let his thought be thus limited. He does not want practice to be equated with theory.

He is inwardly starved. He considers life to be a lost cause from the outset. He would rather be excused from this big game, but remains loyal to its rules. He knows that 'though man does not do what he wants, he is responsible for his life'. And that 'it does not matter what has been made of us; what matters is what we ourselves make of what has been made of us'. Sometimes he thinks himself an existentialist; at other times – just a marxist who has revolted. But he knows that 'death transforms life into destiny'. He has read Malraux's *La Condition Humaine*.

This attitude of the modern Hamlet is a defence of his inner freedom. This Hamlet fears, most of all, a clear-cut definition. But act he must. Ophelia may have a hair-do like Leonardo's 'Lady with a Weasel', or her hair may be let down loose; she may wear a pigtail, or a pony-tail. But she, too, knows that life is a hopeless business from the start. So she does not want to play her game with life at too high a stake. It is the events that compel her to overplay. Her boy-friend has been involved in high politics. She has slept with him. But she is a daughter of a minister of the crown; an obedient daughter. She agrees to her conversation with Hamlet being overheard by her father. Maybe she wants to save Hamlet. But she falls into the trap herself. The events have driven her into a blind alley from which there is no way out. An ordinary girl, who loved her boy, has been given by the scenario of history – a tragic part.

IV

Traditional nineteenth-century hamletology devoted itself almost exclusively to the study of the problem of who Hamlet really was. The traditional scholars charge Shakespeare with having written an untidy, inconsistent and badly constructed masterpiece. Whereas modern essays consider *Hamlet* from a theatrical standpoint. *Hamlet* is not a philosophical, moral or psychological treatise; it is a piece for the theatre, that is to say, a scenario with parts. If this is so, then one must begin with Fortinbras, who plays a decisive role, as far as the scenario of *Hamlet* is concerned.

Let us imagine a modern producer starting analytical rehearsals of *Hamlet*. He has seated his actors round a table and told them: 'We are going to do a play by Shakespeare called *Hamlet*. We will try to do it as honestly as we can. That means we are not going to alter the text. We will try to give as much text as can be put over in three and a half hours. We will reflect on every cut. We will try to show a modern *Hamlet*. We will try to break with nineteenth-century naturalism, and be content with a back-cloth, rostrum and two chairs on either side of the stage. We will endeavour to design colourful renaissance costumes. But these costumes will be worn by us, modern people. You must not throw your hands up in the air, walk on tiptoes, or on stilts. The world shown in this scenario is cruel, but every one of us has experienced the cruelty of the world. Some people revolt against this cruelty, others accept it as a law; but both are crushed by it.'

An elderly actor who is to play Polonius will, perhaps, ask at this point: 'Is *Hamlet* a political play?'

'I don't know,' the producer will probably reply. 'This depends on what Denmark means to these three young people here.' And he will point out a young girl, who is to play Ophelia, the young actor, who is just trying on the green costume of Laertes, and – Hamlet, who is sitting anxiously in the corner looking at his silver medallion. Then, maybe, the producer will be lost in thought for a while and say quietly to himself: 'Perhaps it depends on who our Fortinbras will be?'

In all modern analyses of *Hamlet* (H. Granville-Barker, F. Fergusson, J. Paris) the character of Fortinbras has been brought to the foreground. In structural interpretations *Hamlet* is a drama of analogical situations, a system of mirrors, in which the same problem is in turn reflected tragically, pathetically, ironically and grotesquely: three sons who have lost their fathers, one after the other, or Hamlet's and Ophelia's madness.

In predominantly historical interpretations *Hamlet* is a drama of power and heredity. In the first instance, Fortinbras is one of Hamlet's 'doubles', *'alter egos'*, 'mediums'. In the other – he is the heir to the throne of Denmark; the man who has broken the chain of crime and revenge, who has restored order to the Danish kingdom. This order may be understood as the restoration of moral law, or as the 'neue Ordnung in Europa'. The ending of the tragedy has been interpreted in both ways. For if one wishes to place *Hamlet's* moral conflicts in an historical context, no matter whether renaissance or modern, one cannot ignore the part played by Fortinbras.

The difficulty is that in the text of the play Fortinbras is only broadly sketched. On the stage he appears only twice: for the first time in Act Four, when he and his troops are on the way to Poland; for the second time – when he comes to claim the throne after the general slaughter. But young Fortinbras is mentioned many times. His father has been killed in a duel by Hamlet's father. The fathers of all the young people in this play – Hamlet, Laertes and Ophelia – have been murdered. Spectators get confused when tracing the history of young Fortinbras. From the prologue we learn that he wants to wage war against Denmark; then he fights with the Poles for a piece of land hardly worth having; at the end he appears in Elsinore. It is he who speaks the final words of this cruel drama.

Who is this young Norwegian prince? We do not know. Shakespeare does not tell us. What does he represent? Blind fate, the absurdity of the world, or the victory of justice? Shakespearian scholars have made a case for all these interpretations in turn. The producer has to decide. Shakespeare has only told us his name. But the name is significant: Fortinbras – 'forte braccio'. Fortinbras, the man of the strong arm. A young and strong fellow. He comes and says: 'Take away these corpses. Hamlet was a good boy, but he is dead. Now I shall be your king. I have just remembered that I happen to have certain rights to this crown.' Then he smiles and is very pleased with himself.

A great drama has been concluded. People fought, plotted,

killed one another, committed crimes for love, and went mad
for love. They told amazing things about life, death and human
fate. They set traps for each other, and fell into them. They defended their power, or revolted against power. They wanted to
build a better world, or just save themselves. They all stood for
something. Even their crimes had a certain greatness. And then
a vigorous young lad comes, and says with a charming smile:
'Take away these corpses. Now I shall be your king.'

Troilus and Cressida – Amazing and Modern

To start with there is the *buffo* tone. The great Achilles, the heroic Achilles, the legendary Achilles wallows in bed with his male tart – Patroclus. He is a homosexual, he is boastful, stupid, and quarrelsome like an old hag. Only Ajax, a chicken-brained heap of flesh, is more stupid than he. The whole camp laughs at these two giants, envious of each other. They are both cowards. But Shakespeare is not content with all this. Achilles and Patroclus play in their tent at mimicking the kings and generals. Often in Shakespeare clowns imitate princes. But here the mockery is even more cruel and spares no one. Heroes imitate clowns, and they are clowns. Only the real clown is not a clown. He makes clowns of princes. He is wiser. He hates and sneers.

> Agamemnon is a fool to offer to command Achilles; Achilles is a fool to be commanded by Agamemnon; Thersites is a fool to serve such a fool; and Patroclus is a fool positive.   (II, 3)

The fools' circle is now closed. Even Nestor and Ulysses are for a while engulfed by this universal foolery; they are a couple of old prattlers, unable to win the war without the help of two morons.

And Troy? An old procurer and a young girl watch the warriors and the King's sons return from a sortie fought outside the city walls. For them the war does not exist. They have not noticed it. All they see is marching men. In Troy there is also Helen. Shakespeare shows her only in one scene, but even before she has been shown Pandarus has told us how she embraced Troilus in a 'compass'd window' and plucked hairs from his youthful beard. The *buffo* tone has changed; it is more subtle now, but no less ironic. In the Greek camp we have seen red-faced fools, big, fat, heavy barbarians mimicking one another. In Troy we meet smart courtiers with their small talk. Parody is still there, but its subject has changed. Paris kneels at Helen's knees as in a courtly romance. Page-boys play the lute or the viol. But Paris calls the lady from a medieval romance simply – 'Nell'. Lovely Nell, Greek queen and the cause of the Trojan war, cracks jokes like a whore from a London tavern. The *buffo* tone, the great parody, the anachronisms and contemporary allusions, all this amazes us in a work written a year after *Hamlet*. Offenbach's *La Belle Hélène* of 1601. But Shakespeare's *Troilus and Cressida* is not *La Belle Hélène*.

For it is not the *buffo* tone that is the most amazing, but its sudden break, or rather its fusion with a most bitter philosophy and passionate poetry. In the Greek camp no one has any illusions. Everybody knows that Helen is a whore, that the war is being fought over a cuckold and a hussy. The Trojans know it too. Priam and Cassandra know it, even Paris knows it, certainly Hector knows it. Both parties know it. And what of it? The war has been going on for seven years, and it will go on. Helen is not worth one drop of Greek or Trojan blood spilt in battle. But what of it? And what does 'is not worth' mean?

Menelaus is a cuckold, Helen is a tart, Achilles and Ajax are buffoons. But the war is not buffoonery. Trojans and Greeks die in it, Troy will perish in it. Heroes call on gods, but there are no gods in *Troilus and Cressida*. There are no gods and there is no fate. Why then is war being waged? On either side it is not just fools who are taking part in it. Nestor, Ulysses, even Agamemnon, are no fools. Neither Priam, nor Hector, nor even Troilus – who hankers after the absolute – is a fool. In no other play of Shakespeare's, perhaps, do the characters analyse themselves and the world quite so violently and passionately. They want to choose in full awareness. They philosophize, but it is not an easy or apparent philosophy. Nor is it just rhetoric.

The great dispute about the sense and cost of war, about the existence and cost of love, goes on from the opening to the final scene of *Troilus and Cressida*. It is a dispute constantly punctuated by buffoonery. One can call it something else: it is a dispute about the existence of a moral order in a cruel and irrational world. Hamlet, the Prince of Denmark, has faced the same trial.

The war goes on. Trojans and Greeks kill each other. If war is just butchery, the world in which war exists is absurd. But the world goes on, and one has to give it a purpose in order to preserve the sense of the world's existence and a scale of values. Helen is a whore, but Helen has been abducted with Priam's permission and that of the Trojan leaders. Helen's cause has become Troy's cause. Helen has become the symbol of love and beauty. Helen will become a whore only when the Trojans return her to Menelaus and admit themselves that she is a whore, not worth dying for. How much is a jewel worth? A trader weighs it on scales. But a jewel can be worth something else; worth the price of passion it has aroused; the price it has in the eyes of the person who wears it; the price given to it.

Hector knows all about Helen, and almost all about war. He knows that according to the law of nature and the law of the land Helen ought to be returned to the Greeks; that it would be common sense to give her back. But he knows also that to give Helen back would mean a loss of face, an admission that a jewel is weighed on scales and worth only as much as tradesmen give for it in gold; that traders and *nouveau-riche* ship-owners are right in thinking that everything, including love, loyalty and even honour, can be bought. The war has lasted seven years. People have died for Helen. To give Helen back would be to deprive those deaths of any meaning. Hector makes a deliberate choice. He is not a young enthusiast, like Troilus; or a crazy lover, like Paris. He knows that the Greeks are stronger and that Troy can be destroyed. He chooses against reason, and against himself. To him reason seems a tradesman's affair. Hector knows he must choose between the physical and moral destruction of Troy. Hector cannot give Helen back.

This dispute is not carried on in a void. *Troilus and Cressida* is from the outset a modern play, a sneering political pamphlet. Troy was Spain, the Greeks were the English. The war went on for a long time after the defeat of the Invincible Armada, and the end was not in sight. The Greeks are down-to-earth, heavy and brutal. They know that the war is being fought over a cuckold and a hussy, and they do not have to make themselves believe that they die for the sake of loyalty and honour. They are part of another, a new world. They are tradesmen. They know how to count. To them the war really makes no sense. The Trojans insist on their ridiculous absolutes and a medieval code of combat. They are anachronistic. But from this it does not follow that they do not know how to defend themselves; or that they must surrender. The war is pointless, but a pointless war, too, has to be won. This is a proof of Shakespeare's realism. Ulysses is a realist, a practical man, a rationalist. He even knows mathematics. In his great speech he refers to Euclid's axiom: 'That's done; – as near as the extremest ends of parallels.' (I, 3)

Ulysses the rationalist is also an ideologist, who constructs a system to suit his practice. He invokes the entire medieval cosmogony and theology. He speaks about the hierarchic principle which rules the universe, the sun and the planets, the stars and the earth. This heavenly hierarchy is paralleled on earth by a hierarchy of class and rank. Hierarchy is a law of nature; its violation is equal to the victory of force over law, anarchy over order. Not only feudal mystics try to find a purpose for this war, fought over a cuckold and a tart. Rationalists also defend the war. Here lies the bitter wisdom and the deep irony of *Troilus and Cressida*.

Hector has been idealized into a knight of the medieval crusades. Having noticed that Achilles' 'arms are out of use', he gives up the duel. Achilles has no such feudal scruples. He avails himself of the moment when Hector has laid aside his sword and taken off his helmet, and murders him, helped by his Myrmidons. Troy shall fall, as Hector has fallen. She is anachronistic with her illusions about honour and loyalty, in the new Renaissance world where power and money win. Hector is killed by the stupid, base and cowardly Achilles. No one and nothing can save the sense of this war.

War has been ridiculed. Love will be ridiculed too. Helen is a tart, Cressida will be sent to the Greek camp and will become a tart. The transfer of Cressida to the Greek camp is not only part of the action of the play; it is also a great metaphor.

Cressida is one of the most amazing Shakespearian characters, perhaps just as amazing as Hamlet. And, like Hamlet, she has many aspects and cannot be defined by a single formula.

This girl could have been eight, ten, or twelve years old when the war started. Maybe that is why war seems so normal and ordinary to her that she almost does not notice it and never talks about it. Cressida has not yet been touched, but she knows all about love, and about sleeping with men; or at any rate she thinks she knows. She is inwardly free, conscious and daring. She belongs to the Renaissance, but she is also a Stendhal type akin to Lamiel, and she is a teen-age girl of the mid-twentieth century. She is cynical, or rather would-be cynical. She has seen too much. She is bitter and ironic. She is passionate, afraid of her passion and ashamed to admit it. She is even more afraid of feelings. She distrusts herself. She is our contemporary because of this self-distrust, reserve, and need of self-analysis. She defends herself by irony.

In Shakespeare there never exists a character without a situation. Cressida is seventeen. Her own uncle procures her for Troilus and brings a lover to her bed. Cynical Cressida wants to be more cynical than her uncle; bitter Cressida scoffs at confidences; passionate Cressida is the first to provoke a kiss. And it is at this point that she loses all her self-confidence, becomes affectionate, blushing and shy; she is now her age again.

> I would be gone: –
> Where is my wit? I know not what I speak.   (III, 2)

This is one of Shakespeare's most profound love scenes. The Balcony scene in *Romeo and Juliet*, set all in one key, is just a bird's love song. Here we have everything. There is conscious cruelty in this meeting of Troilus and Cressida. They have been brought together by a procurer. His chuckle accompanies them on the first night of their love.

There is no place for love in this world. Love is poisoned

from the outset. These war-time lovers have been given just one
night. And even that night has been spoilt. It has been deprived
of all its poetry. It has been defiled. Cressida had not noticed the
war. The war reached her at the break of dawn, after her first
night with Troilus.

> Prithee, tarry; –
> You men will never tarry. –
> O foolish Cressid! – I might have still held off,
> And then you would have tarried.   (IV, 2)

Pandarus had procured Cressida like a parcel of goods. Now
like goods, she will be exchanged with the Greeks for a captured
Trojan general. She has to leave at once, the very morning after
her first night. Cressida is seventeen. An experience like this is
enough. Cressida will go to the Greeks. But it will be a different
Cressida. Until now she has known love only in imagination.
Now she has come to know it in reality. During one night. She
is violently awakened. She realizes that the world is too vile and
cruel for anything to be worth defending. Even on her way to
the Greek camp, Diomedes makes brutal advances to her. Then
she is kissed in turn by the generals and princes, old, great and
famous men: Nestor, Agamemnon, Ulysses. She has realized
that beauty arouses desire. She can still mock. But she already
knows she will become a tart. Only before that happens, she has
to destroy everything, so that not even memory remains. She is
consistent.

Before her departure for the Greek camp she exchanges with
Troilus a glove for a sleeve. Never mind these medieval props.
She could equally well have exchanged rings with Troilus.
Details are not important. What matters is the pledge of faith
itself. That very evening Diomedes will ask Cressida for
Troilus's sleeve. And Cressida will give it to him. She did not
have to give it. She could have become Diomedes's mistress
without doing so. And yet she could not. First she had to kill
everything in herself. Cressida went to bed with Diomedes, as
Lady Anne went to bed with Richard who had killed her
husband and father.

In this tragicomedy there are two great parts for clowns: the sweet clown Pandarus in Troy, and the bitter clown Thersites in the Greek camp. Pandarus is a kind-hearted fool who wants to do his best for everybody, and make the bed for every couple. He lives as if the world were one great farce. But cruelty will reach him as well. The old procurer will weep. But his cry will evoke neither pity nor compassion.

Only the bitter fool, Thersites, is free from all illusions. This born misanthrope regards the world as a grim grotesque:

> Would I could meet that rogue Diomed! I would croak like a raven; I would bode, I would bode, Patroclus will give me anything for the intelligence of this whore: the parrot will not do more for an almond than he for a commodious drab. Lechery, lechery; still wars and lechery; nothing else holds fashion: a burning devil take them! (V, 2)

Let us imagine a different ending for *Othello*. He does not murder Desdemona. He knows she could have been unfaithful; he also knows he could murder her. He agrees with Iago: if Desdemona could be unfaithful, if he could believe in her infidelity, and if he could murder her, then the world is base and vile. Murder becomes unnecessary. It is enough to leave.

In tragedy the protagonists die, but the moral order is preserved. Their death confirms the existence of the absolute. In this amazing play Troilus neither dies himself, nor does he kill the unfaithful Cressida. There is no catharsis. Even the death of Hector is not fully tragic. Hero that he is, he pays for a noble gesture and dies surrounded by Myrmidons, stabbed by a boastful coward. There is irony in his death, too.

The grotesque is more cruel than tragedy. Thersites is right. But what of it? Thersites is vile himself.

'Macbeth', or Death-Infected

What bloody man is that?   (*Macbeth*, I, 2)

The Grand Mechanism of *Richard III* operates also in *Macbeth*, perhaps even more brutally. Having suppressed a rebellion, Macbeth is placed near the throne. He can become a king, so he must become a king. He kills the rightful sovereign. He then must kill the witnesses of the crime, and those who suspect it. He must kill the sons and friends of those he has killed. Later he must kill everybody, for everybody is against him:

> Send out moe horses, skirr the country round;
> Hang those that talk of fear. – Give me mine armour.   (V, 3)

In the end he will be killed himself. He has trod the whole way up and down the grand staircase of history.

The plot of *Macbeth* does not differ from those of the Histories. But plot summaries are deceptive. Unlike in Shakespeare's historical plays, history in *Macbeth* is not shown as the Grand Mechanism. It is shown as a nightmare. Mechanism and nightmare are just different metaphors to depict the same struggle for power and the crown. But the differing metaphors reflect a difference of approach; and even more than that: different philosophies. History, shown as a mechanism, fascinates by its very terror and inevitability. Whereas nightmare paralyses and terrifies. In *Macbeth* history, as well as crime, has been shown through personal experience. It is a matter of decision, choice and compulsion. Crime is committed on personal responsibility and has to be executed with one's own hands. Macbeth murders Duncan himself.

History in *Macbeth* is confused the way nightmares are; and, as in a nightmare, everyone is enveloped by it. Once the mechanism has been put in motion, one is apt to be crushed by it. One wades through the nightmare, which gradually rises up to one's throat.

Says Macbeth:

> I am in blood
> Stepp'd in so far, that, should I wade no more,
> Returning were as tedious as go o'er. (III, 4)

History in *Macbeth* is sticky and thick like a brew or blood. After a prologue with the three witches, the action proper begins with Duncan's words:

> What bloody man is that? (I, 2)

Everyone in this play is steeped in blood; victims as well as murderers. The whole world is stained with blood. Says Duncan's son, Donalbain:

> There's daggers in men's smiles: the near in blood,
> The nearer bloody. (II, 3)

Blood in *Macbeth* is not just a metaphor; it is real blood flowing out of murdered bodies. It leaves its stains on hands and faces, on daggers and swords.

Says Lady Macbeth:

> A little water clears us of this deed:
> How easy is it, then! (II, 2)

But this blood cannot be washed off hands, faces, or daggers. *Macbeth* begins and ends with slaughter. There is more and more blood, everyone walks in it; it floods the stage. A production of *Macbeth* not evoking a picture of the world flooded with blood would inevitably be false. There is something abstract about the Grand Mechanism. Richard's cruelties mean death sentences. Most of them are executed off stage. In *Macbeth*, death, crime, murder are concrete. So is history in this play: it is concrete, palpable, physical and suffocating; it means the death-rattle, the raising of the sword, the thrust of the dagger. *Macbeth* has been called a tragedy of ambition, and a tragedy of terror. This is not true. There is only one theme in *Macbeth*: murder.

History has been reduced to its simplest form, to one image and one division: those who kill and those who are killed.

Ambition means in this play the intention and planning of murder. Terror means memory of murders that have been committed, and fear of new crimes that are inevitable. The great and true murder, with which history begins, is the murder of a king. Then one just has to kill; until the killer is himself killed. The new king will be the man who has killed a king. This is the pattern of *Richard III* and other 'royal dramas', as well as of *Macbeth*. The huge steam-roller of history has been put in motion and crushes everybody in turn. In *Macbeth*, however, this murder-cycle does not possess the logic of a mechanism, but reminds one rather of a frighteningly growing nightmare.

> *Macbeth*. What is the night?
> *Lady Macbeth*. Almost at odds with morning, which is which.
>   (III, 4)

Most scenes take place at night; at all hours of the night, in fact: there is late night, midnight, and the small hours of the dawn. Night is ever-present, invoked and recalled obtrusively; by metaphors: 'O, never shall sun that morrow see!' (I, 5); by means of action: servants carry torches, light them and put them out; by sudden prosaic statements of fact:

> Get on your nightgown   (II, 2.)

It is a night from which sleep has been banished. In no other Shakespearian tragedy is there so much talk about sleep. Macbeth has murdered sleep, and cannot sleep any more. In all Scotland no one can sleep. There is no sleep, just nightmares.

> . . . when in swinish sleep
> Their drenched natures lie as in a death . . .   (I, 7)

Not only do Macbeth and Lady Macbeth struggle with this uneasy sleep, which does not bring forgetfulness, but with daytime thoughts of crime. It is the same sort of nightmare that torments Banquo.

> A heavy summons lies like lead upon me,
> And yet I would not sleep: merciful powers,
> Restrain in me the cursed thoughts that nature
> Gives way to in repose!   (II, 1)

Both sleep and food have been poisoned. In Macbeth's world – the most obsessive of all worlds created by Shakespeare – murder, thoughts of murder and fear of murder pervade everything. In this tragedy there are only two great parts, but the third *dramatis persona* is the world. We remember the faces of Macbeth and Lady Macbeth more readily, because we see more of them than of the others. But all faces have the same grimace, expressing the same kind of fear. All bodies are just as tormented. Macbeth's world is tight, and there is no escape. Even nature in it is nightmarishly impenetrable and close, consisting of mud and phantoms.

> *Banquo.* The earth hath bubbles, as the water has,
> . . . whither are they vanished?
> *Macbeth.* Into the air; and what seem'd corporal melted
> As breath into the wind.   (I, 3)

Witches in *Macbeth* are part of the landscape and are formed of the same matter as the world. They squeak at crossroads and incite to murder. The earth shivers as if in a fever, a falcon has been pecked to death in flight by an owl, horses break out of enclosures in a mad rush, fighting and biting one another. In the world of *Macbeth* there is no margin left for love, or friendship; not even for desire. Or rather, lust, too, has been poisoned with the thought of murder. There are many dark issues between Macbeth and Lady Macbeth. Each great Shakespearian character has many aspects, and lends himself, or herself, to more than one interpretation. In this particular union, in which there are no children, or they have died, Lady Macbeth plays a man's part. She demands murder from Macbeth as a confirmation of his manhood, almost as an act of love. In all Lady Macbeth's speeches there returns the same obsessive theme:

>   From this time
>   Such I account thy love.
>
>   .   .   .   .
>
>   When you durst do it, then you were a man.   (I, 7)

These two are sexually obsessed with each other, and yet have
suffered a great erotic defeat. But this is not the most important
factor in the interpretation of the tragedy, although it may be
decisive for the interpretation of their parts by the two principal
actors.

There is no tragedy without awareness. Richard III is aware
of the Grand Mechanism. Macbeth is aware of the nightmare.
In the world upon which murder is being imposed as fate, compulsion and inner necessity, there is only one dream: of a
murder that will break the murder cycle, will be the way out of
nightmare, and will mean liberation. For the thought of
murder that has to be committed, murder one cannot escape
from, is even worse than murder itself.

Says Macbeth:

>   If it were done – when 'tis done – then 'twere well
>   It were done quickly: if th' assassination
>   Could trammel up the consequence . . .
>   . . . that but this blow
>   Might be the be-all and the end-all here,
>   But here upon this bank and shoal of time,
>   We'ld jump the life to come.   (I, 7)

The terrorist Chen in Malraux's *La Condition Humaine* utters one
of the most terrifying sentences written in the mid-twentieth
century: 'A man who has never killed is a virgin.' This sentence
means that killing is cognition, just as, according to the Old
Testament, the sexual act is cognition; it also means that the
experience of killing cannot be communicated, just as the experience of the sexual act cannot be conveyed. But this sentence
means also that the act of killing changes the person who has
performed it; from then on he is a different man living in a
different world.

Says Macbeth after his first murder:

>   ... from this instant,
> There's nothing serious in mortality:
> All is but toys: renown and grace is dead;
> The wine of life is drawn ...   (II, 3)

Macbeth has killed in order to put himself on a level with the world in which murder potentially and actually exists. Macbeth has killed not only to become king, but to reassert himself. He has chosen between Macbeth, who is afraid to kill, and Macbeth, who has killed. But Macbeth, who has killed, is a new Macbeth. He not only knows that one can kill, but that one must kill.

> *Edmund.* .... know thou this, that men
> Are as the time is: to be tender-minded
> Does not become a sword ...
>
> . . . .
>
> *Officer.* I cannot draw a cart, nor eat dried oats;
> If it be man's work, I'll do't.   (V, 3)

The above fragment is taken from *King Lear*. Edmund orders assassins to hang Cordelia in prison. Murder is man's work. What can a man do? This Nietzschean question has been put for the first time in *Macbeth*.

> *Lady Macbeth.* Art thou afeard
> To be the same in thine own act and valour
> As thou art in desire?
>
> . . . .
>
> *Macbeth.* Prithee, peace:
> I dare do all that may become a man;
> Who dares do more is none.
> *Lady Macbeth.* What beast was't, then,
> That made you break this enterprise to me?   (I, 7)

This dialogue takes place before the murder of Duncan. After the murder Macbeth will know the answer. Not only can a man kill; a man is he who kills, and only he. Just as the animal which barks and fawns is a dog. Macbeth calls the assassins and orders them to kill Banquo and his son.

> *First Murderer.* We are men, my liege.

Macbeth. Ay, in the catalogue ye go for men;
    As hounds, and greyhounds, mongrels, spaniels, curs,
    Shoughs, water-rugs, and demi-wolves, are clept
    All by the name of dogs . . .

. . . .

Second Murderer. We shall, my lord,
    Perform what you command us.   (III, 1)

This for Macbeth is one end of experience. It can be called the 'Auschwitz experience'. A threshold has been reached past which everything is easy: '. . . all is but toys.' But this is only part of the truth about Macbeth. Macbeth has killed the King, because he could not accept a Macbeth who would be afraid to kill a king. But Macbeth, who has killed, cannot accept the Macbeth who has killed. Macbeth has killed in order to get rid of a nightmare. But it is the necessity of murder that makes the nightmare. A nightmare is terrifying just because it has no end. 'The night is long that never finds the day.' (IV, 3.) The night enveloping Macbeth is deeper and deeper. Macbeth has murdered for fear, and goes on murdering for fear. This is another part of the truth about Macbeth, but it is still not the whole truth.

In its psychology, *Macbeth* is, perhaps, the deepest of Shakespeare's tragedies. But Macbeth himself is not a character, at least not in the sense of what was meant by a character in the nineteenth century. Lady Macbeth is such a character. Everything in her, except craving for power, has been burnt out. She is empty, and goes on burning. She is taking her revenge for her failure as lover and mother. Lady Macbeth has no imagination; and for that reason she accepts herself from the outset, and later cannot escape from herself. Macbeth does have imagination, and from the moment of the first murder he asks himself the same sort of questions that Richard III has asked himself:

            To be thus is nothing;
      But to be safely thus.   (III, 1)

From the first scenes onwards Macbeth defines himself by negation. To himself he is not the one who is, but rather the one

who is not. He is immersed in the world as if in nothingness;
he exists only potentially. Macbeth chooses himself, but after
every act of choice he finds himself more terrifying, and more
of a stranger. '. . . . all that is within him does condemn itself for
being there'. (V, 2.) The formulas by which Macbeth tries to
define himself are amazingly similar to the language of the
existentialists. 'To be' has for Macbeth an ambiguous, or at
least a double, meaning; it is a constant exasperating contradiction between existence and essence, between being 'for itself'
and being 'in itself'.

He says:

> . . . and nothing is
> But what is not.   (I, 3)

In a bad dream we are, and are not, ourselves, at the same
time. We cannot accept ourselves, for to accept oneself would
mean accepting nightmare for reality, to admit that there is
nothing but nightmare, that night is not followed by day.

Says Macbeth after the murder of Duncan: 'To know my
deed, 'twere best not know myself.' (II, 2.) Macbeth recognizes
that his existence is apparent rather than real, because he does
not want to admit that the world he lives in is irrevocable. This
world is to him a nightmare. For Richard 'to be' means to capture the crown and murder all pretenders. For Macbeth 'to be'
means – to escape, to live in another world, where:

> Rebellion's head, rise never . . .
> . . . and our high-plac'd Macbeth
> Shall live the lease of nature, pay his breath
> To time and mortal custom.   (IV, 1)

The plot and the order of history, in Shakespeare's Histories
and in *Macbeth*, do not differ from each other. But Richard
accepts the order of history and his part in it. Macbeth dreams
about a world where there will be no more murders, and all
murders will have been forgotten; where the dead will have
been buried in the ground once and for all, and everything will
begin anew. Macbeth dreams of the end of nightmare, while
sinking in it more and more. He dreams of a world without

crime, while becoming enmeshed in crime more and more deeply. Macbeth's last hope is that the dead will not rise:

> *Lady Macbeth.* But in them nature's copy's not eterne.
> *Macbeth.* There's comfort yet; they are assailable;
>   Then be thou jocund.   (III, 2)

But the dead do rise. The appearance at the banquet of murdered Banquo's ghost is one of the most remarkable scenes in *Macbeth*. Banquo's ghost is visible to Macbeth alone. Commentators see in this scene an embodiment of Macbeth's fear and terror. There is no ghost; it is a delusion. But Shakespeare's *Macbeth* is not a psychological drama of the second half of the nineteenth century. Macbeth has dreamed of a final murder to end all murders. Now he knows: there is no such murder. This is the third and last of Macbeth's experiences. The dead do return. 'The sequence of time is an illusion . . . We fear most the past that returns.' This aphorism by S. J. Lec has something of the atmosphere of *Macbeth*:

> If charnel-houses and our graves must send
> Those that we bury back, our monuments
> Shall be the maws of kites.   (III, 4)

Macbeth, the multiple murderer, steeped in blood, could not accept the world in which murder existed. In this, perhaps, consists the gloomy greatness of this character, and the true tragedy of Macbeth's history. For a long time Macbeth did not want to accept the reality and irrevocability of nightmare, and could not reconcile himself to his part, as if it were somebody else's. Now he knows everything. He knows that there is no escape from nightmare, which is the human fate and condition, or – in more modern language – the human situation. There is no other.

> They have tied me to a stake; I cannot fly,
> But, bear-like, I must fight the course.   (V, 7)

Before his first crime, which was the murder of Duncan, Macbeth had believed that death could come too early, or too late. 'Had I but died an hour before this chance, I had liv'd a blessed time.' (II, 3.) Now Macbeth knows that death does not change anything, that it cannot change anything, that it is just as absurd as life. No more, no less. For the first time Macbeth is not afraid. 'I have almost forgot the taste of fears.' (V, 5.)

There is nothing to be afraid of any more. He can accept himself at last, because he has realized that every choice is absurd, or rather – that there is no choice.

> Out, out, brief candle!
> Life's but a walking shadow; a poor player,
> That struts and frets his hour upon the stage,
> And then is heard no more: it is a tale
> Told by an idiot, full of sound and fury,
> Signifying nothing. (V, 5)

In the opening scenes of the tragedy there is talk about the thane of Cawdor, who had betrayed Duncan and become an ally of the King of Norway. After the suppression of the rebellion he was captured and condemned to death.

> . . . nothing in his life
> Became him like the leaving it; he died
> As one that had been studied in his death,
> To throw away the dearest thing he owed,
> As 'twere a careless trifle. (I, 4)

The thane of Cawdor does not appear in *Macbeth*. All we know of him is that he has been guilty of treason and executed. Why is his death described so emphatically and in such detail? Why did Shakespeare find it necessary? After all, his expositions are never wrong. Cawdor's death, which opens the play, is necessary. It will be compared to Macbeth's death. There is something Senecan and stoic about Cawdor's cold indifference to death. Faced with utter defeat Cawdor saves what can still be saved: a noble attitude and dignity. For Macbeth attitudes are of no importance; he does not believe in human dignity any more. Macbeth has reached the limits of human experience. All he has left is contempt. The very concept of man has crumbled to pieces, and there is nothing left. The end of *Macbeth*, like the endings of *Troilus and Cressida*, or *King Lear*, produces no *catharsis*. Suicide is either a protest, or an admission of guilt.

Macbeth does not feel guilty, and there is nothing for him to protest about. All he can do before he dies is to drag with him into nothingness as many living beings as possible. This is the last consequence of the world's absurdity. Macbeth is unable to blow the world up. But he can go on murdering till the end.

> Why should I play the Roman fool, and die
> On my own sword? whiles I see lives, the gashes
> Do better upon them.   (V, 8)

The Two Paradoxes of 'Othello'

Iago. He, in good time, must his lieutenant be,
    And I, God bless the mark, his worship's ancient.
Roderigo. By heaven I rather would have been his hangman. (I, 1)
Gratiano. Torments will ope your lips. (V, 2)
Othello. That's he that was Othello; here I am. (V, 2)

I

There is much in *Othello* that we find revolting. Those elements
in particular that until recently were most highly valued. 'Not
his greatest work, but his best play', writes the commentator
and latest editor of *Othello*, and adds: 'in the narrow sense of
'theatre' probably much his best'.[1] Perhaps, but for what kind
of theatre?

Thomas Rymer, whose taste was classical, in the French
sense of the word, wrote towards the close of the seventeenth
century:

> The moral, sure, of this Fable is very instructive. First, This may
> be a caution to all Maidens of Quality, how, without their
> Parents' consent they run away with Blackamoors. Secondly, This
> may be a warning to all good Wives that they may look well to
> their Linnen. Thirdly, This may be a lesson to Husbands, that
> before their Jealousie be Tragical, the proofs may be Mathe-
> matical. . . . But the tragical part is, plainly none other, than a
> Bloody Farce, without salt or savour.[2]

Ducis, whose adaptation of *Othello* was produced in Paris in
1792, must have taken a similar view of the tragedy. It was the
first year of the Republic, but Ducis thought that Shakespeare,
in spite of the Revolution, was still too violent and cruel for the
French taste. In contrast with the English tradition, he substi-

[1] *Othello*, ed. by M. R. Ridley. *The Arden Shakespeare*, London, 1958.

[2] Thomas Rymer, 'Short View of Tragedy', in *Critical Works of Thomas Rymer*, ed. by Curt A. Zimansky, New Haven, London, 1956, pp. 132, 164.

tuted an Arab for a Negro. His Othello had a yellow complexion, in order – as he put it – not to frighten the eyes of women. Desdemona did not lose her handkerchief, for a handkerchief was part of ladies' lingerie and even the very word could not possibly be uttered from the stage. Desdemonas of the *Convention nationale* were allowed only to lose their diadems. Othello did not strangle Desdemona; that would be too vulgar. Ducis substituted the dagger for the pillow. But there was still the ending to deal with: revolutionary audiences did not fancy bloody scenes. At the point when Othello raised his arm to deal Desdemona a mortal blow, the Venetian envoy rushed into the bedchamber, shouting: '*Barbare, que fais-tu?*' Ducis provided two endings for the play, one happy, the other unhappy.

Othello was produced again in France in 1829 in Alfred de Vigny's translation. The *Moor of Venice* paved the way for *Hernani*. From then on *Othello* turned out to be the most 'nineteenth-century play' of Shakespeare. Not only was it the most romantic of the plays; *Othello* fitted all the nineteenth-century theatres: it was the best-made play, an opera, a melodrama. *Othello* had local colour, exhibited great characters and passions, and was a historical, psychological, realistic play. It was indeed 'Shakespeare's best stage play'.

In his *Diary of a Journey in England*, Karol Sienkiewicz made the following entry, dated 28th August, 1820:

I went to the theatre to see *Othello*. It is one of Shakespeare's finest tragedies, and Kean is at his best in it. . . . In the fifth act there is a terrible scene. The curtain rises on the second scene and in the background is a bed and on it Desdemona asleep, everything in the proper order: she wears a nightcap and lies covered with a quilt. There is a curtain over the bed and beside it a little stool, a night table; they even said that a chamber pot could be seen under the bed. Othello enters holding a lamp; he puts it down on the dressing-table. Desdemona is still asleep. Othello also holds a naked sword. He comes to kill Desdemona, having endured heavy torments of jealousy . . .

A tragedy of jealousy fitted perfectly into the framework of English domestic drama where, according to a tradition inherited from the eighteenth century, the middle-class Desdemona wore a nightcap; but it was also in keeping with romantic melodrama in which the protagonist used to be presented in turn as a primitive and passionate Negro, or as a noble and dignified descendant of Arab kings. *Othello*, thus conceived, was a ready-made 'oriental' opera, waiting for its composer. Verdi wrote it in 1887, and it is surely not by chance that *Othello* is perhaps the only really successful opera among those adapted from Shakespeare's plays.

As a matter of fact, there was not much difference in those days between an operatic and a dramatic production of *Othello*. In the second act of the opera a chorus of Cypriots sang in honour of Desdemona; Act Three ended with a finale in which the whole ensemble, ballet included, took part. Of all Shakespeare's plays, *Othello* was the most suited for a grand and magnificent display: the opera, combined with ballet, about a jealous man of the Orient, gradually turned into an historical spectacle, in which Venice was represented 'like the real thing'.

These tendencies found their fullest expression in the Russian theatre. The tragedy of jealousy became there a tragedy of betrayed confidence, in which Othello fell victim not only to Iago's intrigues, but to the envy of the Doge and the entire Venetian senate. For this purpose one had to represent Venice and Cyprus. The social and historical background became more important than the protagonists of the tragedy. Stanislavsky produced *Othello* for the first time as a young man, but it is his project for the *mis en scène* sent in 1930 from Nice to the Moscow Art Theatre that has been remembered in theatre history. This project was also published.[1]

Stanislavsky turned the orchestra pit into a canal for gondolas. In the first scene they appeared twice: Roderigo and Iago arrived in a gondola; then Brabantio with members of his household set out in a gondola in search of Othello. Stanislavsky advised that the gondolier's oar should be made of metal and its paddle end filled with water, so that when raised

---

[1] It was published in an English translation as *Stanislavsky Rehearses Othello* in 1948.

it could give a characteristic splash. In Act Two he introduced silent figures of Turkish Cypriots, who waited anxiously for the arrival of ships and then dispersed in panic on realizing that it was the Venetian fleet that was coming. In commentaries designed for actors he described in detail Roderigo's unsuccessful courtship of Desdemona and her meetings with Othello, on Sunday mornings, when she was returning from church in her gondola. He even knew what flowers Othello threw into her gondola and how Roderigo's unsuccessful serenade in front of Desdemona's house ended. In fact, he knew everything about Desdemona and Othello, from their births to the moment the tragedy began.

Then, after the opera we had the novel: Verdi's *Othello* was followed by Dumas' *Othello*. However, it was *Othello* seen as a novel that suddenly revealed how arbitrary, vague and contradictory the story was. Shakespearian scholars had known this for a long time. Granville-Barker and Stoll had observed the parallel running of Shakespeare's double time in this particular play. Only for Othello does the night of jealousy last from midnight to dawn. Iago, Roderigo and Desdemona need weeks for the action to be accomplished. Weeks are required for Desdemona to have the physical possibility of infidelity, or for a ship to reach Venice from Cyprus with news of victory and arrive back in Cyprus with the appointment of a new governor.

Stanislavsky brought to its final conclusion the tendency prevalent in all European theatres since the nineties, towards the realistic representation of Shakespeare in historical 'authentic' costume. The theatre of yesterday always repeats interpretations dating from the day before yesterday. The tragedy of jealousy and the tragedy of betrayed confidence, the operatic *Othello* and the *Othello* out of an historical romance, still exert their influence on us today.

II

In what setting does Othello's tragedy unfold itself? The question sounds absurd. The first act takes place in Venice, the remaining four in Cyprus. Venice and Cyprus had already been depicted by means of an open change; later it seemed that the revolving stage would solve every difficulty. Each scene could now have a new set. In the English theatres of the early nineteenth century *Othello* was mostly set in contemporary middle-class interiors. Only later did it gradually become an historical costume play. The naturalistic theatre even managed to reproduce St Mark's Square on the stage in its entirety. *Othello* has been identified with nineteenth-century stage design to such an extent that of all Shakespeare's plays it is the most difficult to visualize on a bare stage. However, Venice and Cyprus in *Othello* are no more real than cities and countries in all the other tragedies and comedies of Shakespeare. Cyprus and Venice are no less and no more real than Elsinore, Bohemia, Illyria, the forest of Dunsinane, or the cliffs of Dover from which blind Gloster wanted to hurl himself into the abyss.

> Excellent wretch, perdition catch my soul,
> But I do love thee, and when I love thee not,
> Chaos is come again.   (III, 3)

The action of *Othello*, like that of all the other great tragedies of Shakespeare, really takes place only on the Elizabethan stage which is also the *Theatrum Mundi*. On that stage, as in *Hamlet* and in *King Lear*, the world is unhinged, chaos returns and the very order of Nature is threatened.

> If she be false, O, then heaven mocks itself,
> I'll not believe it.   (III, 3)

> On horror's head horrors accumulate:
> Do deeds to make heaven weep, all earth amaz'd.   (III, 3)

Even the firmament is shaken, the balance of the heavenly spheres disturbed, as if madness descended on people from the stars:

> It is the very error of the moon,
> She comes more near the earth than she was wont,
> And makes men mad.   (V, 2)

And then, Desdemona having been murdered, apocalyptic night falls on Othello's world:

> Methinks it should be now a huge eclipse
> Of sun and moon, and that the affrighted globe
> Should yawn at alteration. (V. 2)

A simultaneous eclipse of the sun and the moon is a vision of the end of the world found in Baroque painting. Night falls on Othello. Not only a night without sun and moon. As in *King Lear* and *Macbeth*, the sky is empty.

> Are there no stones in heaven
> But what serves for the thunder? (V, 2)

Othello, like *King Lear* and *Macbeth*, is the tragedy of man under an empty heaven. At the close of the play Iago is exposed to torture. But it is really Othello who, from Act Two onwards, is put on the rack. He steps downwards, like Lear, Macbeth, or Gloster; and like them is brought to the ultimate point. He exhausts fully one of the human experiences. As in *King Lear* and *Macbeth*, in *Othello* the plummet has gone down to the bottom, darkness has been fully sounded. Fundamental questions about the meaning, or meaninglessness, of the world can only be answered at the end of the road, at the lowest depths.

Wilson Knight was the first to reveal the music of *Othello*.[1] But he denied *Othello* universality. In comparison with *King Lear* and *Macbeth*, *Othello* is to him a play that does not achieve the power of symbol and remains completely literal. For Mr Knight *Othello* is not a cosmic tragedy. I prefer the view of Victor Hugo, in spite of his unbearable romantic rhetoric:

Now what is Othello? He is night. An immense fatal figure. Night is amorous of day. Darkness loves the dawn. The African adores the white woman. Desdemona is Othello's brightness and frenzy! And then how easy to him is jealousy! He is great, he is dignified, he is majestic, he soars above all heads, he has as an escort bravery, battle, the braying of trumpets, the banner of war, renown, glory; he is radiant with twenty victories, he is studded with stars, this Othello: but he is black. And thus how soon, when jealous, the hero becomes a monster, the black becomes the Negro! How speedily has night beckoned to death![2]

[1] G. Wilson Knight, 'The Othello Music', in *The Wheel of Fire*, London, 1959.
[2] Victor Hugo, *William Shakespeare*, trans., by A. Baillot, London, 1864, p. 208.

The above fragment is not devoid of a genuine theatrical vision; it almost seems to fit Sir Laurence Olivier's latest interpretation of the part of Othello.

> Iago near Othello is the precipice near the landslip. 'This way!' he says in a low voice. The snare advises blindness. The being of darkness guides the black. Deceit takes upon itself to give what light may be required by night. Jealousy uses falsehood as the blind man his dog. Iago the traitor, opposed to whiteness and candour, Othello the Negro, what can be more terrible. These ferocities of the darkness act in unison. These two incarnations of the eclipse comprise together, the one roaring, the other sneering, the tragic suffocation of light. Sound this profound thing. Othello is the night, and being night, and wishing to kill, what does he take to slay with? Poison? the club? the axe? the knife? No, the pillow. To kill is to lull to sleep. Shakespeare himself perhaps did not take this into account. The creator sometimes, almost unknown to himself, yields to his type, so much is that type a power. And it is thus that Desdemona, spouse of the man Night, dies stifled by the pillow, which has had the first kiss, and which has the last sight.[1]

Olivier's Othello enters the stage with the step of a dancer, holding a rose in his mouth. Olivier's Othello stifles Desdemona among kisses.

III

Iago has always caused more difficulties to commentators than any other Shakesperian character. For the romantics he was simply the genius of evil. But even Mephistopheles must have his own reasons for what he does. Especially in the theatre. Iago hates Othello, just as he hates everybody. Commentators observed long ago that there is something disinterested in his hate. Iago hates first, and only then seems to invent reasons for his hate. Coleridge's description hits the nail on the head: 'the motive-hunting of a motiveless malignity.' Thwarted ambition, jealousy of his wife, of Desdemona, of all women and all men: his hate constantly looks for nourishment to feed itself on and

[1] *Op. cit.* pp. 208–9.

D

is never satisfied. But if hate looks for reasons to justify itself,
what are the arguments it uses?

There are two other excellent descriptions of Iago. Carlyle
called him 'an inarticulate poet', Hazlitt 'an amateur of tragedy
in real life'. Iago is not satisfied with devising the tragedy; he
wants to play it through, distributes parts all round, and takes
part in it himself.

Iago is a diabolical stage manager, or rather – a machiavellian stage manager. His motives for acting are ambiguous
and hidden, his intellectual reasons clear and precise. He formu-
lates them in the early scenes when, for instance, he soliloquizes:
'Our bodies are gardens, to the which our wills are gardeners.'
(I, 3.)

The demonic Iago was an invention of the romantics. Iago is
no demon. Like Richard III, he is a contemporary careerist, but
on a different scale. He, too, wants to set in motion a real
mechanism, make use of genuine passions. He does not want to
be cheated. 'We cannot all be masters, nor all masters Cannot be
truly follow'd.' (I, 1.) This is not a demonic statement, but rather
one which is obvious to the point of vulgarity. 'Preferment
goes by letter and affection.' (I, 1.) This is not a demonic statement either. Iago is an empiricist, he does not believe in ideo-
logies and has no illusions: 'Reputation is an idle and most false
imposition, oft got without merit, and lost without deserving.'
(II, 3.)

Of course, Iago is a machiavellian, but machiavellism
merely means for him a generalized personal experience. Fools
believe in honour and love. In reality there is only egoism and
lust. The strong are able to subordinate their passions to ambition. One's own body can also be an instrument. Hence
Iago's contempt for everything that benumbs a man, from
moral precepts to love.

> I never found a man that knew how to love himself: ere I would
> say I would drown myself, for the love of a guinea-hen, I would
> change my humanity with a baboon.   (I, 3)

Iago believes in will-power. One can make everything of oneself, and of other people. Others, too, are only an instrument. They can be moulded like clay. Iago, like Richard III, despises people even more than he hates them.

Says Iago: The world consists of villains and fools; of those who devour and those who are devoured. People are like animals; they copulate and eat each other. The weak do not deserve pity, they are just as abominable, only more stupid than the strong. The world is vile.

Says Othello: The world is beautiful and people are noble. There exist in it love and loyalty.

— If we strip *Othello* of romantic varnish, of everything that is opera and melodrama, the tragedy of jealousy and the tragedy of betrayed confidence become a dispute between Othello and Iago; a dispute on the nature of the world. Is this world good or bad? What are the limits of suffering, what is the ultimate purpose of the few brief moments that pass between birth and death?

Like Richard III, Iago sets in motion the mechanism of vileness, envy and stupidity, and like him, he will be destroyed. The world, in which Othello can believe in Desdemona's infidelity, in which treachery is possible, in which Othello murders Desdemona, in which there is no friendship, loyalty, or faith, in which Othello – by agreeing to the murder of Cassio – has consented to a secret assassination, such a world is bad. Iago is an accomplished stage manager.

> Thou has set me on the rack. (III, 3)

He has proved that the world consists of fools and villains. He has destroyed all around him, and himself. He goes to be tortured in a tragedy devised by himself. He has proved that neither the world nor himself deserves any pity. Richard's defeat confirms the working of the Grand Mechanism; just as Iago's failure does. The world is vile. He was right. And the very fact that he was right proved his undoing. This is the first paradox.

IV

In the last scene Iago is silent. Why should he talk? Everything has become clear. The world has fallen, but for Othello, not for him. They will crush his bones, but he can triumph. The torture and death of Iago do not restore justice; they do not serve any purpose, and happen outside the play, as it were, even in the literal sense. But Iago wins not only on the intellectual plane of the tragedy; he wins in its very fabric and texture, in its language.

In Act Three Othello crawls up to Iago's feet, foaming at the mouth in a fit. Shakespeare is never afraid of cruelty. Gloster has his eyes torn out, Lear goes mad. The magnificent, proud, beautiful Othello has to degrade himself, physically. Othello's world, he himself, everything will dissolve, as if eaten away by acid. (This is how Wilson Knight has described it.)

> O now for ever
> Farewell the tranquil mind, farewell content:
> Farewell the plumed troop, and the big wars,
> That makes ambition virtue: O farewell,
> Farewell the neighing steed, and the shrill trump,
> The spirit-stirring drum, the ear-piercing fife;
> The royal banner, and all quality,
> Pride, pomp, and circumstance of glorious war!
> And, O ye mortal engines, whose wide throats
> The immortal Jove's great clamour counterfeit;
> Farewell, Othello's occupation's gone!   (III, 3)

Othello is endowed by Shakespeare with all the attributes of feudal heroics found in knightly epic and romance. There is enchanting poetry here, but at the same time a decaying set of values. To start with, there is royal blood:

> I fetch my life and being
> From men of royal siege.   (I, 2)

Next, there are the heroic stereotypes, inherited from Roman rhetoric:

> The tyrant custom, most grave senators,
> Hath made the flinty and steel couch of war
> My thrice-driven bed of down.   (I, 3)

And then, there are the elements of fairy tale, dream, legend. Iago is all reality, everyday life, pure matter. Othello belongs to a different world, the world of the exotic that ranges from the adventures of Ulysses to the expeditions of Renaissance sailors. He talks to Desdemona:

> ... of the Cannibals, that each other eat,
> The Anthropophagi, and men whose heads
> Do grow beneath their shoulders ...   (I, 3)

With Othello, the bare Elizabethan stage has been filled with the seascape of all the oceans.

>   Like to the Pontic sea,
> Whose icy current, and compulsive course,
> Ne'er feels retiring ebb, but keeps due on
> To the Propontic, and the Hellespont:
> Even so my bloody thoughts, with violent pace
> Shall ne'er look back, ne'er ebb to humble love,
> Till that a capable and wide revenge
> Swallow them up.   (III, 3)

The system of values in *Othello* disintegrates together with the play's poetry and language. But there is another language, another rhetoric in this tragedy. Iago uses it. In Iago's semantic sphere there stand out, as word-slogans, word-clues, evocative words – names of things and animals arousing abhorrence, fear, disgust. Iago talks about glues, baits, nets, poisons, drugs, enemas, pitch and sulphur, plague and pestilence.

> So will I turn her virtue into pitch,
> And out of her own goodness make the net
> That shall enmesh 'em all.   (II, 3)

Even more characteristic is the bestiary invoked by Iago. It contains helpless and powerless animals ('drown thyself? drown cats and blind puppies'. I, 3), symbols and allegories of stupidity and ugliness (guinea-hens, baboons), lust and lewdness ('as prime as goats, as hot as monkeys, As salt as wolves in pride'. III, 3.)

Othello's speech is gradually reduced to mumbling. The pathos and poetry of feudal heroics are destroyed in language and in imagery. This has already been observed by Mr Knight. Not only shall Othello crawl at Iago's feet; he shall talk his language. These broken sentences are at the same time one of the earliest interior monologues – in the modern sense of the word – that we find in drama.

> Lie with her, lie on her? – We say lie on her, when they belie her, – lie with her, zounds, that's fulsome! Handkerchief – confessions – handkerchief! To confess, and be hanged for his labour. First, to be hanged, and then to confess; I tremble at it. Nature would not invest herself in such shadowing passion without some instruction. It is not words that shake me thus. Pish! Noses, ears and lips. Is't possible? – Confess? – Handkerchief? – O devil!   (IV, 1)

Othello will now rave incessantly about whoring and breeding, fire and sulphur, cords, knives and poison. He will invoke the same bestiary. Iago spoke of jackdaws looking for prey; Othello will now be haunted by the image of 'the raven o'er the infected house'. (IV, 1.) He will take over from Iago all his obsessions, as if he were unable to break away from the images of monkeys and goats, mongrels and lewd bitches. 'Exchange me for a goat,' he says. (III, 3.) Even while he is ceremoniously receiving Lodovico, he cannot contain himself: 'You are welcome, sir, to Cyprus . . . Goats and monkeys.' (IV, 1.)

Caroline Spurgeon in her catalogue of Shakespearian images compared the bestiaries of *Othello* and *King Lear*. In both tragedies animals appear in the semantic sphere of suffering and cruelty; suffering that has to be endured, torments that have to be inflicted. In *King Lear* there are magnificent and fierce beasts of prey: tiger, vulture, boar; in *Othello* – reptiles and insects.[1] The action of the tragedy takes place in the course of two long nights, at least according to the clock of the passions. The internal landscape of *Othello*, in which the leading characters of the tragedy are more and more deeply submerged, the landscape of their dreams, erotic obsessions and fears, is the landscape of

[1] Caroline Spurgeon, *Shakespeare's Imagery*, Cambridge, 1935, pp. 335–6.

darkness; of the earth without sun, stars and moon; a dungeon full of spiders, blindworms and frogs.

> I had rather be a toad,
> And live upon the vapour in a dungeon. (III, 3)

And again:

> The fountain, from the which my current runs,
> Or else dries up, to be discarded thence,
> Or keep it as a cistern, for foul toads
> To knot and gender in! (IV, 2)

The difference between the animal sphere of *Othello* and *King Lear* is not only one of degree. The animal symbolism of *Othello* serves to degrade the human world. Man is an animal. But what sort of animal?

> *Man* – the description of man, in which are contained the kinds almost alike, such as baboon, ape and others which are many.

This is a note by Leonardo, very similar in intention and the choice of comparisons. Man can be described as an animal. A bloodthirsty and cowardly, deceitful and cruel animal. Man, considered as an animal, inevitably rouses revulsion.

> As little a web as this will ensnare as great a fly as Cassio. (II, 1)

This is the most significant image in the tragedy. Flies and spiders, spiders and flies. Cassio, Roderigo, Othello – all are flies for Iago. Small flies and big flies. The white Desdemona, too, will turn into a black fly. Othello will take over all Iago's obsessions.

> *Desdemona.* I hope my noble lord esteems me honest.
> *Othello.* O, ay, as summer's flies are in the shambles,
>   That quicken even with blowing. (IV, 2)

The image of flies returns in *King Lear*, in a sentence that contains one of man's ultimate experiences:

> As flies to wanton boys, are we to the gods;
> They kill us for their sport. (*Lear*, IV, 1)

To whom can a fly appeal? What can justify the suffering of a

fly? Does a fly deserve pity? Can a fly ask men for compassion?
Can men ask the gods for compassion?

> Thou, nature, art my goddess; to thy law
> My services are bound.   (*Lear*, I, 2)

These words are spoken by Edmund in *King Lear*. In the great
Shakespearian tragedies we are witness to an earthquake. Both
human orders have fallen; the feudal hierarchy of loyalty, as
well as the naturalism of the Renaissance. The world's history
is just that of spiders and flies.

> *Iago* (*Spider*). 'Tis in ourselves, that we are thus, or thus. (I, 3)
> *Iago* (*Spider*). Heaven is my judge, not I for love and duty,
>   But seeming so, for my peculiar end.   (I, 1)
> *Iago* (*Spider*). I follow him to serve my turn upon him.   (I, 1)
> *Othello* (*Fly*). My parts, my title, and my perfect soul,
>   Shall manifest me rightly.   (I, 2)
> *Desdemona* (*Fly*). Good night, good night: God me such usage send,
>   Not to pick bad from bad, but by bad mend!   (IV, 3)

Othello not only came to find himself in Iago's semantic sphere,
but in 'a close-shut murderous room' (Bradley). Othello, like
King Lear, is put to the torture and driven to madness.

> And let her rot, and perish, and be damned to-night, for she shall
> not live; no, my heart is turn'd to stone; I strike it, and it hurts my
> hand: O, the world has not a sweeter creature, she might lie by an
> emperor's side, and command him tasks. . . . Hang her, I do but
> say what she is: so delicate with her needle, an admirable musician.
> . . . I will chop her into messes.   (IV, 1)

Othello talks the language of the mad Lear. All kinds of
rhetoric have been smashed to pieces. And so have people.
Othello, like King Lear, like Macbeth in his last scene, has
found himself in the area of the absurd.

V

They talk about her even before she has appeared. They shout
that she has run away with a Negro. Her image is already being
shown in the sphere of animal eroticism:

> . . . an old black ram
> Is tupping your white ewe.   (I, 1)

The prologue of *Othello* is a brutal one. Iago and Roderigo want to anger Brabantio. This, however, does not explain the obstinacy with which animal comparisons are used. They are there by design. The union of Othello and Desdemona is presented from the very first moment as the mating of animals.

> . . . you'll have your daughter cover'd with a Barbary horse; you'll have your nephews neigh to you; you'll have coursers for cousins, and gennets for germans.   (I, 1)

Othello is black, Desdemona is white. Victor Hugo, in the fragment quoted above, wrote about the symbolism of black and white, of day and night. But Shakespeare had been more specific than the romantics; more material and carnal. Bodies in *Othello* are not only tormented; they also attract each other.

> . . . your daughter, and the Moor, are now making the beast with
> two backs.   (I, 1)

The image of the animal with two backs, one white, the other black, is one of the most brutal and, at the same time, most fascinating representations of the sexual act.[1] But there is in it also the atmosphere of modern eroticism, with its longing for pure physicality, its fascination with 'being different', its breaking of sexual taboo. That is why its area is so often black and white. Othello is fascinated by Desdemona but Desdemona is much more strongly fascinated by Othello.

> . . . and she, in spite of nature,
> Of years, of country, credit, everything,
> To fall in love with what she fear'd to look on?   (I, 3)

She has given up everything. She is in a hurry. She does not want a single empty night any more. She will follow Othello to Cyprus.

[1] I quote from Antonin Artaud; '. . . all true freedom is dark, and infallibly identified with sexual freedom which is also dark, although we do not know precisely why . . . And that is why all the great Myths are dark . . .' (Antonin Artaud, *The Theater and Its Double*, translated by Mary Richards, Grove Press, New York, 1958.)

That I did love the Moor, to live with him,
My downright violence, and scorn of fortunes,
May trumpet to the world.   (I, 3

In the days of Kean, Desdemona used to go to bed in a nightcap
Modern Desdemonas not infrequently still wear that Victorian
nightcap. Heine felt uneasy about Desdemona having mois
hands. He wrote that sometimes he felt sad at the thought tha
perhaps Iago was partially right. Heine interpreted Shakespear
with far greater pungency than Schlegel, Tieck and all the
other sentimental Germans. He compared *Othello* to *Titu
Andronicus*. 'In both the passion of a beautiful woman for ar
ugly Negro is represented with particular relish,' he wrote.[1]

Desdemona is two to four years older than Juliet; she coulc
be Ophelia's age. But she is much more of a woman than eithe
of them. Heine was right. Desdemona is obedient and stubborr
at the same time. She is obedient to the point where passior
begins. Of all Shakespeare's female characters she is the mos
sensuous. More silent than Juliet or Ophelia, she seem
absorbed in herself, and wakes only to the night.

Nature would not invest herself in such shadowing passion
without some instruction.   (IV 1

She does not even know that she disturbs and – promises by hei
very presence. Othello only later learns about it, but Iago knows
this from the outset. Desdemona is faithful, but must have
something of the slut in her. Not *in actu* but *in potentia*. Otherwise the drama could not work, because Othello would be ridiculous. Othello must not be ridiculous. Desdemona is sexually
obsessed with Othello, but all men – Iago, Cassio, Roderigo – are
obsessed with Desdemona. They remain in her erotic climate.

The wine she drinks is made of grapes; if she had been blest, she
would never have lov'd the Moor. Didst thou not see her paddle
with the palm of his hand? . . . They met so near with their lips
that their breaths embrac'd together.   (II, 1

In Othello's relation to Desdemona a violent change now

[1] Heinrich Heine, *Shakespeares Mädchen und Frauen mit Erläuterungen*, Leipzig
1839.

occurs; a change that cannot be explained fully by Iago's intrigues. It is as if Othello were suddenly horrified by Desdemona. Robert Speaight in his reflections on Othello wonders where their marriage was consummated. In Venice, or only in Cyprus, the night when Iago made Cassio drunk.[1] Such a question may sound absurd when applied to a Shakespearian tragedy, with its double time of events and synthetic motivation. But, perhaps because Shakespeare leaves no motivation out, this question touches on a dark sphere in Othello's relations with Desdemona. Othello behaves as if he found a different Desdemona from the one he expected. 'She that so young could give out such a seeming . . .' (III, 3.) It is as if the outburst of sensuality in a girl who not long ago listened to his tales with her eyes lowered, amazed and horrified him.

> His bed shall seem a school, his board a shrift . . .   (III, 3)

From the very first night Desdemona felt herself a lover and a wife. Eroticism was her vocation and joy; eroticism and love, eroticism and Othello are one and the same. Her Eros is a substance of light. But for Othello Eros is a trap. It is as if, after the first night, he got lost in darkness, where love and jealousy, lust and disgust were inextricably bound together.

The more violently Desdemona becomes engrossed by love, the more of a slut she seems to Othello; a past, present, or future slut. The more she desires, the better she loves, the more readily Othello believes that she can, or has, betrayed him.

Iago sets all the world's evil in motion and falls victim to it in the end. Desdemona is the victim of her own passion. Her love testifies against her, not for her. Love proves her undoing. This is the second paradox.

In no other great Shakespearian drama, with the possible exception of *King Lear*, is the word 'nature' uttered so frequently as in *Othello*.

> It is a judgement maim'd, and most imperfect,
> That will confess perfection so would err
> Against all rules of nature . . .   (I, 3)

---

[1] Robert Speaight, *Nature in Shakespearian Tragedy*, London, 1955.

This idea is repeated several times, almost in the same words:

> And yet how nature erring from itself –   (III, 3)

What is nature? What is against nature? Desdemona deceived her father. In *King Lear* we look at daughters with the eyes of the exiled old man. We hear his curses. In *Othello* the viewpoint is different. Othello and Desdemona stand in the foreground. Brabantio does not rouse our compassion. But only for the time being: his words will later be repeated by Othello:

> Look to her, Moor, have a quick eye to see:
> She has deceiv'd her father, may do thee.   (I, 3)

Respect for father, husband, family, class and estate is consistent with nature. Social order is natural. Everything that destroys it is against nature. Eroticism is nature, too. But nature can be good or evil. Eroticism is nature depraved. The theme of *Othello*, like that of *Macbeth* and *King Lear*, is the Fall. The Renaissance tale of the cunning villain and the jealous husband has been changed into a medieval morality.

> *Othello.* Why, what art thou?
> *Desdemona.* Your wife, my lord, your true and loyal wife.
> *Othello.* Come, swear it, damn thyself,
>   Lest, being like one of heaven, the devils themselves
>   Should fear to seize thee, therefore be double-damn'd,
>   Swear thou art honest.
> *Desdemona.* Heaven doth truly know it.
> *Othello.* Heaven truly knows, that thou art false as hell.   (IV, 2)

Angel turns into devil. After animal symbolism, in which eroticism has been enclosed, this is, in frequency, the second semantic sphere of the tragedy. *Othello's* landscape consisted of the earth without moon and stars, then of the world of reptiles and insects. Now the setting, as in medieval theatre, consists of two gates: of heaven and hell. Even the sober and down-to-earth Emilia turns into a gate-keeper of hell:

> . . . you, mistress,
> That have the office opposite to Saint Peter,
> And keeps the gates in hell . . .   (IV, 2)

In front of the two gates Othello utters his great closing speeches before he kills himself:

> . . . when we shall meet at count,
> This look of thine will hurl my soul from heaven,
> And fiends will snatch at it.   (V, 2)

But in fact *Othello* is no more a morality, or a mystery, than it is an opera or a melodrama. Nature is depraved and cannot be trusted. Eros is nature and cannot be trusted either. There is no appeal to nature, or her laws. Nature is evil, not only to Othello, but also to Shakespeare. It is just as insane and cruel as history. Nature is depraved but, unlike in a medieval morality, it is not redeemed. There is no redemption. Angels turn into devils. All of them.

> Turn thy complexion there;
> Patience, thy young and rose-lipp'd cherubin,
> I here look grim as hell!   (IV, 2)

It is the mad Lear, who continues the argument:

> Behold yond simpering dame,
> Whose face between her forks presages snow,
> That minces virtue, and does shake the head
> To hear of pleasure's name;
> The fitchew nor the soiled horse goes to't
> With a more riotous appetite.
> Down from the waist they are Centaurs,
> Though women all above:
> But to the girdle do the gods inherit,
> Beneath is all the fiends';
> There's hell, there's darkness, there's the sulphurous pit,
> Burning, scalding, stench, consumption.   (*Lear*, IV, 6)

Othello and Lear stay in the same sphere of madness. Nature has been put on trial. Once again Shakespeare's hatred of nature forecasts that of Swift. Nature is depraved, above all in its reproductive function. Love tales, stories of lovers and married couples, are just as ruthless and cruel as the histories of kings, princes and usurpers. In both, dead bodies are carried away from the empty stage.

VI

All the landscapes of *Othello*, gestures, rhetoric – the last also in
its gradual destruction – belong to the poetics of the Baroque.
I visualize Othello, Desdemona and Iago in black and gold,
dipped in Rembrandtian darkness. Light falls on their faces.
The first crowd scene, when Brabantio with his retinue sets out
in search of Othello, always reminds me of the Night Watch.

> Keep up your bright swords, for the dew will rust 'em.
>
> (I, 2)

Othello is a tragedy of gestures. This, too, is part of the
Baroque. But the gestures are stayed, held in the air, as it were.
Everyone is motionless for a moment. I would have Othello's
final gestures held in the same way. Let him approach Desdemona lying on her bed. And let him draw back. He knows now
that Iago has won the final argument. The world is sufficiently
vile, if she could have betrayed him, if he has come to believe in
her infidelity, if he could believe in it even.

> . . . to be once in doubt,
> Is once to be resolv'd.   (III, 3)

Othello does not have to kill Desdemona. The play would be
more cruel if, in that final and decisive moment, he just left her.
Cressida does not die after her act of betrayal, nor does Troilus
kill himself. Their play ends on a mocking tone.

Othello kills Desdemona in order to save the moral order, to
restore love and faith. He kills Desdemona to be able to forgive
her, so that the accounts be settled and the world returned to its
equilibrium. Othello does not mumble any more. He desperately wants to save the meaning of life, of his life, perhaps
even the meaning of the world.

> And say besides, that in Aleppo once,
> Where a malignant and a turban'd Turk
> Beat a Venetian, and traduc'd the state,
> I took by the throat the circumcised dog,
> And smote him thus.   (V, 2)

Othello's death can save nothing. Desdemona is dead, and so is the world of feudal loyalty. The *condottieri* are anachronistic, together with their enchanting poetry, with their rhetoric, their pathos and their gestures. One such gesture is Othello's suicide.

Desdemona is dead, as are the stupid fool Roderigo and the prudent Emilia. Soon Othello will die. All of them die: the noble ones and the villains; the level-headed ones and the madmen; the empiricists and the absolutists. All choices are bad.

> *Desdemona.* Would'st thou do such a deed, for all the world?
> *Emilia.* Why, would not you?
> *Desdemona.* No, by this heavenly light!
> *Emilia.* Nor I neither, by this heavenly light,
>   I might do it as well in the dark.
> *Desdemona.* Would'st thou do such a thing for all the world?
> *Emilia.* The world is a huge thing, it is a great price,
>   For a small vice.   (IV, 3)

Iago keeps silent. Probably even on the rack he will not utter a word. He has won all the arguments; but only the intellectual ones. In all great Shakespearian dramas, from *Hamlet* and *Troilus and Cressida* onwards, the moral order and the intellectual order are in conflict with one another. They will remain so up to *The Winter's Tale* and *The Tempest*. The world is as Iago sees it. But Iago is a villain. Like our world, Shakespeare's world did not regain its balance after the earthquake. Like our world, it remained incoherent. In Shakespeare's *Othello* everybody loses in the end.

'King Lear,' or Endgame

King Lear. Dost thou call me fool, boy?
Fool. All thy other titles thou hast given away; that thou wast born
  with.   (*King Lear*, I, 4)
We are all born mad. Some remain so. (*Waiting for Godot,* II)

The attitude of modern criticism to *King Lear* is ambiguous and
somehow embarrassed. Doubtless *King Lear* is still recognized
as a masterpiece, beside which even *Macbeth* and *Hamlet* seem
tame and pedestrian. *King Lear* is compared to Bach's *Mass in
B Minor*, to Beethoven's *Fifth* and *Ninth* Symphonies, to
Wagner's *Parsifal*, Michelangelo's *Last Judgement*, or Dante's
Purgatory and *Inferno*. But at the same time *King Lear* gives one
the impression of a high mountain that everyone admires, yet
no one particularly wishes to climb. It is as if the play had lost
its power to excite on the stage and in reading; as if it were out
of place in our time, or, at any rate, had no place in the modern
theatre. But the question is: what is modern theatre?

The apogee of *King Lear*'s theatrical history was reached no
doubt in the romantic era. To the romantic theatre *King Lear*
fitted perfectly; but only conceived as a melodrama, full of
horrors, and dealing with a tragic king, deprived of his crown,
conspired against by heaven and earth, nature and men. Charles
Lamb might well laugh at early nineteenth-century performances in which a miserable old man wandered about the stage
bare-headed, stick in hand, in an artificial storm and rain. But
the theatre was soon to attain the full power of illusion.
Diorama, scene changes effected by means of new stage
machinery, without bringing the curtain down, made it
possible suddenly, almost miraculously, to transform a Gothic
castle into a mountainous region, or a blood-red sunset into a
stormy night. Lightning and thunder, rain and wind, seemed

like the real thing. It was easy for the romantic imagination to find its favourite landscape: gloomy castles, hovels, deserted spots, mysterious and awe-inspiring places, towering rock gleaming white in the moonlight.[1] *King Lear* was also in keeping with the romantic style of acting, since it offered scope for sweeping gestures, terrifying scenes, and violent soliloquies, loudly delivered, so popular with Kean and his school. The actor's task was to demonstrate the blackest depths of the human soul. Lear's and Gloster's unhappy fate was to arouse pity and terror, to shock the audience. And so it did. Suffering purified Lear and restored his tragic greatness. Shakespeare's *King Lear* was the 'black theatre' of romanticism.

Then came the turn of the historical, antiquarian and realistic Shakespeare. Stage designers were sent to Rome to copy features of the Forum for sets to *Julius Caesar*. Crowds of extras were dressed in period costume. Copies were made of medieval dress, renaissance jewellery, Elizabethan furniture. Sets became more and more solid and imposing. The stage was turned into a large exhibition of historical props. A balcony had to be a real balcony, a palace – a real palace, a street – a real street. Real trees were substituted for the old painted landscape.

At that time attempts were also made to set *King Lear* in a definite historical period. With the help of archaeologists, celtic burial places were reconstructed on the stage. Lear became an old druid. Theatrical machinery was more and more perfect, so that storm, wind and rain could drown the actors' voices more and more effectively. As a result of the odd marriage between new and perfected theatre techniques with the archaeological reconstruction of a celtic tomb, only the plot remained

---

[1] The reviewer for *John Bull* in 1838 depicted the set for the contemporary Macready production: 'The castles are heavy, sombre, solid; their halls adorned with trophies of the chase and instruments of war; druid circles rise in spectral loneliness out of the heath, and the "dreadful pother" of the elements is kept up with a verisimilitude which beggars all that we have hitherto seen attempted. Forked lightnings, now vividly illumine the broad horizon, now faintly coruscating in small and serpent folds, play in the distance; the sheeted element sweeps over the foreground, and then leave it in pitchy darkness; and wind and rain howl and rush in "tyranny of the open night"'. I quote this from *King Lear in Our Time* by Maynard Mack, Methuen, 1966.

of Shakespeare's play. In such a theatre Shakespeare was indeed out of place: he was untheatrical.

The turn of the century brought a revolution in Shakespearian studies. For the first time his plays began to be interpreted through the theatre of his time. A generation of scholars were busy on patiently recreating the Elizabethan stage, style of acting and theatrical traditions. Granville-Barker in his famous *Prefaces to Shakespeare* showed, or at least tried to show, how *Lear* must have been played at the Globe. The return to the so-called 'authentic' Shakespeare began. From now on the storm was to rage in Lear's and Gloster's breast rather than on the stage. The trouble was, however, that the demented old man, tearing his long white beard, suddenly became ridiculous. He should have been tragic, but he no longer was.

Nearly all Shakespeare's expositions have an amazing speed and directness in the way conflicts are shown and put into action, and the whole tone of the play is set. The exposition of *King Lear* seems preposterous if one is to look in it for psychological verisimilitude. A great and powerful king holds a competition of rhetoric among his daughters as to which one of them will best express her love for him, and makes the division of his kingdom depend on its outcome. He does not see or understand anything: Regan's and Goneril's hypocrisy is all too evident. Regarded as a person, a character, Lear is ridiculous, naïve and stupid. When he goes mad, he can only arouse compassion, never pity and terror.

Gloster, too, is naïve and ridiculous. In the early scenes he seems a stock character from a comedy of manners. Robert Speaight compares him to a gentleman of somewhat old-fashioned views who strolls on a Sunday along St James's Street complete with bowler hat and umbrella.[1] Nothing about him hints at the tragic old man whose eyes will be gouged out. It is true that Polonius in *Hamlet* is also a comic figure, who later is stabbed to death. But his death is grotesque, too, while Lear and Gloster are to go through immense suffering.

Producers have found it virtually impossible to cope with the

[1] See R. Speaight, *Nature in Shakespearian Tragedy*, London, 1955.

plot of *King Lear*. When realistically treated, Lear and Gloster were too ridiculous to appear tragic heroes. If the exposition was treated as a fairy tale or legend, the cruelty of Shakespeare's world, too, became unreal. Yet the cruelty of *Lear* was to the Elizabethans a contemporary reality, and has remained real since. But it is a philosophical cruelty. Neither the romantic, nor the naturalistic theatre was able to show that sort of cruelty; only the new theatre can. In this new theatre there are no characters, and the tragic element has been superseded by the grotesque. The grotesque is more cruel than tragedy.

The exposition of *King Lear* is as absurd, and as necessary, as in Dürrenmatt's *Visit* is the arrival at Güllen of multi-million-airess Claire Zachanassian and her entourage, including a new husband, a couple of eunuchs, a large coffin, and a panther in a cage. The exposition of *King Lear* shows a world that is to be destroyed.

Since the end of the eighteenth century no other dramatist has had a greater impact on European drama than Shakespeare. But theatres in which Shakespeare's plays have been produced, were in turn influenced by contemporary plays. Shakespeare has been a living influence in so far as contemporary plays, through which his dramas were interpreted, were a living force themselves. When Shakespeare is dull and dead on the stage, it means that not only the theatre but also plays written in that particular period are dead. This is one of the reasons why Shakespeare's universality has never dated.

The book devoted to 'Shakespeare and the new drama' has not yet been written. Perhaps it is too early for such a book to appear. But it is odd how often the word 'Shakespearian' is uttered when one speaks about Brecht, Dürrenmatt, or Beckett. These three names stand, of course, for three different kinds of theatrical vision, and the word 'Shakespearian' means something different in relation to each of them. It may be invoked to compare with Dürrenmatt's full-bloodedness, sharpness, lack of cohesion, and stylistic confusion; with Brecht's epic quality; or with Beckett's new *Theatrum mundi*. But every one of these three kinds of drama and theatre has more similarities to Shakespeare

and medieval morality plays than to nineteenth-century drama,
whether romantic or naturalistic. Only in this sense can the new
theatre be called anti-theatre.

A striking feature of the new theatre is its grotesque quality.
Despite appearances to the contrary, this new grotesque has not
replaced the old drama and comedy of manners. It deals with
problems, conflicts and themes of tragedy, such as: human fate,
the meaning of existence, freedom and inevitability, the discrepancy between the absolute and the fragile human order.
Grotesque means tragedy rewritten in different terms. Maurice
Regnault's statement: 'the absence of tragedy in a tragic world
gives birth to comedy' is only seemingly paradoxical. The
the grotesque exists in a tragic world. Both the tragic and the
grotesque visions of the world are composed as it were of
same elements. In a tragic and grotesque world, situations are
imposed, compulsory and inescapable. Freedom of choice and
decision are part of this compulsory situation, in which both the
tragic hero and the grotesque actor must always lose their
struggle against the absolute. The downfall of the tragic hero is
a confirmation and recognition of the absolute; whereas the
downfall of the grotesque actor means mockery of the absolute
and its desecration. The absolute is transformed into a blind
mechanism, a kind of automaton. Mockery is directed not only
at the tormentor, but also at the victim, who believed in the
tormentor's justice, raising him to the level of the absolute.
The victim has consecrated his tormentor by recognizing himself as victim.

In the final instance tragedy is an appraisal of human fate, a
measure of the absolute. The grotesque is a criticism of the
absolute in the name of frail human experience. That is why
tragedy brings *catharsis*, while grotesque offers no consolation
whatsoever. 'Tragedy,' wrote Gorgias of Leontium, 'is a
swindle in which the swindler is more just than the swindled, and
the swindled wiser than the swindler.' One may travesty this
aphorism by saying that grotesque is a swindle in which the
swindled is more just than the swindler, and the swindler wiser
than the swindled. Claire Zachanassian in Dürrenmatt's *Visit* is

wiser than Ill, but Ill is more just than she is. Ill's death, like Polonius's death in *Hamlet*, is grotesque. Neither Ill, nor the inhabitants of Güllen, are tragic heroes. The old lady, with her artificial breasts, teeth and limbs, is not a goddess, she hardly even exists, she might almost have been invented. Ill and the people of Güllen find themselves in a situation in which there is no room for tragedy, but only for grotesque. 'Comedy' – writes Ionesco in his *Expérience du théâtre* – 'is a feeling of absurdity, and seems more hopeless than tragedy; comedy allows no way out of a given situation.'[1]

The tragic and the grotesque worlds are closed, and there is no escape from them. In the tragic world this compulsory situation has been imposed in turn by the Gods, Fate, the Christian God, Nature, and History that has been endowed with reason and inevitability.

On the other side, opposed to this arrangement, there was always man. If Nature was the absolute, man was unnatural. If man was natural, the absolute was represented by Grace, without which there was no salvation. In the world of the grotesque, downfall cannot be justified by, or blamed on, the absolute. The absolute is not endowed with any ultimate reasons; it is stronger, and that is all. The absolute is absurd. Maybe that is why the grotesque often makes use of the concept of a mechanism which has been put in motion and cannot be stopped. Various kinds of impersonal and hostile mechanisms have taken the place of God, Nature and History, found in the old tragedy. The notion of an absurd mechanism is probably the last metaphysical concept remaining in modern grotesque. But this absurd mechanism is not transcendental any more in relation to man, or at any rate to mankind. It is a trap set by man himself into which he has fallen.

The scene of tragedy has mostly been a natural landscape. Raging nature witnessed man's downfall, or – as in *King Lear* – played an active part in the action. Modern grotesque usually takes place in the midst of civilization. Nature has evaporated from it almost completely. Man is confined to a room and

[1] E. Ionesco, *Expérience du théâtre*, 'Nouvelle Revue Française', February, 1958

surrounded by inanimate objects. But objects have now been raised to the status of symbols of human fate, or situation, and perform a similar function to that played in Shakespeare by forest, storm, or eclipse of the sun. Even Sartre's hell is just a vast hotel consisting of rooms and corridors, beyond which there are more rooms and more corridors. This hell 'behind closed doors' does not need any metaphysical aids.

Ionesco's hell is arranged on similar lines. A new tenant moves into an empty flat. Furniture is brought in. There is more and more furniture. Furniture surrounds the tenant on all sides. He is surrounded already by four wardrobes but more are brought in. He has been closed in by furniture. He can no longer be seen. He has been brought down to the level of inanimate objects, and has become an object himself.

In Beckett's *Endgame* there is a room with a wheel-chair and two dustbins. A picture hangs face to the wall. There is also a staircase, a telescope and a whistle. All that remains of nature is sand in the dustbins, a flea, and the part of man that belongs to nature: his body.

> *Hamm.* Nature has forgotten us.
> *Clov.* There's no more nature.
> *Hamm.* No more nature! You exaggerate.
> *Clov.* In the vicinity.
> *Hamm.* But we breathe, we change! We lose our hair, our
>   teeth! Our bloom! Our ideals!
> *Clov.* Then she hasn't forgotten us.   (p. 16)

It can easily be shown how, in the new theatre, tragic situations become grotesque. Such a classic situation of tragedy is the necessity of making a choice between opposing values. Antigone is doomed to choose between human and divine order, between Creon's demands, and those of the absolute. The tragedy lies in the very principle of choice by which one of the values must be annihilated. The cruelty of the absolute lies in demanding such a choice and in imposing a situation which

---

[1] All quotations from Beckett are given in the author's own translation. Page references in quotations from *Endgame* and *Act Without Words* apply to the Faber & Faber edition of 1958.

excludes the possibility of a compromise, and where one of the alternatives is death. The absolute is greedy and demands everything; the hero's death is its confirmation.

The tragic situation becomes grotesque when both alternatives of the choice imposed are absurd, irrelevant or compromising. The hero has to play, even if there is no game. Every move is bad, but he cannot throw down his cards. To throw down the cards would also be a bad move.

It is this situation that Dürrenmatt's Romulus finds himself in. He is the last emperor of a crumbling empire. He will not alter the course of history. History has made a fool of him. He can either die in a spectacular fashion, or lie on his bed and wait to be butchered. He can surrender, compose speeches, or commit suicide. In his position as the last Roman emperor, every one of these solutions is compromising and ridiculous. History has turned Romulus into a clown, and yet demands him to treat her seriously. Romulus has only one good move to make: consciously to accept the part of a clown and play it to the end. He can breed chickens. In this way the historical inevitability will have been made a fool of. The absolute will have been flouted.

Antigone is a tragedy of choice, *Oedipus* a tragedy of 'unmerited guilt' and destiny. The gods loyally warn the protagonist that fate has destined him to be a patricide and his own mother's husband. The hero has full freedom of decision and action. The gods do not interfere; they just watch and wait until he makes a mistake. Then they punish him. The gods are just, and punish the hero for a crime he has indeed committed, and only after he has committed it. But the protagonist *had* to commit a crime. Oedipus wanted to cheat fate, but did not and could not escape it. He fell into a trap, made his mistake, killed his father and married his mother. What is to happen will happen.

The tragedy of Oedipus may, perhaps, be posed as a problem belonging to the game theory. The game is just, i.e. at the outset both partners must have the same chances of losing or winning, and both must play according to the same rules. In its game with Oedipus Fate does not invoke the help of the gods, does not change the laws of nature. Fate wins its game without recourse to miracles.

The game must be just, but at the same time must be so arranged that the same party always wins; so that Oedipus always loses.

Let us imagine an electronic computer which plays chess and calculates any number of moves in advance. A man *must* play chess with an electronic computer, cannot leave or break the game, and *has* to lose the game. His defeat is just, because it is effected according to the rules of the game; he loses because he has made a mistake. But he could not have won.

A man losing the chess-game with an electronic computer, whom he himself has fed with combinatorial analysis and rules, whom he himself has 'taught' to play, is not a tragic hero any more. If he plays that chess-game from the moment he was born until he dies, and if he has to lose, he will at most be the hero of a tragi-grotesque. All that is left of tragedy is the concept of 'unmerited guilt', the inevitable defeat and unavoidable mistake. But the absolute has ceased to exist. It has been replaced by the absurdity of the human situation.

The absurdity does not consist in the fact that man-made mechanisms are under certain conditions stronger, and even wider, than he. The absurdity consists in that they create a compulsory situation by forcing him into a game in which the probability of his total defeat constantly increases. The Christian view of the end of the world, with the Last Judgement and its segregation of the just and the unjust, is pathetic. The end of the world caused by the atomic bomb is spectacular, but grotesque just the same. Such an end of the world is intellectually unacceptable, either to Christians or to Marxists. It would be a silly ending.

The comparison between fate's game with Oedipus, and a game of chess with an electronic computer, is not precise enough. An automatic device to play chess, even if it could compute any number of moves, need not win all the time. It would simply more often win than lose. But among automatic devices that really exist one could find a much better example. There is

machine for a game similar to tossing coins for 'heads or tails'.
put a coin on the table the way I like, with 'heads' or 'tails' on
top. The machine does not see the coin, but it has to predict
how I have put it. If it gives the right answer, it wins. I inform
the machine whether it has given the right answer. I put down
the coin again, and so on. After a time the machine begins to
win by giving the right answers more and more often. It has
memorized and learned my system; it has deciphered me, as it
were. It foresees that after three 'heads' I will put down two
'tails'. I change the system, and play using a different method.
The blind machine learns this one too, and begins to win again.
I am endowed with free will and have the freedom of choice. I
can put down 'heads' or 'tails'. But in the end, like Oedipus, I
must lose the game.

There is a move by which I do not lose. I do not put the coin
on the table, I do not choose. I simply toss it. I have given up
the system, and left matters to chance. Now the machine and
I have even chances. The possibility of win and lose, of 'heads'
or 'tails' is the same. It amounts to fifty-fifty. The machine
wanted me to treat it seriously, to play rationally with it, using
a system, a method. But I do not want to. It is I who have now
seen through the machine's method.

The machine stands for fate, which acts on the principle of
the law of averages. In order to have even chances with fate I
must become fate myself; I must chance my luck; act with a
fifty-fifty chance. A man who, when playing with the machine,
gives up his free will and freedom of choice, adopts an attitude
to fate similar to that which Dürrenmatt's Romulus adopted
with regard to historical necessity. Instead of putting the coin
with 'heads' on top a hundred times in succession, or 'heads'
and 'tails' in turn, or two 'tails' after ten 'heads', he would just
toss the coin. That kind of man most certainly is not a tragic
hero. He has adopted a clownish attitude to fate. Romulus is
such a man.

In modern tragedy, fate, gods and nature have been replaced
by history. History is the only framework of reference, the final
authority to accept or reject the validity of human actions. It is

unavoidable and realizes its ultimate aims; it is objective
'reason', as well as objective 'progress'. In this scheme of things
history is a theatre with actors, but without an audience. No one
watches the performance, for everybody is taking part. The
script of this grand spectacle has been composed in advance and
includes a necessary epilogue, which will explain everything.
But, as in the *commedia dell'arte*, the text has not been written
down. The actors improvise and only some of them foresee
correctly what will happen in the following acts. In this particular theatre the scene changes with the actors; they are constantly setting it up and pulling it down again.

Actors are often wrong, but their mistakes have been foreseen
by the scenario. One might even say that mistakes are the basis
of the script, and that it is thanks to them that the action unfolds.
History contains both the past and the future. Actors from previous scenes keep coming back, repeating old conflicts, and
want to play parts that are long since over. They needlessly
prolong the performance and have to be removed from the
stage. They arrived too late. Other actors have arrived too early
and start performing a scene from the next act, without noticing
that the stage is not yet ready for them. They want to speed up
the performance, but this cannot be done: every act has to be
performed in its proper order. Those who arrive too early are
also removed from the stage.

It is these parts that nineteenth-century philosophy and
literature considered tragic. For Hegel the tragic heroes of
history were those who came too late. Their reasons were noble
but one-sided. They had been correct in the previous era, in the
preceding act. If they continue to insist on them, they must be
crushed by history. The Vendée was for Hegel an example of
historical tragedy. Count Henry in Krasiński's *Undivine Comedy*
is a Hegelian tragic hero.

Those who came too early, striving in vain to speed up the
course of history, are also history's tragic heroes. Their
reasons, too, are one-sided; they will become valid only at the
next historical phase, in the succeeding act. They failed to
understand that freedom is only the conscious recognition of

necessity. Consequently they were annihilated by historical necessity, which solves only those problems that are capable of solution. The Paris Commune is an example of this kind of historical tragedy. Pancrace in the *Undivine Comedy* is a tragic hero of history thus conceived.

The grotesque mocks the historical absolute, as it has mocked the absolutes of gods, nature and destiny. It does so by means of the so-called 'barrel of laughs', a popular feature of any funfair: a score of people or more try to keep their balance while the upturned barrel revolves round its axis. One can only keep one's balance by moving on the bottom in the opposite direction to, and with the same speed as, the barrel's movement. This is not at all easy. Those who move too fast or too slow in relation to the barrel's movement are bound to fall. The barrel brings them up, then they roll downwards trying desperately to cling to the moving floor. The more violent their gestures and their grip on the walls, the more difficult it is for them to get up, and the more funny they look.

The barrel is put in motion by a motor, which is transcendental in relation to it. However, one may easily imagine a barrel that is set in motion by the people inside it: by those who manage to preserve their balance and by those who fall over. A barrel like this would be immanent. Its movements would, of course, be variable: sometimes it would revolve in one direction, sometimes in the other. It would be even more difficult to preserve one's balance in a barrel like this: one would have to change step all the time, move forwards and backwards, faster or slower. In such an immanent barrel many more people would fall over. But neither those who fall because they move too fast, nor those who fall because they move too slow, are tragic heroes. They are just grotesque. They will be grotesque even if there is no way out of this immanent barrel. The social mechanism shown in most of Adamov's plays is very much like the barrel of laughs.

The world of tragedy and the world of grotesque have a similar structure. Grotesque takes over the themes of tragedy and poses the same fundamental questions. Only its answers are different. This dispute about the tragic and grotesque interpretation of human fate reflects the everlasting conflict of two philosophies and two ways of thinking; of two opposing attitudes defined by the Polish philosopher Leszek Kolakowski as the irreconcilable antagonism between the priest and the clown. Between tragedy and grotesque there is the same conflict for or against such notions as eschatology, belief in the absolute, hope for the ultimate solution of the contradiction between moral order and everyday practice. Tragedy is the theatre of priests, grotesque is the theatre of clowns.

This conflict between two philosophies and two types of theatre becomes particularly acute in times of great upheaval. When established values have been overthrown, and there is no appeal to God, Nature, or History from the tortures inflicted by the cruel world, the clown becomes the central figure in the theatre. He accompanies the exiled trio – the King, the nobleman and his son – on their cruel wanderings through the cold endless night which has fallen on the world; through the 'cold night' which, as in Shakespeare's *King Lear*, 'will turn us all to fools and madmen'.

II

After his eyes have been gouged out, Gloster wants to throw himself over the cliffs of Dover into the sea. He is led by his own son, who feigns madness. Both have reached the depths of human suffering; the top of 'the pyramid of suffering', as Juliusz Slowacki has described *King Lear*. But on the stage there are just two actors, one playing a blind man, the other playing a man who plays a madman. They walk together.

> *Gloster*. When shall I come to the top of that same hill?
> *Edgar*. You do climb up it now: look, how we labour.
> *Gloster*. Methinks the ground is even.
> *Edgar*. Horrible steep.
>   Hark, do you hear the sea?
> *Gloster*. No, truly.   (IV, 6)

It is easy to imagine this scene. The text itself provides stage directions. Edgar is supporting Gloster; he lifts his feet high pretending to walk uphill. Gloster, too, lifts his feet, as if expecting the ground to rise, but underneath his foot there is only air. This entire scene is written for a very definite type of theatre, namely pantomime.

This pantomime only makes sense if enacted on a flat and level stage.

Edgar feigns madness, but in doing so he must adopt the right gestures. In its theatrical expression this is a scene in which a madman leads a blind man and talks him into believing in a non-existing cliff. In another moment a landscape will be sketched in. Shakespeare often creates a landscape on an empty stage. A few words, and the diffused, soft afternoon light at the Globe changes into night, evening, or morning. But no other Shakespearian landscape is so exact, precise and clear, as this one. It is like a Brueghel painting: thick with people, objects and events. A little human figure hanging half-way down the cliff is gathering samphire. Fishermen walking on the beach are like mice. A ship seems a little boat, a boat is floating like a buoy.

It is this abyss of Shakespeare's imagination that Slowacki makes the hero of his *Kordian* look into:

> Come! Here, on the top stand still. Your head will whirl,
> When you cast your eyes on the abyss below your feet.
> Crows flying there half-way no bigger are than beetles.
> And there, too, someone is toiling, gathering weed.
> He looks no bigger than a human head.
> And there on the beach the fishermen seem like ants . . .

This accurate landscape created on an empty stage is not meant to serve as part of the décor, or to replace the non-existent settings. Slowacki understood perfectly the dramatic purpose of this scene:

> Oh, Shakespeare! Spirit! You have built a mountain
> Higher than that created by God.
> For you have talked of an abyss to a man blind . . .

The landscape is now just a score for the pantomime. Gloster

and Edgar have reached the top of the cliff. The landscape is
now below them.

> Give me your hand: – you are now within a foot
> Of the extreme verge: for all beneath the moon
> Would I not leap upright.   (*King Lear*, IV, 6)

In Shakespeare's time the actors probably put their feet forward
through a small balustrade above the apron-stage, immediately
over the heads of the 'groundlings'. But we are not concerned
here with an historical reconstruction of the Elizabethan stage.
It is the presence and importance of the mime that is significant.
Shakespeare is stubborn. Gloster has already jumped over the
precipice. Both actors are at the foot of a non-existent cliff. The
same landscape is now above them. The mime continues.

> *Gloster.* But have I fall'n, or no?
> *Edgar.* From the dread summit of this chalky bourn.
>   Look up a-height; – the shrill-gorg'd lark so far
>   Cannot be seen or heard: do but look up.   (IV, 6)

The mime creates a scenic area: the top and bottom of the cliff,
the precipice. Shakespeare makes use of all the means of anti-
illusionist theatre in order to create a most realistic and concrete landscape. A landscape which is only a blind man's
illusion. There is perspective in it, light, men and things, even
sounds. From the height of the cliff the sea cannot be heard, but
there is mention of its roar. From the foot of the cliff the lark
cannot be heard, but there is mention of its song. In this landscape sounds are present by their very absence: the silence is
filled with them, just as the empty stage is filled with the cliff.

The scene of the suicidal leap is also a mime. Gloster kneels
in a last prayer and then, in accordance with the tradition of the
play's English performances, falls over. He is now at the
bottom of the cliff. But there was no height; it was an illusion.
Gloster knelt down on an empty stage, fell over and got up. At
this point disillusion follows.[1]

---

[1] Compare the analysis of this scene in G. Wilson Knight's most original study
of the grotesque elements in *King Lear*, treated somewhat differently than in my
essay: '*King Lear*' *and the Comedy of the Grotesque* (in *The Wheel of Fire*, London,
1957).

The non-existent cliff is not meant just to deceive the blind man. For a short while we, too, believed in this landscape and in the mime. The meaning of this parable is not easy to define. But one thing is clear: this type of parable is not to be thought of outside the theatre, or rather outside a certain kind of theatre. In narrative prose Edgar could, of course, lead the blind Gloster to the cliffs of Dover, let him jump down from a stone and make him believe that he was jumping from the top of a cliff. But he might just as well lead him a day's journey away from the castle and make him jump from a stone on any heap of sand. In film and in prose there is only the choice between a real stone lying in the sand and an equally real jump from the top of a chalk cliff into the sea. One cannot transpose Gloster's suicide attempt to the screen, unless one were to film a stage performance. But in the naturalistic, or even stylized theatre, with the precipice painted or projected on to a screen, Shakespeare's parable would be completely obliterated.

The stage must be empty. On it a suicide, or rather its symbol, has been performed. Mime is the performance of symbols. In Ionesco's *Le Tueur sans Gages* the Architect, who is at the same time the commissioner of police, shows Berenger round the *Cité Radieuse*. On an empty stage Berenger sniffs at non-existent flowers and taps non-existent walls. The Radiant City exists and does not exist, or rather it has existed always and everywhere. And that is why it is so terrifying. Similarly, the Shakespearian precipice at Dover exists and does not exist. It is the abyss, waiting all the time. The abyss, into which one can jump, is everywhere.

By a few words of dialogue Shakespeare often turned the platform stage, the inner stage, or the gallery into a London street, a forest, a palace, a ship, or a castle battlement. But these were always real places of action. Townspeople gathered outside the Tower, lovers wandered through the forest, Brutus murdered Caesar in the Forum. The white precipice at Dover performs a different function. Gloster does not jump from the top of the cliff, or from a stone. For once, in *King Lear*, Shakespeare shows the paradox of pure theatre. It is the

same theatrical paradox that Ionesco uses in his *Le Tueur san*
Gages.

In the naturalistic theatre one can perform a murder scene, o
a scene of terror. The shot may be fired from a revolver or a toy
pistol. But in mime there is no difference between a revolve
and a toy pistol: in fact neither exist. Like death, the shot is onl
a performance, a parable, a symbol.

Gloster, falling over on flat, even boards, plays a scene from
a great morality play. He is no longer a court dignitary whos
eyes have been gouged out because he showed mercy to th
banished king. The action is no longer confined to Elizabetha
or Celtic England. Gloster is Everyman, and the stage become
the medieval *Theatrum Mundi*. A biblical parable is now enacted
the one about the rich man who became a beggar, and the blin
man who recovered his inner sight when he lost his eyes. Every
man begins his wanderings through the world. In medieva
mystery plays the stage was also empty, but in the backgroun
there were four mansions, four gates representing Eartl
Purgatory, Heaven and Hell. In *King Lear* the stage is empt
throughout: there is nothing, except the cruel earth, wher
man goes on his journey from the cradle to the grave. Th
theme of *King Lear* is an inquiry into the meaning of th
journey, into the existence or non-existence of Heaven an
Hell.

From the middle of the second act to the end of the fourt
act, Shakespeare takes up a biblical theme. But this new *Book*
Job, or new Dantean *Inferno*, was written towards the close o
the Renaissance. In Shakespeare's play there is neither Christia
heaven, nor the heaven predicted and believed in by humanist
King Lear makes a tragic mockery of all eschatologies: of th
heaven promised on earth, and the heaven promised after deatl
in fact – of both Christian and secular theodicies; of cosmogor
and of the rational view of history; of the gods and natur
goodness, of man made in the 'image and likeness'. In *King Lea*
both the medieval and the renaissance orders of establishe
values disintegrate. All that remains at the end of this gigant
pantomime is the earth – empty and bleeding. On this eartl

[handwritten annotation: No reference to the actual lines note. seene]

through which a tempest has passed leaving only stones, the King, the Fool, the Blind Man and the Madman carry on their distracted dialogue.

The blind Gloster falls over on the empty stage. His suicidal leap is tragic. Gloster has reached the depths of human misery; so has Edgar, who pretends to be Mad Tom in order to save his father. But the pantomime performed by actors on the stage is grotesque, and has something of a circus about it. The blind Gloster who has climbed a non-existent height and fallen over on flat boards, is a clown. A philosophical buffoonery has been performed, of the sort found in modern theatre.

> Whistle from left wing.
> He (the man) does not move.
> He looks at his hands, looks round for scissors, sees them, goes and picks them up, starts to trim his nails, stops, runs his finger along blade of scissors, goes and lays them on small cube, turns aside, opens his collar, frees his neck and fingers it.
> The small cube is pulled up and disappear in flies, carrying away rope and scissors.
> He turns to take scissors, sees what has happened.
> He turns aside, reflects.
> He goes and sits down on big cube.
> The big cube is pulled from under him. He falls. The big cube is pulled up and disappears in flies.
> He remains lying on his side, his face towards auditorium, staring before him. (*Act Without Words*, pp. 59–60)

The *Act Without Words* closes Beckett's *Endgame*, providing as it were its final interpretation. Remaining vestiges of characters, action and situation have been further reduced here. All that remains is a situation which is a parable of universal human fate. A total situation. Man has been thrown on to the empty stage. He tries to escape into the wings, but is kicked back. From above a tree with some leaves, a jug of water, tailoring scissors, and some cubes are pulled down on ropes. The man tries to hide in the shade of the leaves, but the tree is pulled up. He tries to catch hold of the jug, but it rises into the air. He attempts suicide, but this, too, proves impossible. 'The bough folds down against trunk' (p. 59). The man sits down and

E

thinks. The jug and the tree appear again. The man does not move.

In this ending to *Endgame* the forces external to man – gods, fate, the world – are not indifferent, but sneering and malicious. They tempt him all the time. These forces are stronger than he. Man must be defeated and cannot escape from the situation that has been imposed on him. All he can do is to give up; refuse to play blindman's buff. Only by the possibility of refusal can he surmount the external forces.

It is easy to see how close to the Bible this parable is, even in its metaphors: a palm, its shadow, water. The force above and beyond man is strongly reminiscent of the Old Testament God. This is also a *Book of Job*, but without an optimistic ending.

This new *Book of Job* is shown in buffo, as a circus panto-mime. *Act Without Words* is performed by a clown. The philo-sophical parable may be interpreted as tragedy or grotesque, but its artistic expression is grotesque only. Gloster's suicide attempt, too, is merely a circus somersault on an empty stage. Gloster's and Edgar's situation is tragic, but it has been shown in pantomime, the classic expression of buffoonery. In Shake-speare clowns often ape the gestures of kings and heroes, but only in *King Lear* are great tragic scenes shown through clowning.

It is not only the suicide mime that is grotesque. The accom-panying dialogue is also cruel and mocking. The blind Gloster kneels and prays:

> O you mighty gods!
> This world I do renounce, and, in your sights,
> Shake patiently my great affliction off:
> If I could bear it longer, and not fall
> To quarrel with your great opposeless wills,
> My snuff and loathed part of nature should
> Burn itself out. If Edgar live, O, bless him!   (IV, 6)

Gloster's suicide has a meaning only if the gods exist. It is a protest against undeserved suffering and the world's injustice. This protest is made in a definite direction. It refers to eschato-logy. Even if the gods are cruel, they must take this suicide into consideration. It will count in the final reckoning between gods and man. Its sole value lies in its reference to the absolute.

But if the gods, and their moral order in the world, do not exist, Gloster's suicide does not solve or alter anything. It is only a somersault on an empty stage. It is deceptive and unsuccessful on the factual as well as on the metaphysical plane. Not only the pantomime, but the whole situation is then grotesque. From the beginning to the end. It is waiting for a Godot who does not come.

> *Estragon.* Why don't we hang ourselves?
> *Vladimir.* With what?
> *Estragon.* You haven't got a bit of rope?
> *Vladimir.* No.
> *Estragon.* Then we can't.
> *Vladimir.* Let's go.
> *Estragon.* Wait, there's my belt.
> *Vladimir.* It's too short.
> *Estragon.* You could hang on to my legs.
> *Vladimir.* And who'd hang on to mine?
> *Estragon.* True.
> *Vladimir.* Show all the same. (*Estragon loosens the cord that holds up his trousers which, much too big for him, fall about his ankles. They look at the cord.*) That might do at a pinch. But is it strong enough?
> *Estragon.* We'll soon see. Here. (*They each take an end of the cord and pull. It breaks. They almost fall.*)
> *Vladimir.* Not worth a curse.   (*Waiting for Godot*, II)

Gloster did fall, and he got up again. He has made his suicide attempt, but he failed to shake the world. Nothing has changed. Edgar's comment is ironical:

> . . . had he been where he thought,
> By this had thought been past.   (IV, 6)

If there are no gods, suicide makes no sense. Death exists in any case. Suicide cannot alter human fate, but only accelerate it. It ceases to be a protest. It is a surrender. It becomes the acceptance of the world's greatest cruelty – death. Gloster has finally realized:

>   . . . henceforth I'll bear
>   Affliction till it do cry out itself
>   'Enough, enough', and die.   (IV, 6)

And once again in the last act:

>   No further, sir; a man may rot even here.   (V, 2)

After his grotesque suicide the blind Gloster talks to the deranged Lear. Estragon and Vladimir carry on a very similar
conversation, interrupted by the despairing cries of the blind
Pozzo, who has fallen down and cannot get up. Pozzo would
find it easiest to understand Gloster:

> . . . one day I went blind, one day we'll go deaf, one day we were
> born, one day we shall die . . . They give birth astride of a grave,
> the light gleams an instant, then it's night once more.
>   (*Waiting for Godot*, II)

Shakespeare had said as much, in fewer words:

>   Men must endure
>   Their going hence, even as their coming hither.
>   Ripeness is all.   (V, 2)

But it was Ionesco who put it most briefly of all, in his *Tueur
sans Gages*: 'We shall all die, this is the only serious alienation.'

III

The theme of *King Lear* is the decay and fall of the world. The
play opens like the Histories, with the division of the realm and
the King's abdication. It also ends like the Histories, with the
proclamation of a new king. Between the prologue and the
epilogue there is a civil war. But unlike in the Histories and
Tragedies, the world is not healed again. In *King Lear* there is no
young and resolute Fortinbras to ascend the throne of Denmark; no cool-headed Octavius to become Augustus Caesar; no
noble Malcolm to 'give to our tables meat, sleep to our nights'.
In the epilogues to the Histories and Tragedies the new monarch invites those present to his coronation. In *King Lear* there

will be no coronation. There is no one whom Edgar can invite to it. Everybody has died or been murdered. Gloster was right when he said: 'This great world shall so wear out to nought.' Those who have survived – Edgar, Albany and Kent – are, as Lear has been, just 'ruin'd pieces of nature'.

Of the twelve major characters one half are just and good, the other – unjust and bad. It is a division just as consistent and abstract as in a morality play. But this is a morality play in which everyone will be destroyed: noble characters along with the base ones, the persecutors with the persecuted, the torturers with the tortured. Vivisection will go on until the stage is empty. The decay and fall of the world will be shown on two levels, on two different kinds of stage, as it were. One of these may be called Macbeth's stage, the other – Job's stage.

Macbeth's stage is the scene of crime. At the beginning there is a nursery tale of two bad daughters and one good daughter. The good daughter will die hanged in prison. The bad daughters will also die, but not until they have become adulteresses, and one of them also a poisoner and murderess of her husband. All bonds, all laws, whether divine, natural or human, are broken. Social order, from the kingdom to the family, will crumble into dust. There are no longer kings and subjects, fathers and children, husbands and wives. There are only huge renaissance monsters, devouring one another like beasts of prey. Everything has been condensed, drawn in broad outlines, and the characters are hardly marked. The history of the world can do without psychology and without rhetoric. It is just action. These violent sequences are merely an illustration and an example, and perform the function of a black, realistic counterpart to 'Job's stage'.

For it is Job's stage that constitutes the main scene. On it the ironic, clownish morality play on human fate will be performed. But before that happens, all the characters must be uprooted from their social positions and pulled down, to final degradation. They must reach rock-bottom. The downfall is not merely a philosophical parable, as Gloster's leap over the supposed precipice is. The theme of downfall is carried through by

Shakespeare stubbornly, consistently, and is repeated at least four times. The fall is at the same time physical and spiritual, bodily and social.

At the beginning there was a king with his court and ministers. Later, there are just four beggars wandering about in a wilderness, exposed to raging winds and rain. The fall may be slow, or sudden. Lear has at first a retinue of a hundred men, then fifty, then only one. Kent is banished by one angry gesture of the King. But the process of degradation is always the same. Everything that distinguishes a man – his titles, social position, even name – is lost. Names are not needed any more. Every one is just a shadow of himself; just a man.

> *King Lear*. Doth any here know me? – Why, this is not Lear:
>   Doth Lear walk thus? speak thus? . . .
>
>   .   .   .   .
>   Who is it that can tell me who I am? –
> *Fool*. Lear's shadow.   (I, 4)

And once more the same question, and the same answer. The banished Kent returns in disguise to his King.

> *King Lear*. How now! what art thou?
> *Kent*. A man, sir.   (I, 4)

A naked man has no name. Before the morality commences, everyone must be naked. Naked like a worm.

> Then Job arose, and rent his mantle, and shaved his head, and fell down upon the ground, and worshipped.
> And said, Naked came I out of my mother's womb, and naked shall I return thither.   (*Book of Job*, I, 20–21)

Biblical imagery in this new *Book of Job* is no mere chance. Edgar says that he will with his 'nakedness out-face the winds and persecutions of the sky' (II, 3). This theme returns obstinately, and with an equal consistency:

> I'the last night's storm I such a fellow saw;
> Which made me think a man a worm.   (IV, 1)

A downfall means suffering and torment. It may be a physical or spiritual torment, or both. Lear will lose his wits; Kent will be put in the stocks; Gloster will have his eyes gouged out and will attempt suicide. For a man to become naked, or rather to become nothing but man, it is not enough to deprive him of his name, social position and character. One must also maim and massacre him both morally and physically. Turn him – like King Lear – into a 'ruin'd piece of nature', and only then ask him who he is. For it is the new renaissance Job who is to judge the events on 'Macbeth's stage'.

A Polish critic, Andrzej Falkiewicz, has observed this process of maiming and mutilating man, not in Shakespeare, but in modern literature and drama.[1] He compares it to the peeling of an onion. One takes off the skin, and then peels off the layers of onion one by one. Where does an onion end and what is in its core? The blind man is a man. the madman is a man, the doting old man is a man. Man and nothing but man. A nobody, who suffers, tries to give his suffering a meaning or nobility, who revolts or accepts his suffering, and who must die.

> O gods! Who is't can say, 'I am at the worst'?
> I am worse than e'er I was.
>
> . . . .
>
> And worse I may be yet: the worst is not
> So long as we can say 'This is the worst.'   (IV, 1)

Vladimir and Estragon talk to each other in a very similar fashion. They gibber, but in that gibber there are remnants of the same eschatology:

Vladimir. We're in no danger of ever thinking any more.
Estragon. Then what are we complaining about?
Vladimir. Thinking is not the worst.
Estragon. Perhaps not. But at least there's that.
Vladimir. That what?
Estragon. That's the idea, let's ask other questions.
Vladimir. What do you mean, at least there's that?
Estragon. That much less misery.
Vladimir. True.

[1] A. Falkiewicz, *Theatrical Experiment of the Fifties*, 'Dialog', No. 9, 1959 (in Polish).

Estragon. Well? If we gave thanks for our mercies?
Vladimir. What is terrible is to *have* thought.

                                        (*Waiting for Godot*, II)

Pozzo is proud and pompous when in the first part of *Waiting for Godot* he leads on a rope the starving Lucky. Their relation is still that of master and servant, the exploiter and the exploited. When they appear for the second time Pozzo is blind and Lucky is dumb. They are still joined by the same rope. But now they are just two men.

'Tis the times' plague, when madmen lead the blind. (IV, 1)

Almost as in Brueghel's famous picture, Edgar is leading the blind Gloster to the precipice at Dover. This is just the theme of *Endgame*; Beckett was the first to see it in *King Lear*; he eliminated all action, everything external, and repeated it in its skeleton form.

Clov cannot sit down, the blind Hamm cannot get up, moves only in his wheel-chair, and passes water only by means of a catheter. Nell and Nagg have 'lost their shanks' and are almost breathing their last in dustbins. But Hamm continues to be the master, and his wheel-chair brings to mind a throne. In the London production he was dressed in a faded purple gown and wiped his face with a blood-red handkerchief. He was, like King Lear, a degraded and powerless tyrant, a 'ruin'd piece of nature'. He was a King Lear, the scene in Act Four, where Lear meets the blind Gloster and after a great frantic monologue gives the order that one of his shoes be taken off, as it pinches him. It is the same pinching shoe that one of the clowns in *Waiting for Godot* will take off at the beginning of the scene.

This is the cruel and mocking 'peeling of an onion', Shakespearian and modern alike. The onion is peeled to the very last, to the suffering 'nothing'. This is the theme of the fall. The concept of man has been reduced and all situations have shrunk to the one ultimate, total and concentrated human fate. To Vladimir's question 'What is in this bag?' the blind Pozzo replies: 'Sand.' Clov in *Endgame* lifts the lid of the dustbin in

order to find out what is happening to Nagg. 'He's crying,' he
reports. To this Hamm replies: 'Then he's living.'

He's crying, then he's living. English critics have regarded
it as Beckett's reply to the Cartesian formula of man, which was
in itself a reduction of the theological formula. But in fact
Beckett simply repeats after Shakespeare:

> . . . we came crying hither.
>
> . . . .
>
> When we are born, we cry that we are come
> To this great stage of fools.   (IV, 6)

The world is real, and the shoe really pinches. Suffering is also
real. But the gesture with which the ruin of a man demands that
his pinching shoe be taken off is ridiculous. Just as ridiculous as
blind Gloster's somersault on the flat empty stage.

The biblical Job, too, is the ruin of a man. But this ruin
constantly talks to God. He curses, imprecates, blasphemes. Ultimately he admits that God is right. He has justified his sufferings and ennobled them. He included them in the metaphysical
and absolute order. The *Book of Job* is a theatre of the priests.
Whereas in both the Shakespearian and Beckettian *Endgames*
the *Book of Job* is performed by clowns. But here, too, the gods
are invoked throughout by all the characters; by Lear, Gloster,
Kent, even Albany:

> *King Lear*. By Jupiter, I swear, no.
> *Kent*. By Juno, I swear, ay.   (II, 4)

At first gods have Greek names. Then they are only gods, great
and terrifying judges high above, who are supposed to intervene sooner or later. But the gods do not intervene. They are
silent. Gradually the tone becomes more and more ironical.
The ruin of a man invoking God is ever more ridiculous. The
action becomes more and more cruel, but at the same time
assumes a more and more clownish character:

> By the kind gods, 'tis most ignobly done
> To pluck me by the beard.   (III, 7)

Defeat, suffering, cruelty have a meaning even when the gods
are cruel. Even then. It is the last theological chance to justify
suffering. The biblical Job knew about it well when he called
on God:

> If the scourge slay suddenly, he will laugh at the trial of the
> innocent.   (*Book of Job*, IX, 23)

From the just God, one can still appeal to the unjust God. Says
Gloster after his eyes have been gouged out:

> As flies to wanton boys, are we to the gods, –
> They kill us for their sport.   (IV, 1)

But as long as gods exist, all can yet be saved:

> Hearken unto this, O Job: stand still, and consider the wond-
> rous works of God.   (*Book of Job*, XXXVII, 14)

The Bible is Beckett's favourite reading. After all, the passage
sounds like the dialogue in *Endgame*.

> *Clov.* They said to me, Here's the place, raise your head and look
> at all that beauty. That order! They said to me, Come now
> you're not a brute beast, think upon these things and you'll
> see how all becomes clear. And simple! They said to me,
> What skilled attention they get, all these dying of their wounds.
> *Hamm.* Enough!
> *Clov.* I say to myself – sometimes, Clov, you must learn to suffer
> better than that if you want them to weary of punishing you.
> I say to myself – sometimes, Clov, you must be there better
> than if you want them to let you go – one day.   (pp. 50–51)

Clov is a clown, but he is more unhappy than Hamm. Clov's
gabble is still eschatological, just as Lucky's is in *Waiting for
Godot*. In this dialogue of 'human ruins' Hamm alone has
realized the folly of all suffering. He has one reply to make to
eschatology: 'Take it easy . . . Peace to our . . . arses.' Both
couples: Pozzo who has been made blind, and Lucky who has
been made dumb, on the one hand, Hamm who cannot get up,
and Clov who cannot sit down, on the other, have been taken
from the Endgame of *King Lear*:

King Lear. Read.
Gloster. What, with the case of eyes?

. . . .

King Lear. What, art mad? A man may see how this world goes
   with no eyes. Look with thine ears.   (IV, 6)

These are biblical parables. The blind see clearly, madmen tell
the truth. After all, they are all mad. 'There are four of them,'
writes Camus, 'one by profession, one by choice, two by the
suffering they have been through. They are four torn bodies,
four unfathomable faces of the same fate.'[1] The Fool accompanies Lear on the cold night of madness; Edgar takes the
blind Gloster through a grotesque suicide. Lear's invocations of
the gods are countered by the Fool's scatological jokes;
Gloster's prayers by Edgar's clownish demonology:

   Fraterretto calls me, and tells me Nero is an angler in the lake of
   darkness. – Pray, innocent, and beware of the foul fiend. (. . .) The
   foul fiend bites my back. (. . .) Pur! the cat is gray.   (III, 6)

But Edgar's demonology is no more than a parody, a travesty of
contemporary Egyptian dream books and books on witchcraft;
a great and brutal gibe, in fact. He gibes at himself, at Job, conversing with God. For above 'Job's stage', there is in *King Lear*
only 'Macbeth's stage'. On it people murder, butcher and
torture one another, commit adultery and fornication, divide
kingdoms. From the point of view of a Job who has ceased to
talk to God, they are clowns. Clowns who do not yet know
they are clowns.

   King Lear. . . . come, come; I am a king!
         My masters, know you that.
   Gentleman. You are a royal one, and we obey you.
   King Lear. Then there's life in't. Nay, an you get it, you shall get it
      by running. Sa, sa, sa, sa.   (IV, 6)

The zero hour has come. Lear has come to understand it at last.
Just as blind Hamm came to understand everything, although
he was bound to his wheel-throne. And Pozzo, when he turned
blind and fell over his sand-filled bags:

[1] A. Camus, *Le Mythe de Sisyphe*, Paris, 1942.

Pozzo. I woke up one fine day as blind as Fortune . . .
Vladimir. And when was that?
Pozzo. I don't know . . . Don't question me! The blind have no
notion of time. The things of time are hidden from them too.
(*Waiting for Godot*, II)

And this is how King Lear ends his final frantic tirade:

No rescue? What, a prisoner? I am even
The natural fool of fortune.   (IV, 6)

In a moment he will run off the stage. Before that happens he
will ask for his pinching shoe to be taken off. He is a clown
now, so he can afford to do this. On 'Job's stage' four clowns
have performed the old medieval *sotie* about the decay and fall
of the world. But in both Shakespearian and Beckettian *Endgames* it is the modern world that fell; the renaissance world, and
ours. Accounts have been settled in a very similar way.

IV

The original clown was Harlequin. There is something in him
of an animal, a faun and a devil. That is why he wears a black
mask. He rushes about and seems to transform himself into
different shapes. The laws of space and time do not seem to
apply to him. He changes his guises in a flash and can be in
several places at once. He is a demon of movement. In Goldoni's
play *The Servant of Two Masters,* as produced by the Piccolo
Teatro of Milan, Harlequin, sitting on the edge of a wooden
platform, plucked a hair from his head, lengthened or shortened
it, pulled it through his ears, or put it on his nose and kept it
rigid in the air. Harlequin is a prestidigitator. He is a servant
who really does not serve anybody and jockeys everybody
away. He sneers at merchants and lovers, at marquesses and
soldiers. He makes fun of love and ambition, of power and
money. He is wiser than his masters, although he seems only to
be more clever. He is independent, because he has realized that
the world is simply folly.

Puck in *A Midsummer Night's Dream* is a popular goblin of

English folklore, a Robin Goodfellow. But he is also the Harlequin of the renaissance *commedia dell'arte*. He, too, is a quick-change artist, a prestidigitator and producer of the comedy of errors. He confuses the couples of lovers and causes Titania to caress an ass's head. In fact, he makes them all ridiculous, Titania and Oberon no less than Hermia and Lysander, Helena and Demetrius. He exposes the folly of love. He is accident, fate, chance. Chance happens to be ironical, though it does not know about it itself. Puck plays practical jokes. He does not know what he has done. That is why he can turn somersaults on the stage, just as Harlequin does.

Buffoonery is a philosophy and a profession at the same time. Touchstone and Feste are professional clowns. They wear jesters' attire, and are in the service of the prince. They have not ceased to be Harlequins and are not above pantomime. But they do not produce the performance any more; they do not even take part in it, but just comment on it. That is why they are jeering and bitter. The position of a jester is ambiguous and abounds in internal contradictions, arising out of the discrepancy between profession and philosophy. The profession of a jester, like that of an intellectual, consists in providing entertainment. His philosophy demands of him that he tell the truth and abolish myths. The Fool in *King Lear* does not even have a name, he is just a Fool, pure Fool. But he is the first fool to be aware of the fool's position:

> *Fool.* Prithee, nuncle, keep a schoolmaster that can teach thy fool to lie: I would fain learn to lie.
> *King Lear.* An you lie, sirrah, we'll have you whipp'd.
> *Fool.* I marvel what kin thou and thy daughters are: they'll have me whipp'd for speaking true, thou'lt have me whipp'd for lying; and sometimes I am whipp'd for holding my peace. I had rather be any kind o'thing than a fool: and yet I would not be thee, nuncle; thou hast pared thy wit o'both sides, and left nothing i'th'middle.   (I, 4)

A fool who has recognized himself for a fool, who has accepted the fact that he is only a jester in the service of the prince, ceases to be a clown. But the clown's philosophy is based on the

assumption that every one is a fool; and the greatest fool is he
who does not know he is a fool: the prince himself. That is why
the clown has to make fools of others; otherwise he would not
be a clown. The clown is subject to alienations because he is a
clown, but at the same time he cannot accept the alienation; he
rejects it when he becomes aware of it. The clown has the social
position of the bastard, as described many times by Sartre. The
bastard is a bastard for as long as he accepts his bastard's
position and regards it as inevitable. The bastard ceases to be a
bastard when he does not consider himself a bastard any more.
But at this point the bastard must abolish the division into
bastards and legitimate offspring. He then enters into opposi-
tion against the foundations of social order, or at least exposes
them. Social pressures want to limit the Clown to his part of a
clown, to pin the label 'clown' on him. But he does not accept
this part. On the contrary: he constantly pins that label on
others:

> *King Lear.* Dost thou call me fool, boy?
> *Fool.* All thy other titles thou hast given away; that thou wast
> born with.
> *Kent.* This is not altogether fool, my lord.
> *Fool.* No, faith, lords and great men will not let me; if I had a
> monopoly out, they would have part on't: and ladies too, they
> will not let me have all fool to myself; they'll be snatching.
>
> (I, 4)

This is the opening of the 'clowns' play', performed on 'Job's
stage'. In his very first scene, the Fool offers Lear his fool's cap.
For buffoonery is not only a philosophy, it is also a kind of
theatre. To us it is the most contemporary aspect of *King Lear*.
Only it has to be seen and interpreted properly. For this reason
one must reject all the romantic and naturalistic accessories; the
opera and melodrama about the old man who, driven out by
his daughters, wanders about bareheaded in a storm and goes
mad as a result of his misfortunes. But, as in the case of Hamlet,
there is method in this madness. Madness is in *King Lear* a
philosophy, a conscious crossing over to the position of the
Clown. Leszek Kolakowski writes:

The Clown is he who, although moving in high society, is not part of it, and tells unpleasant things to everybody in it; he, who disputes everything regarded as evident. He would not be able to do all this, if he were part of that society himself; then he could at most be a drawing-room scandal-monger. The Clown must stand aside and observe good society from outside, in order to discover the non-evidence of evidence, the non-finality of its finality. At the same time he must move in good society in order to get to know its sacred cows, and have occasion to tell the unpleasant things (. . .) The philosophy of Clowns is the philosophy that in every epoch shows up as doubtful what has been regarded as most certain; it reveals contradictions inherent in what seems to have been proved by visual experience; it holds up to ridicule what seems obvious common sense, and discovers truth in the absurd.[1]

Let us now turn to *King Lear*:

> *Fool*. Give me an egg, nuncle, and I'll give thee two crowns.
> *King Lear*. What two crowns shall they be?
> *Fool*. Why, after I have cut the egg i'th'middle, and eat up the meat, the two crowns of the egg. When thou clovest thy crown i'th'middle, and gavest away both parts, thou borest thine ass on thy back o'er the dirt. (. . .) now thou art an O without a figure: I am better than thou art now; I am a fool, thou art nothing. (I, 4)

After the crown had been torn off his head, Richard II asked for a mirror. He cast a look at it, and broke the mirror. He saw in the mirror his own unchanged face; the same that had belonged to a king. This amazed him. In *King Lear* the degradation occurs gradually, step by step. Lear divided his kingdom and gave away his power, but wanted to remain a king. He believed that a king could not cease to be a king, just as the sun could not cease to shine. He believed in pure majesty, in the pure idea of kingship. In historical dramas royal majesty is deprived of its sacred character by a stab of the dagger, or by a brutal tearing off of the crown from a living king's head. In *King Lear* it is the Fool who deprives majesty of its sacredness.

Lear and Gloster are adherents of eschatology; they

---

[1] L. Kolakowski, *The Priest and the Clown – Reflections on the Theological Heritage in Modern Thinking*, 'Twórczość', No. 10, 1959, pp. 82–3 (in Polish).

desperately believe in the existence of absolutes. They invoke the gods, believe in justice, appeal to laws of nature. They have fallen off 'Macbeth's stage', but remain its prisoners. Only the Fool stands outside 'Macbeth's stage', just as he has stood outside 'Job's stage'. He is looking on apart and does not follow any ideology. He rejects all appearances, of law, justice, moral order. He sees brute force, cruelty and lust. He has no illusions and does not seek consolation in the existence of natural or supernatural order, which provides for the punishment of evil and the reward of good. Lear, insisting on his fictitious majesty, seems ridiculous to him. All the more ridiculous because he does not see how ridiculous he is. But the Fool does not desert his ridiculous, degraded king, and accompanies him on his way to madness. The Fool knows that the only true madness is to recognize this world as rational. The feudal order is absurd and can be described only in terms of the absurd. The world stands upside down:

> When usurers tell their gold i'the field;
> And bawds and whores do churches build;
> Then shall the realm of Albion
> Come to great confusion:
> Then comes the time, who lives to see't,
> That going shall be us'd with feet.   (III, 2)

Hamlet escaped into madness not only to confuse informers and deceive Claudius. Madness to him was also a philosophy, a criticism of pure reason, a great, ironic clearing of accounts with the world, which has left its orbit. The Fool adopts the language Hamlet used in the scenes in which he feigned madness. There is nothing left in it now of Greek and Roman rhetoric, so popular in the Renaissance; nothing left of the cold and noble Senecan indifference to inevitable destiny. Lear, Gloster, Kent, Albany, even Edmund, still use rhetoric. Fool's language is different. It abounds in biblical travesties and inverted medieval parables. One can find in it splendid baroque surrealist expressions, sudden leaps of imagination, condensations and epitomes, brutal, vulgar and scatological comparisons. His rhymes are like limericks. The Fool uses dialectics, paradox and an absurd kind of humour. His language is that of our modern grotesque. The same grotesque that exposes the absurdity of apparent reality and of the absolute by means of a great and universal *reductio ad absurdum*.

> *King Lear.* O me, my heart, my rising heart! – but, down.
> *Fool.* Cry to it, nuncle, as the cockney did to the eels when she put'em i'the paste alive; she knapp'd 'em o'the coxcombs with a stick, and cried, 'Down, wantons, down!' 'Twas her brother that, in pure kindness to his horse, butter'd his hay.   (II, 4)

The Fool appears on the stage when Lear's fall is only beginning. He disappears by the end of Act III. His last words are: 'And I'll go to bed at noon.' He will not be seen or heard again. A clown is not needed any more. King Lear has gone through the school of clown's philosophy.[1] When he meets Gloster for the last time, he will speak the Fool's language and look at 'Macbeth's stage' the way the Fool has looked at it: 'They told me I was everything; 'tis a lie, – I am not ague-proof.' (IV, 6.)

[1] Maynard Mack, in his book *King Lear in Our Time*, found in the play the archetypal theme of the Abasement of the Proud King as is also found in *King Robert of Sicily*. 'In the finest of all the retellings of this archetype,' he wrote, 'the repudiated king is not driven out but made the court Fool and compelled to take his food with the palace dogs.' . . . In this version, the king's repentance comes when he has gone in the usurping angel's retinue to Rome, where to his dismay his former fellow-rulers, the Emperor and Pope, do not recognize him at all, and suppose him to be a mad fool. In a moment of insight the king sees a likeness between himself and the great Nebuchadnezzar who was also brought low and lived in a desert for many years on roots and grass. He is moved to repentance and in his humble prayer acknowledges himself to be only 'thy fool, Lord.' Now the angel asks the question again, and the reply comes: 'A fool.' Professor Mack emphasizes the pattern of the abasement, but it seems to me that much more relevant to the Shakespearian vision is the mutual relationship between a fool and a king.

Let Rome in Tiber Melt

>   . . . saucy lictors
> Will catch at us, like strumpets; and scald rimers
> Ballad us out o'tune: the quick comedians
> Extemporally will stage us, and present
> Our Alexandrian revels.   (*Anthony and Cleopatra*, V, 2)

The exposition of *Anthony and Cleopatra* is one of the most magnificent, even among Shakespeare's expositions. It is extremely short, yet contains everything. The theme, the characters, the world they live in, and the dimension of the tragedy. The great lovers have not yet appeared. Only Anthony's friends are on the stage, talking:

>   . . . you shall see in him
> The triple pillar of the world transform'd
> Into a strumpet's fool: behold and see.

Enter Anthony and Cleopatra. And a frenzied dialogue begins; a dialogue where every word tells:

> *Cleopatra.* If it be love indeed, tell me how much.
> *Anthony.* There's beggary in the love that can be reckon'd.
> *Cleopatra.* I'll set a bourn how far to be beloved.
> *Anthony.* Then must thou needs find out new heaven, new earth.
>   (I, 1)

At that instant, without the tension slowing down for one second, the Attendant enters. He speaks just one sentence: 'News, my good lord, from Rome.' A few more violent sentences, a dozen lines or so, and Anthony bursts out. He throws the world a challenge:

> Let Rome in Tiber melt, and wide arch
> Of the ranged empire fall! Here is my space.
> Kingdoms are clay: our dungy earth alike
> Feeds beast as man: the nobleness of life
> Is to do thus.   (*Embracing*)

This could be the opening of a tragedy by Racine, the only difference being its choppy rhetoric. We are not allowed to rest for an instant. But the theme and aura of tragedy are similar to Racine's. The royal lovers, heaven and earth. The earth which cannot contain them, the heaven which they cannot change. The world is hostile. Heaven and earth have to fall so that love can triumph. But heaven and earth are stronger than Anthony and Cleopatra. The royal lovers have to surrender, or choose death.

This one situation would provide Racine with enough material for an entire tragedy. And he would do with just one room in Cleopatra's palace. In it the action of the whole play would take place. Racine would do with the messenger from Rome and a pair of confidants for Anthony and Cleopatra. The world would find them in that one room of theirs. Over it would be just the heavens, cruel, empty, unalterable and silent. All the possibilities of escape and revolt would be discussed and exhausted in the space of five acts. The messenger would travel to and from Rome several times. Every time he would ask for Anthony's return. The world would be just as relentless and merciless as the heavens. The tragedy could work itself out in twelve or six hours, or even in one. Indeed, it would happen out of time. *Hic et nunc*. The story, with all the antecedents and everything that is external in relation to the tragedy itself, would be told by the confidants. To Racine only Anthony and Cleopatra would matter; perhaps Cleopatra alone. The whole tragedy would be condensed to the one last hour of choice; to the one hour in which Anthony and Cleopatra decide to choose death.

Time, space and history are to Racine no more than ideas, abstract terms. Kant expressed a similar view when he said: 'The starry sky above me, the moral law within me.' But Racine's heroes rebel against the law, and the law kills them. Shakespeare's tragedy of Anthony and Cleopatra encompasses ten years, and the whole historic world is its place of action. Time in this tragedy is real, and it weighs heavily. Space is even more concrete than in Shakespeare's other plays. Shakespeare's stage is always the world. But in this instance the world is not a metaphor; it is solid and differentiated, it is historical and geographical. Action takes place successively in Alexandria, Rome, Sicily, on the battlefield of Actium, then in Athens, and again in Rome and Egypt. These are not just place-names. His world is full of people, objects and events; as on a huge canvass by Rubens, every place in it has been filled. In the centre there are the great lovers, raging, loving, despairing, cursing each other, or entwined in a fiery embrace. But immediately around them, at their side, there are the generals, proconsuls, soldiers, messengers, eunuchs, court ladies, parades of slaves and military parades, tables loaded with meat and wine, ships and galleys, feasts and marches, councils and great battles, seas, sands, streets of Rome, landscapes and architecture, noise and music.

Shakespeare's world is historical not only because he remains more or less true to facts and dates. History in *Anthony and Cleopatra* is present not only as material for the plot. The names of generals and geographical terms are taken from Plutarch. But Plutarch's world, compared to Shakespeare's, is flat. Heroes and history exist in Plutarch side by side. In Shakespeare history itself is the drama. Caesar had destroyed Pompey; Brutus had assassinated Caesar; Anthony had crushed Brutus. Three men have divided the world among themselves: Anthony, Octavius – who has assumed the name of Caesar – and Lepidus. Against them has risen Sextus Pompey, son of the great Pompey. Anthony, through his legates, orders Pompey to be murdered. The younger Caesar has imprisoned Lepidus and ordered him to be murdered. Only two remain:

> Then, world, thou hast a pair of chaps, no more;
> And throw between them all the food thou hast,
> They'll grind the one the other.   (III, 5)

This is Shakespeare. The world is varied and multifarious, but the world is small. Too small for three rulers. Too small even for two. Either Anthony, or Caesar, must die. *Anthony and Cleopatra* is a tragedy about the smallness of the world. This is something not found in Plutarch. Plutarch's world is not tragic.

Generals and rulers are good or bad, wise or stupid, prudent or mad. Anthony was mad, and he lost. The younger Caesar was prudent, and he triumphed. History happens to be cruel, because tyrants happen to be cruel. But the world is arranged rationally; in the end virtue and reason win. The world is a great place, after all.

In *Anthony and Cleopatra* the world is little. It seems much smaller than in Plutarch. It is narrow and everything seems to be nearer. The Messenger says:

> Thy biddings have been done; and every hour,
> Most noble Caesar, shalt thou have report
> How 'tis abroad. (I, 4)

This sentence, too, is absent in Plutarch. Not only did Shakespeare read *Lives of the Noble Grecians and Romans* in North's contemporary version. He viewed the world through the experiences of the late Renaissance. In *Anthony and Cleopatra* the sun still encircles the earth, but the earth has already become a tiny globule, lost and of no importance in the universe.

> His face was as the heavens; and therein stuck
> A sun and moon, which kept their course, and lighted
> The little O, the earth. (V, 2)

The world is small, because one cannot escape it. The world is small because it can be won. The world is small, because to master it, chance, or a helping hand, or a skilful blow will do. Three men have divided the world among themselves. Another man, who wanted to resist them, has already humbled himself. He gives a feast and invites the triumvirs to his galley. They drink. Lepidus gets drunk first. He falls down on to the deck. A servant throws him over his shoulder and carries the 'pillar of the world' out. The officers look at their generals:

> *Enobarbus.* A'bears the third part of the world . . .
> *Menas.* The third part, then, is drunk. (II, 7)

This is the first confrontation. But on board the same galley another confrontation takes place, even more cruel and violent. The triumvirs are drunk, and Pompey is recalled from the feast by one of his followers. The man suggests that the sails be raised, and the throats of the three rulers of the world cut.

It is one of the greatest scenes in *Anthony and Cleopatra*: another scene not found in Plutarch, but taken straight from the experience of the Renaissance; a scene strikingly modern. Pompey refuses. But how does he do it? By reproaching Menas for not having done it himself; for asking his approval before and not after the deed:

> Ah, this thou shouldst have done,
> And not have spoke on't! In me 'tis villainy;
> In thee't had been good service.   (II, 7)

Racine's heroes possess a complete freedom of choice. Heaven is always silent, the world does not seem to exist. They are alone. They are devoured by passion, but are transparent to themselves. The deed is done, or will be done; it belongs to the antecedents of tragedy, or will be accomplished in its last scene. They are consumed by it throughout five acts. They prepare for it as for a leap into an abyss. They analyse it in all its aspects in fluent alexandrines. And the alexandrine will never be broken. Like the alexandrine, the heroes are noble and transparent.

Shakespeare's characters are – with the possible exception of Hamlet – a puzzle and a surprise to themselves. His protagonists are torn apart by passion, but in a different manner from Racine's heroes. The world is always there and constantly exerts its pressure, from the opening to the final scene. They too exercise a choice, but it is a choice through action. The theme of *Anthony and Cleopatra* could be taken from Racine: dignity and love cannot be reconciled with the struggle for power which forms the matter of history. But neither the world nor the struggle for power is shown in the abstract. The heroes are restless, like big animals in a cage. The cage gets smaller and smaller, and they writhe more and more violently.

Cleopatra is twenty-nine years old at the opening of the tragedy and thirty-nine years old at its close. Anthony is forty-three in the first scene and fifty-three in his last scene. This is not just a matter of historical chronology. *Romeo and Juliet* is a tragedy of first love. For these young lovers, in their abandon, the world does not exist. That is, perhaps, why they choose death so easily. *Anthony and Cleopatra* is the story of love as experienced by mature adults. Even their embrace is bitter: they know it as a challenge and that they will have to pay for it. A seed of hate is inherent from the start in this love of the royal lovers. Neither Anthony nor Cleopatra want to give up their inner freedom; they accept love as if under duress, and want to gain the upper hand over their partner.

Anthony breaks away from Cleopatra, returns to Rome, concludes a marriage of convenience. He fights, but not with himself; he fights for the mastery of the world. He returns to Egypt again, and suffers a decisive defeat. He is beaten. Cleopatra wants to keep him, and to retain Egypt for herself. She mobilizes all her resources, tries all possibilities; she is both brave and cowardly; faithful and ready to betray when she must, if she can sell herself to the new Caesar and save her kingdom. In Shakespeare's world even rulers do not have the freedom of choice. History is not an abstract term, but a practical mechanism. Cleopatra loses, in the same way as Anthony. She does not lose the battle with her own passion; she loses as a queen. She can only be a captive of the new Caesar and take part in his triumph as its main attraction.

Cleopatra can stay with Anthony. But Cleopatra loves Anthony – one of the pillars of the world; Anthony the invincible general. Anthony, who has lost, who has been defeated, is not Anthony. Anthony can stay with Cleopatra. But Anthony loves Cleopatra – goddess of the Nile. Cleopatra, who will be a captive of Caesar's, who will be pointed at in the streets of Rome, is no more Cleopatra.

Anthony and Cleopatra make their final choice only after their defeat – the choice which for Racine would be in itself a subject for a five-act tragedy. In Shakespeare it is a compulsory choice. But a compulsory choice does not detract from his heroes' greatness. Anthony and Cleopatra become the great lovers only in acts four and five. And not just great lovers. They pronounce judgement on the world. At the close of the play the theme of the exposition returns. Heaven and earth are too small for love. Anthony's words will be repeated by Cleopatra just before her death:

> 'Tis paltry to be Caesar;
> . . . .
>   . . . it is great
> To do that thing that ends all other deeds;
> Which shackles accidents, and bolts up change;
> Which sleeps, and never palates more the dug,
> The beggar's nurse and Caesar's.   (V, 2)

In *Richard III* the entire kingdom turned out to be worth less than a horse. A swift horse may save one's life. Anthony and Cleopatra do not want to flee, and have nowhere to escape to. 'Kingdoms are but ashes.' In both these great plays, power and those who wield it have been judged. And there will be no appeal. When a hero of Racine's kills himself, the tragedy is over, and, simultaneously, the world and history cease to exist. In fact they have never existed. When Anthony and Cleopatra kill themselves, the tragedy is over, but history and the world go on existing. The funeral oration over the corpses of Anthony and Cleopatra is spoken by the victorious triumvir, Octavius, the future Augustus Caesar. A very similar oration over Hamlet's body has been spoken by Fortinbras. He is still talking, but the stage is empty. All the great ones have gone. And the world has become flat.

'Coriolanus',
or
Shakespearian Contradictions

> You have deserved nobly of your country, and you have
> not deserved nobly . . . You have been a scourge to her
> enemies, you have been a rod to her friends; you have not,
> indeed, loved the common people.   (*Coriolanus*, II, 3)

I

Among all the great Shakespearian plays, *Coriolanus* has been
one of the least frequently performed. The play has had few
enthusiasts and admirers, although among their number were
Coleridge, Swinburne, Brecht[1] and Leon Schiller. But most
people were discouraged, revolted, or – at best – unmoved by
it. The play had not been a success in Shakespeare's lifetime,
and in the three centuries that followed; nor is it in our times.
It has been called a bleak tragedy, or a monodrama. In *Coriolanus*
there is no enchanting poetry, no music of the spheres; there
are no great lovers, or superb clowns; no raging elements, or
monsters conceived in imagination, but more real than actual
experience itself. There is only an historical chronicle, dry as a
bone, though violently dramatized. There is also a monumen-
talized hero, who can rouse all sorts of emotions, but never
sympathy.

However, *Coriolanus* is not really a monodrama. In fact, the
tragedy has two protagonists, although one of them has many
heads and many names. I will not describe him at once, but
rather begin with the assertion that Coriolanus is never alone,

[1] Brecht was preparing a production of *Coriolanus*, or rather its adapted version. His reading of the play was anti-traditional and didactic. He saw in it a
drama of the people betrayed by their fascist leader.

at least, in the physical and dramatic sense. In twenty-five scenes of the play, out of twenty-nine, crowds are present. Twelve scenes take place in the streets of Rome, in the Forum, and on the Capitol; two scenes at Corioli; ten – on fields of battle and in military camps. The crowd is nameless rather than having many names. Characters are called: First Citizen, Second Citizen, Third Citizen; First Senator, Second Senator; First Sentinel, Second Sentinel; First Officer, Second Officer; First Conspirator, Second Conspirator. The characters of military and political leaders are only very broadly outlined. They emerge for a moment from the crowd and are lost in it again. There are also Coriolanus's mother, wife and son. But even they do not have a life of their own, and simply serve as background to the situations in which the tragedy will be developed.

No doubt the dryness of *Coriolanus* must have had a discouraging effect on readers and audiences. The play is, indeed, harsh and austere. But the austerity of dramatic matter does not sufficiently explain the dislike almost universally felt for so long with regard to one of Shakespeare's most profound works. In my view the reasons for this dislike must be looked for elsewhere. It resulted from the ambiguity of *Coriolanus* – political, moral, and, in the last resort, philosophical. It was the sort of ambiguity difficult to swallow.

Coriolanus, as written by Shakespeare, could not wholly satisfy either aristocrats, or republicans; the friends of the people, or its enemies. The play annoyed those who believed in the masses, and those who despised them; those who recognized the purpose and didactics of history, and those who laughed at it; those who saw mankind as a mound of termites, and those who saw only lone individual termites painfully experiencing the tragedy of existence. *Coriolanus* did not fit in with any historical and philosophical conception current in the eighteenth and nineteenth centuries.

Coriolanus could not please either classicists or romanticists. To the first it seemed incoherent, vulgar and brutal; to the latter it was too bitter, flat and dry. The case of *Troilus and Cressida* repeated itself here: that was another Shakespearian play suffering from misapprehension; a play, whose philosophical essence, in spite of all the apparent differences, is very much akin to *Coriolanus*. In both plays ideas are violently and ironically contrasted with practice; this does not, however, result in recognizing practice as the final and only standard of value.

Coriolanus is only seemingly a monodrama, or a tragedy on an ancient theme. No doubt the play could be considered in terms of *polis* or *urbs* – a city state – protagonist, fate. The hero breaks the moral law, the city is threatened with destruction. The hero must choose between his life and the city. He chooses death. The city has been saved and erects a temple to Fortune. Rome is the city, Coriolanus the hero. But fate, as visualized by Shakespeare, although it pursues, corners and breaks the hero in the mode of the Greek furies, has a modern aspect. Fate is represented here by the class struggle. Rome is a city-state. But it is a Rome of plebeians and patricians.

The action of *Coriolanus* takes place after the expulsion of the kings in the half-legendary times of the early Roman republic. The story is briefly described by Livy, and Plutarch gives a detailed account of it in his *Lives of the Noble Grecians and Romans*. The English version by Sir Thomas North was published in 1579. It is from this translation that Shakespeare took the plot, characters and outline of events.

Rome has been engaged in warfare with neighbouring peoples. In Rome itself a struggle of the poor against the rich is going on. Plutarch has this to say about it:

> The Senate did favour the rich against the people, who did complain of the sore oppression of usurers, of whom they borrowed money. For those that had little, were yet spoiled of that little they had by their creditors, for lack of ability to pay the usury: who offered their goods to be sold to them that would give most. And such as had nothing left, their bodies were laid hold on, and they were made their bondmen . . . The Senate would give no care to them, but made as though they had forgotten their former promise, and suffered them to be made slaves and bondmen to their creditors, and besides, to be turned out of all that ever they had: they fell then even to flat rebellion and mutiny, and to stir up dangerous tumults within the city.

Wars have made the patricians rich. They have gained land and slaves. But they cannot carry on war without the plebeians. The plebeians have gained the right to elect their tribunes and to participate in government. The bravest of the Romans is Caius Marcius of an old patrician family. Having captured the town of Corioli from a mountain people called the Volscians he has been given the name Coriolanus. He has rendered Rome meritorious services. He is a great general, and on his body there are twenty-seven scars from wounds inflicted by the enemy. The patricians nominate Coriolanus for the office of Consul. The nomination has to be approved by the people. Coriolanus is an aristocrat, hates the people and is hated by them. There is famine in Rome. Coriolanus objects to the distribution of grain, unless the plebeians renounce their right to elect tribunes. The angry people refuse to approve Coriolanus's appointment to the consulate. The tribunes accuse him of plotting against the republic. Coriolanus has to stand trial. The people force the patricians to banish Coriolanus from Rome for ever. Coriolanus now dreams of revenge. He goes to the Volscians and proposes to his recent enemies an expedition against Rome. He assumes command of it himself.

This is the first chapter of the Roman legend of Coriolanus. There is in it a republican moral. A leader who despises the people, betrays the country and goes over to the enemy. An ambitious general aiming at dictatorial power is extremely dangerous for the republic. The people have been right to exile Coriolanus. But now the second chapter begins. Coriolanus, at the head of the Volscian army, approaches the gates of Rome. The city has no military leader, is defenceless and doomed to destruction. Plebeians and patricians accuse each other of having driven out Coriolanus. They try to appease him, beg for mercy. All in vain. The Romans then send Coriolanus's wife and mother as envoys. Coriolanus agrees to conclude peace, and retreats with the enemy army from the gates of Rome.

There are two endings to the story. The first, quoted by Livy, is sentimental and idyllic. The grateful Romans erect a temple in honour of Coriolanus's wife and mother, while he himself returns to the Volscians and dies peacefully after a long life. The other ending is far more dramatic. Coriolanus knows that by retreating from Rome he has condemned himself to death. Breaking his contract with the Volscians is a second betrayal. And he is murdered by them as a traitor.

The latter ending is quoted by Plutarch. But the author of the *Lives* does not seem to be aware of the fact that Coriolanus's history contains two morals, contradictory with each other. The moral drawn from the second chapter is very bitter indeed. The city that exiles its leader becomes defenceless. The people can only hate and bite, but are unable to defend their city. The masses are an element, just as blind and destructive as fire or flood. Among this multi-headed and nameless crowd, only Coriolanus was a great man. The country showed itself ungrateful to him. It could not contain him. He was a born ruler. History is cruel and abounds in traps. The great ones fall, the little ones remain.

Plutarch did not see either the tragedy of Coriolanus, or the tragedy inherent in history. In his *Lives* he set the Greek ethical ideal of harmonious personality against the Roman *virtus*. The moral drawn from Coriolanus's biography, as narrated by him, was psychological and empirical:

> A rare and excellent wit untaught, doth bring forth many good and evil things together, as a fat soil that lieth unmanured bringeth forth herbs and weeds ... he was so choleric and impatient, that he would yield to no living creature: which made him churlish, uncivil, and altogether unfit for any man's conversation ... his behaviour was so unpleasant to them by reason of a certain insolent and stern manner he had, which because it was too lordly, was disliked. And to say truly, the greatest benefit that learning bringeth unto men, is this: that it teacheth men that be rude and rough of nature, by compass and rule of reason, to be civil and courteous, and to like better, the mean state than the higher.

So much for Plutarch. Coriolanus's history is virulent, indeed. But it was Shakespeare who first saw the virulence in it. He must have been particularly struck by it, since he made it the main theme of the drama. In the Histories and Tragedies – the latter being more condensed than the former – Shakespeare shows feudal history, its bare and unalterable mechanism, in an absolute form. History is being performed at the apex of the social hierarchy. It is personal and uses names, though the names are few. Only occasionally do frightened townsmen appear. They learn about the sovereign's death, a war, or a *coup d'état*. They view every change of king as an elemental disaster. History takes place above them, but it is they who have to pay for it.

Feudal history could easily find its model and reflection in the story of the Roman emperors. Comparisons between Caesar and Brutus were a frequent theme of renaissance moralizing; stories of tyrants were a favourite plot of pre-Shakespearian and Elizabethan tragedy. Tacitus and Suetonius were quoted more frequently than other Roman authors. Busts of the twelve Caesars decorated the palaces of all the Christian kings.[1] Republican Rome was far more remote and less familiar to the Renaissance. The only comparable contemporary institution was the Venetian Republic, but even she was governed by the Doge and an aristocracy. People of the Renaissance were fascinated by the problem of absolute power; the mechanism by means of which a good prince is transformed into a tyrant. To them it was an everyday affair. It was one of the great Shakespearian themes. But not the only one.

Shakespeare was a far greater innovator in *Julius Caesar* and in *Coriolanus* than in *Anthony and Cleopatra*. In the first two plays he introduced republican Rome into tragedy. No doubt he looked at it through the experiences of the late Renaissance and searched for the confirmation of his bitter, most pessimistic and cruel philosophy of history. But the matter he used was different somehow, and could not be contained in the unchanging circle, where the beginning and end of every reign was marked by the sufferings of the fallen monarch. The metaphor of the grand staircase, climbed by every ruler in turn, with the

[1] See T. J. B. Spencer, *Shakespeare and the Elizabethan Romans*, 'Shakespeare Survey', 10, 1957.

scaffold as the first and the last step, could not be applied to this view of history any longer.

Coriolanus still has a mark of grim greatness, and is crushed by history. But the history that breaks Coriolanus is not royal history any more. It is the history of a city divided into plebeians and patricians. It is the history of class struggle. History in the royal chronicles, and in *Macbeth*, was a Grand Mechanism, which had something demonic in it. History in *Coriolanus* has ceased to be demonic. It is only ironic and tragic. This is another reason why *Coriolanus* is a modern play.

II

The first scene of *Coriolanus* opens with the entry of the mutinous plebeians. The theme, the conflict, the protagonists of the play are all given at the outset:

> *First Citizen.* You are all resolved rather to die than to famish?
> *Citizens.* Resolved! Resolved!
> *First Citizen.* First, you know Caius Marcius is chief enemy to the
>   people. (I, 1)

This is practically the opening of the play. Shakespeare never wastes any time. The situation has been stated. There is famine in Rome; the plebeians demand a reduction of the grain prices. Caius Marcius does not agree to it. The plebeians resolve to kill Marcius. Action begins in the very first minute. Very soon the theme of the play will be stated. The plebeians shout at each other in a rather confused manner, but in their speeches a detailed theory of class division is formulated. It is based on three elementary contrasts: some people work, others feed on their misery; some are poor, others are rich; some are placed low and have to obey, others are placed high and rule. All this is contained in the plebeian exclamations of the first scene:

> The leanness that afflicts us, the object of our misery, is as an inventory to particularize their abundance; our sufferance is a gain to them.

. . . .

They . . . suffer us to famish, and their store-houses cramm'd with grain; make edicts for usury, to support usurers; repeal daily any wholesome act established against the rich; and provide more piercing statutes daily, to chain up and restrain the poor. If the wars eat us not up, they will.   (I, 1)

At this point the patrician Menenius Agrippa enters. He has been sent by the Senate to calm the rebels. Agrippa admits that there is hunger, that there are the rich and the poor. But he takes a different view of causes and effects. The poor starve not because the rich have too much for themselves. The patricians care for the people. Poverty is a judgement of the gods. This is the way the world has been arranged, and no one can change the eternal order:

> For your wants,
> Your suffering in this dearth, you may as well
> Strike at the heaven with your staves as lift them
> Against the Roman state . . .
>
> . . . .
>
>   . . . for the dearth,
> The gods, not the patricians, make it; and
> Your knees to them, not arms, must help.   (I, 1)

Agrippa speaks in verse; the plebeians in prose. Class distinctions have to be observed even by Shakespearian heroes. But it is something more than a mere distinction between verse and prose. Agrippa counters the simple spatial 'top – bottom' metaphor of the plebeians, based on consciousness of class oppression, with a metaphor of society as a great organism. He tells the plebeians the famous story about the revolt of the parts of the body against the stomach. The stomach stands for the Roman Senate, the rebellious parts of the body – for the plebs. Agrippa's fable has already been quoted by Livy and Plutarch. But Shakespeare, as is usual with him, condenses and dramatizes it. Agrippa's fable is also a theory of class division, as seen by the patricians. The brutal dichotomy of the plebeians is opposed by a functional and organic theory. Both theories are shown by Shakespeare in their class functions. They provide means of agitation, as well as justify action. This is just the way they have operated in history.

Agrippa's arguments have had a long political and academic career. They were repeated by Theodoretus of Ciro in the first century of the Christian era ('Masters participate in the cares of their servants, but servants do not participate in the cares of their masters'), as well as by American planters in Franklin D. Roosevelt's time ('We have to take care for the provision of grain, for financing the lease and all such things, while the black farm labourer expects to be provided by us, and has no cares whatsoever for as long as he is maintained by us'). Agrippa's concept of class inter-dependence was proclaimed by the physiocrats ('a perfect entity composed of various parts, necessary to each other'), and by the nineteenth-century papal encyclicals. It was developed by Spencer and Dürkheim into a scientific system of sociology.[1] Shakespeare needed just five minutes to state this theory.

The first scene of *Coriolanus* is not yet over. Agrippa has hardly finished telling his story than Caius Marcius appears. He begins to revile the plebeians in his very first sentence:

> ... What's the matter, you dissentious rogues,
> That, rubbing the poor itch of your opinion,
> Make yourselves scabs? (I, 1)

Agrippa is the ideologue of the patricians, in the sense in which Marx contemptuously used the word 'ideologue'. Agrippa is a tactician and philosopher of opportunism. Marcius is not an ideologist and rejects all tactics. Marcius accepts the class distinction that is superficially in accord with the plebeian view: the antagonistic, vertical division between top and bottom, the occupiers of which feel deadly hate for each other. He tells the senators:

---

[1] All three quotations are based on the work by Stanislaw Ossowski, *Class Structure in Social Consciousness*, Łódź 1957 (in Polish). Ossowski distinguishes three fundamental schemes of class structure: dichotomic, gradational and functional. He quotes Agrippa's fable, but does not mention its part in *Coriolanus*.

> You are plebeians,
> If they be senators: and they are no less,
> When, both your voices blended, the great'st taste
> Most palates theirs. They choose their magistrate;
> And such a one as he, who puts his 'shall',
> His popular 'shall', against a graver bench
> Then ever frown'd in Greece.   (III, 1)

Marcius accepts two of the classic opposites of the plebeian theory: the rich – the poor, the rulers – the governed. But to these two, he adds two more: the noble – the base, the wise – the fools. To him the people are like animals that bite each other, hate the stronger, and cannot remember today what they wanted yesterday:

> . . . What would you have, you curs,
> That like nor peace nor war? the one affrights you,
> The other makes you proud.
>
> . . . .
>
> . . . Who deserves greatness
> Deserves your hate.
>
> . . . .
>
> . . . Trust ye!
> With every minute you do change a mind;
> And call him noble that was now your hate . . .
>
> . . . .
>
> . . . in these several places of the city
> You cry against the noble senate, who,
> Under the gods, keep you in awe, which else
> Would feed on one another . . .   (I, 1)

In Plutarch Marcius also hates the people, mainly because he is consumed by pride, a recluse who does not know how to deal with men. Plutarch really feels himself in sympathy with Agrippa's practical reasoning. Shakespeare mocks Agrippa, at best giving him a part similar to that played in *Hamlet* by Polonius. From the first to the last scene of the tragedy the conflict is between Coriolanus and the people. As in all Shakespeare's great dramas it is a conflict about the conception and moral value of history; a difference of views on how the world is really arranged. Coriolanus, as Shakespeare sees him, is proud and uncontrollable, too. But his actions do not result (or – at any rate – not wholly so) from flaws in his character, or from 'lack of learning', as our good Plutarch would have it. The tragedy of Shakespeare's Coriolanus cannot be defined, or contained in psychological terms. Nor is it a tragedy of a great personality in conflict with the masses, as most commentators maintain. There are no masses in *Coriolanus*. There are just the patricians and the plebeians.

Coriolanus accepts the class contrasts, as the plebeians see them, but it is easy to observe that he alters their character and transfers them into categories of values. The plebeians do not call themselves noble, or the patricians – wicked. They only know they are hungry, because the others are full. Agrippa denies the existence of the hungry and the full, for one cannot say that the hands are hungry when the stomach is full. Coriolanus accepts the division into the hungry and the full, but does so not because it has been the will of the gods. Coriolanus does not believe in gods, and has no need of them. He regards the people as animals who, when well fed, will only grow insolent and attack men. The city will be devoured by rats.

> . . . thus we debase
> The nature of our seats, and make the rabble
> Call our cares fears; which will in time
> Break ope the locks o'the senate, and bring in
> The crows to peck the eagles. (III, 1)

Three theories of class division have been stated and thoroughly discussed, up to their final consequences. Each of them contains an exposition of social reality, and a system of values; each means a different view of the world, and gives a different evaluation, a different reply to two basic questions: how is the world arranged, and how should it be arranged? It is easy to find general terms to define these systems, such as: egalitarianism, solidaritism, the hierarchic system. *Coriolanus* presents a most ruthless and anti-didactic confrontation of these three systems. As is usual for Shakespeare, there is a great system of mirrors, reflecting the people in the eyes of

Coriolanus, as well as Coriolanus and the patricians in the eyes of the people. The last mirror is provided by History. History in drama provides the course of action, inter-relation and the final consequence of events. History can either confirm systems of values, or ridicule and destroy them. If it ridicules and destroys, it is grotesque, or tragic; or even, perhaps – both.

III

The first confrontation is provided by war. The Volscians have attacked Rome. The plebeians are helpless. The situation changes in a flash. The generals assume power, and the rebels withdraw. Agrippa's arguments and his fable seem to be proved right. Caius Marcius triumphs:

> The Volsces have much corn; take these rats thither
> To gnaw their garners.   (I, 1)

The Romans have reached Corioli. The first attack on the town has been repelled, the soldiers flee. Marcius throws insults at deserters, calls the brave ones to him, and attacks again. He pursues the Volscians to the gates, and enters the enemy town single-handed.

> *First Soldier.* Fool-hardiness; not I.
> *Second soldier.* Nor I.
> *First Soldier.* See, they have shut him in.
> *All.* To the pot, I warrant him.   (I, 4)

Shakespeare's battle scenes are accompanied by drum-beats and the sound of trumpets. But there is little noise in them. They take place on an empty stage. Great battles are fought by a handful of soldiers. Of course, at the Globe, red paint was not spared, and swords clattered against each other for long stretches of time. But Shakespeare's battle scenes are neither descriptive nor intended to create a make-believe. Theirs is a dramatic quality of a different, inner kind. Mortal duels are punctuated by bitter philosophic reflection, or by irony. Young Henry is a hero and defeats Percy. But Falstaff would rather pretend to be a corpse; he knows that the main thing is to remain alive. The war is a kings' and generals' war; not a soldiers' war. This is also true of the war in *Coriolanus*.

Corioli has been captured. Marcius has gone through it like a hurricane. Only the carcass of a town has remained, off which the soldiers snatch miserable slices.

First Roman. This will I carry to Rome.
Second Roman. And I this.
Third Roman. A murrain on't; I took this for silver.　　　(I, 5)

Such are the scenes of perennial history, as Shakespeare sees them; scenes written once and for all. They are wide generalizations, and most concrete, at the same time. It is sufficient to imagine this scene, or to re-read it the way it has been written, to realize the deeper causes of Brecht's enthusiasm for *Coriolanus*. *Coriolanus* is a far more emphatic, direct and modern model of the theatre Brecht called epic than Shakespeare's Histories. Mother Courage feeds on war, unaware to the end that it is the war that feeds on her and will take from her everything she has got. Mother Courage is like those soldiers wresting from each other's hands a leaden cup mistaking it for silver. In his last period Brecht often called his epic theatre – 'dialectic'. He looked to Shakespeare for its model. Let us go on. The victorious Roman generals, among them Marcius, enter the streets of the dead town, empty like the Shakespearian stage:

> See here these movers that do prize their hours
> At a crack'd drachma! Cushions, leaden spoons,
> Irons of a doit, doublets that hangmen would
> Bury with those that wore them, these base slaves,
> Ere yet the fight be done, pack up: down with them! –
> And hark, what noise the general makes!　　　(I, 5)

Marcius is clearly and consciously made by Shakespeare to appear heroic. He has Achilles's strength, and a voice more powerful than any man's. The Volscian general calls him Hector, among bragging Romans. Even the style, the similes used to describe Marcius's warlike deeds, are homeric. His mother speaks of Coriolanus:

> With his mail'd hand then wiping, forth he goes,
> Like to a harvest-man, that's task'd to mow
> Or all, or lose his hire. (I, 3)

And this is what the commander-in-chief says of him:

> A carbuncle entire, as big as thou art,
> Were not so rich a jewel. Thou wast a soldier
> Even to Cato's wish, not fierce and terrible
> Only in strokes, but, with thy grim looks and
> The thunder-like percussion of thy sounds,
> Thou madest thine enemies shake, as if the world
> Were feverous and did tremble. (I, 4)

The Volscian general refers to Marcius thus:

> I do not know what witchcraft's in him, but
> Your soldiers use him as the grace 'fore meat,
> Their talk at table, and their thanks at end. (IV, 7)

Marcius is brave. During his first campaign he shielded a wounded soldier with his own body and carried him away from the battlefield; he has been wounded twenty-seven times in the service of Rome; he captured Corioli single-handed. Marcius is selfless. He refuses to accept the tenth part of the booty he is entitled to, and demands that it should be equally distributed among everybody. He does not want to talk about his heroic deeds and does not want others to talk about them.

The war confirms the class hierarchy which Marcius had already perceived in peace-time. Patricians and plebeians behave differently in war. Compared to Marcius, how miserable seem the plebeians, who tremble before the battle, and when the victory is won, snatch from one another cups, spoons and soiled rags.

> ... but for our gentlemen,
> The common file – a plague! – tribunes for them! –
> The mouse ne'er shunn'd the cat as they did budge
> From rascals worse than they. (I, 6)

Marcius is right. Plebeians behave in a war like rats. This is the first mirror: the war as the patricians see it. But even in this

reflection the picture of war is suddenly objectivized, as in
Mother Courage. Shakespeare always carries his confrontations
to their limits. In a war there are not only victors, but also
losers. In the captured town Titus Larcius has assumed military
power:

> Condemning some to death, and some to exile;
> Ransoming him or pitying, threatening the other;
> Holding Corioli in the name of Rome,
> Even like a fawning greyhound in the leash,
> To let him slip at will.   (I, 6)

This is something more than homeric similes. Nor do we find
such a scene in Plutarch. This is a universal representation of
any occupation. Again this scene must be re-read and imagined
as Shakespeare has written it. It questions the whole system of
values defended by Marcius. It represents Brechtian 'objective
dialectic'. It refers to the audience's judgement. Shakespeare's
sense of dramatic irony shows itself in the fact that these words
are spoken by Marcius himself.

Coriolanus contains another amazing speech by Marcius. He
returns in triumph to Rome, is welcomed by his mother and
wife. The wife does not speak one word; she just weeps. Says
Coriolanus:

>   . . . Ah, my dear,
> Such eyes the widows in Corioli wear,
> And mothers that lack sons.   (II, 1)

These words hardly agree with Coriolanus's character. They
are too soft, too sensitive. They sound a jarring note at this
joyous moment. They perform the function of songs in Brecht's
dramatic pieces. Again, they suddenly objectivize, recalling
those who have been defeated. The other mirror is not really
needed any more. But Shakespeare never renounces anything.
He will show the other reflection: war in the eyes of a defeated
general.

> *Aufidius.* The town is ta'en!
> *First soldier.* 'Twill be deliver'd back on good condition.

Aufidius. Condition! –
> I would I were a Roman; for I cannot,
> Being a Volsce, be that I am. – Condition!
> What good condition can a treaty find
> I' the part that is at mercy? (I, 10)

IV

Coriolanus's mother and wife sit on low stools, sew, embroider and wait for news of the war. These low stools on which women used to chatter in the evening can be seen in Stratford even now. In Shakespeare's Rome there is the Forum, the Capitol, the Tarpeian Rock, there are consuls, tribunes, lictors, senate; all the names are taken from Plutarch. Anachronisms – which Ben Jonson had already noted with satisfaction – are few in *Coriolanus*. The most delightful of these is the picture of a Roman hero on the Forum contemptuously waving his big hat before the assembled crowd. Coriolanus in a hat is funny to us, but did not seem funny to an Elizabethan audience.

Shakespeare wrote for the stage of his time. The first Shakespearian productions in antiquarian fashion came only in the middle of the nineteenth century. Shakespeare was concerned with historical truth of a quite different sort.

He did not find scenes from everyday life in Plutarch, but took them from his own experience in London and Stratford. He made them contemporary. He deliberately mixed the high and the low style. He showed the kind of Rome that could not be shown by Corneille, or Racine:

> All tongues speak of him, and the bleared sights
> Are spectacled to see him; your prattling nurse
> Into a rapture lets her baby cry
> While she chats him: the kitchen malkin pins
> Her richest lockram 'bout her reechy neck,
> Clamb'ring the walls to eye him: stalls, bulks, windows,
> Are smother'd up, leads fill'd, ridges hors'd ... (II, 1)

Coriolanus's mother and wife are visited by their neighbour, good mistress Valeria, who wants to take them out for a gossip.

Virgilia does not want to leave the house until her husband returns from the war. She weaves on a loom. Mistress Valeria cracks a joke: 'You would be another Penelope: yet, they say, all yarn she spun in Ulysses' absence did but fill Ithaca full of moths.' (I, 3.) As in *Troilus and Cressida*, the Greek myth has been ironically treated, shown in its everyday aspect. The joke might almost be taken from *La Belle Hélène*. No heroics here, no pathetic expectation of a brave general's return. In this idyllic and ordinary atmosphere of a fine Stratford evening, Volumnia is suddenly and unexpectedly styled a Roman mother, or rather – a Spartan mother. She has an only son, but she would rather see him dead than prove a coward. If she had twelve sons, she would rather lose all twelve: 'I had rather had eleven die nobly for their country than one voluptuously surfeit out of action.' (I, 3.)

The first mirror again. And – as is Shakespeare's custom – a confrontation will follow at once. In this scene, apart from the three women – the Spartan mother, the loving wife and the chattering neighbour – there is also Coriolanus's little son. He does not speak a word. He does not have to. He is being talked about.

> *Valeria.* O' my word, the father's son: I'll swear, 'tis a very pretty boy. O' my troth, I look'd upon him o' Wednesday half an hour together: has such a confirmed countenance, I saw him run after a gilded butterfly; and when he caught it, he let it go again; and after it again; and over and over he comes, and up again; catch'd it again: or whether his fall enraged him, or how 'twas, he did so set his teeth, and tear it: O, I warrant, how he mammock'd it!
> *Volumnia.* One on's father's moods.
> *Valeria.* Indeed, la, 'tis a noble child. (I, 3)

''Tis a noble child.' Shakespeare's irony limits itself to just these words. There is no such scene in Plutarch. Shakespeare has given the Spartan mother a grandson who squashes a 'gilded butterfly' just to amuse himself. This is all. In *Titus Andronicus* – regarded as Shakespeare's most cruel play – young Marcus kills a fly on a plate. Titus, who in the last scene will treat Queen Tamora to a pie baked of her own sons' hearts, cannot look at an innocent fly's death:

> But how, if that fly had a father and mother?
> How would he hand his slender gilded wings,
> And buzz lamenting doings in the air! (III, 2)

King Lear invoked gods to alleviate the world's cruelty. The gods were silent. They turned out to be just as cruel as nature and history. In *Coriolanus* nature and history are rid of all metaphysics. Cruelty is part of the leader's schooling. Coriolanus's son is the grandson of the Spartan mother.

Coriolanus has returned. The patricians want to make him consul. All he must do, according to law and custom, is to appear at the Forum, expose his scars and ask the citizens for approval. Coriolanus refuses. His contempt for the people is too great. He is a soldier and will not lie. He wants to remain true to himself, that is to say – true to nature. Eagles do not lower themselves to the level of rats and crows. Coriolanus wants the world to recognize his greatness. But the world is divided into plebeians and patricians. Coriolanus's hierarchy of nature does not agree with the real world. Rats have no wish to consider themselves worse than eagles.

The Spartan mother begs her son to humble himself and go to the Forum to ask for votes. A stratagem is not inconsistent with honour, it is not shameful to use it in war. The war is not yet over. The enemy is within the city walls. The plebs are the enemy:

> . . . now it lies you on to speak
> To the people; not by your own instruction,
> Nor by the matter which your heart prompts you,
> But with such words that are but rooted in
> Your tongue, though but bastards . . .
> . . . .
> Now, this no more dishonours you at all
> Than to take in a town with gentle words,
> Which else would put you to your fortune, and
> The hazard of much blood. (III, 2)

To the Spartan mother there is no difference between war and peace, between the external and internal enemy. Coriolanus's mother, like the plebeians, sees two classes hating each other, the war between whom never ends. Except that to her Rome means the patricians.

> Rome and her rats are at the point of battle:
> The one side must have bale. (I, 1)

These words are spoken by the same Agrippa who has told the rebellious plebeians the fable of the stomach and the disobedient parts of the body. He, too, calls on Coriolanus, asking him to go to the Forum. Coriolanus will go there, though in spite of himself. In this drama of class hatred Coriolanus is such as the plebeians see him, but the plebeians also conform to Coriolanus's view of them. Shakespeare has no illusions. To have judged the world will not result in the world being changed. A conflagration may cause rupture or terror; but it does not cease to be a fire.

> For the mutable, rank-scented meiny, let them
> Regard me as I do not flatter, and
> Therein behold themselves. (III, 1)

In Juliusz Slowacki's drama, *Kordian*, the Grand Duke Constantine says: 'The people stand there, still, black and muddy. I do not like this people.' The people in *Coriolanus* are black and muddy, but they are not still. They bark like a pack of mongrels deprived of their bone. In the first scene the people want to kill Coriolanus. They later disperse at the first news of war.

The people crowd the streets and throw their caps high in the air to welcome the very same Coriolanus after his victory. They forget everything, and agree to make him consul; all they beg of him is a good word. An hour later, incited by the tribunes, they demand Coriolanus's head and drive him out of the city. Again caps are thrown high in the air. When Coriolanus, at the head of the Volscians, appears at the gates of Rome, the plebeians turn against their own leaders and want to tear them to pieces; they fawn on the patricians and beg for mercy. They are ready to agree to anything in order to save their stinking rags and their lives.

It hath been taught us from the primal state,
That he which is was wish'd until he were;
And the ebb'd man, ne'er lov'd till ne'er worth love,
Comes dear'd by being lack'd. This common body,
Like to a vagabond flag upon the stream,
Goes to and back, lackeying the varying tide.
To rot itself with motion.   (*Anthony and Cleopatra*. I, 4)

This is a quotation from *Anthony and Cleopatra*. It could just as
well come from *Coriolanus*, *Henry VI*, or *Julius Caesar*. In the
great assassination scene the crowd applauds Brutus. But as
soon as Mark Anthony has finished speaking, the plebeians
deplore Caesar's death and turn against his assassins. Shakespeare had seen how London's populace crowded the streets to
welcome Essex with torches, and later thronged to watch his
execution. To Shakespeare the people are only an object of
history, not its actor. They can evoke disgust, pity, or terror;
but they are powerless, they are the sport of those who hold
power in their hands. But the people in Plutarch have their
tribunes. Who are these tribunes? Two London magistrates,
elected by artisans, appear at the Forum:

> *Menenius.* You are ambitious for poor knaves' caps and legs: you
> wear out a good wholesome forenoon in hearing a cause between
> an orange-wife and a fosset-seller; and then rejourn the contro-
> versy of three-pence to a second day of audience. When you are
> hearing a matter between party and party, if you chance to be
> pinch'd with the colic, you make faces like mummers; set up
> the bloody flag against all patience; and, in roaring for a cham-
> ber-pot, dismiss the controversy bleeding, the more entangled
> by your hearing . . .   (II, 1)

It is these two indolent half-wits, proud, violent and petulant,
who represent the people in *Coriolanus*. They are 'the herdsmen
of the beastly plebeians' and stink just as the populace does. They
suffer from scabies and have to scratch themselves all over their
bodies. They are like mongrels. But these mongrels know how
to defend their herd. These two ridiculous tribunes, Brutus and
Sicinius, short and misshapen, envious and suspicious though
they are, possess a class instinct. They ask for news of the war:

Brutus. Good or bad?
Menenius. Not according to the prayer of the people, for they love
   not Marcius.
Sicinius. Nature teaches beasts to know their friends.   (II, 1)

Shakespeare is fascinated not only by the transformation of a
good ruler into a tyrant. He is also fascinated by history. Where
and when is it decided, and who decides it? Does it have a
human face, the name and passions of a prince, or is it just a
sum total of chance, or a mechanism put in motion? In *Coriolanus* history is being played out on a public square. It is these
two little ridiculous tribunes who help to boost it.

> To the Capitol, come;
> We will be there before the stream o' the people;
> And this shall seem, as partly 'tis, their own,
> Which we have goaded onward.   (II, 3)

In the battle scenes soldiers rush across the stage, sword in
hand. Princes place themselves with large banners on opposite
sides of the platform. Generals observe the field of battle from
the upper gallery. Shakespeare appreciates the value of spectacle, but for him spectacle is never an end in itself. He con-
demns war by showing up the feudal butchery. Extras have
already filled the stage. They will represent the people. On the
inner stage, or in the gallery, resplendent senators are seated.
On the apron stage, close to the audience, Coriolanus, Menenius
and two tribunes stand. The latter are not ridiculous any
more.

> We charge you, that you have contriv'd to take
> From Rome all season'd office, and to wind
> Yourself into a power tyrannical;
> For which you are a traitor to the people.   (III, 3)

A seventeenth-century London street has suddenly in our eyes
been transformed into a great scene of popular revolution.
There is no such scene in Plutarch. Shakespeare was the first to
throw the Roman toga of defenders of liberty and the republic
over the shoulders of two stinking and noisy London artisans.
The Jacobins would have recognized themselves better in

Shakespeare's tribunes of the people than on David's huge canvasses:

> *Brutus.* There's no more to be said, but he is banish'd,
>   As enemy to the people and his country:
>   It shall be so.
> *Citizens.* It shall be so, it shall be so.   (III, 3)

In scenes of battle and looting Shakespeare shows the eternal face of war and occupation. The most striking characteristic of Shakespearian tragedies is their historical universality. Shakespeare does not have to be modernized or brought up to date. History fills his plays with ever new contents, and finds its reflection in them, in every age. In the first scene of *Coriolanus* the plebeian theory of class division has been noisily stated. Now they stand opposite each other: the cold and elegant senators, and the plebeians, who shake their fists and raise their clubs. The same scenery will be repeated in many historical situations. At the Capitol and at the Forum, laws of revolution, attitudes and conflicts, are all exposed, sharply like formulas condensed in bits of dialogue. Opposite each other stand, 'top' and 'bottom', Jacobins and Girondists, revolutionary democrats and liberals. The trial of Coriolanus is on.

Says Brutus, or the Jacobins:

>   . . . those cold ways,
>   That seem like prudent helps, are very poisonous
>   Where the disease is violent. – Lay hands upon him,
>   And bear him to the rock.

Says Menenius, or the liberals:

>   Do not cry havoc, where you should but hunt
>   With modest warrant.
>   . . . .
>   Killing our enemies, the blood he hath lost . . .
>   And what is left, to lose it by his country,
>   Were to us all, that do't and suffer it,
>   A brand to the end o' the world.
>   . . . .
>   The service of the foot

Being once gangren'd, is not then respected
For what before it was?

. . . .
                              Proceed by process.

Says the Senator, or the aristocrats:

                              Noble tribunes,
          It is the humane way: the other course
          Will prove too bloody; and the end of it
          Unknown to the beginning.

Says Sicinius, or the Girondists:

                              Noble Menenius,
          Be you, then, as the people's officer. –
          Masters, lay down your weapons.

Says Brutus, or the Jacobins:

                              Go not home.   (III, 1)

The people in *Coriolanus* are stupid and ignorant; they stink and
collect stinking rags on battlefields. The tribunes are small,
deformed and deceitful. Coriolanus is brave, great and noble.
But the people are Rome, and Coriolanus is a traitor to his
country.

> *Sicinius.* What is the city but the people?
> *Citizens.* True,
>   The people are the city.
> *Brutus.* By the consent of all, we were establish'd
>   The people's magistrates.
> *Citizens.* You so remain.   (III, 1)

It is only now that the second, forceful, part of the drama opens.
The plebeians have exiled Coriolanus from Rome. The cowardly
patricians have deserted him. Rome has not appreciated his
bravery and nobility. Rome has proved itself base.

                              Despising
          For you, the city, thus I turn my back:
          There is a world elsewhere.   (III, 3)

But Shakespeare's world is crowded, and there are no empty
spaces in it. There are just patricians, plebeians, and enemies of

Rome. Coriolanus can only choose his place in the world that has been set on fire. He does not, and cannot go away into nowhere, as romantic heroes do. Situations are historically determined, are above and independent of him. Coriolanus will go to the Volscians. History has proved the plebeians right: the enemy of the people has become the enemy of Rome. In the first three acts of *Coriolanus* a bare drama of class attitudes has been played out. One could call it also a drama of historical inevitability. There is in it no discrepancy between social situation and action, or psychology. Coriolanus could be nameless, just as the First, Second and Third Citizens are nameless. He is just an ambitious general, who hates the people and has gone over to the enemy camp when unable to achieve dictatorial power. It is only from the moment of Coriolanus's treason that the world ceases to be clear-cut and arranged according to one principle. History is not a teacher of lay morality any more. The world's contradictions become the next theme of the tragedy. This new theme is no less proper to Shakespeare than the former. Even the style has changed: it is grotesque, pathetic and ironical in turn. Coriolanus mocks himself and the world, as did Hamlet when talking to Polonius. He even describes his dreams. 'The time is out of joint', just as it had been in the kingdom of Denmark.

> *Third Serving-Man.* Where dwell'st thou?
> *Coriolanus.* Under the canopy.
> *Third Serving-Man.* Under the canopy!
> *Coriolanus.* Ay.
> *Third Serving-Man.* Where's that?
> *Coriolanus.* I' th' city of kites and crows.
> *Third Serving-Man.* I' th' city of kites and crows! – What an ass it
>   is!
>   – Then thou dwell'st with daws too?
> *Coriolanus.* No, I serve not thy master.   (IV, 5)

A traitor's role does not fit Coriolanus. He is not determined by his situation, or by his social existence. His inner self does not agree to it. History has declared the plebeians right, but Shakespeare does not admit that history has been right, or at any rate ultimately right. History has proved stronger than Coriolanus; it has caught him and driven him into a blind alley; has made a double traitor of him. History has made fun of Coriolanus, but has not succeeded in breaking him. In Acts Four and Five Coriolanus outgrows both Romans and Volscians, plebeians and patricians. In his defeat there is victory; at least victory in the sense that Conrad's heroes experienced it.

'His nature is too noble for the world,' says Menenius about Coriolanus. While the people's tribune, Brutus, throws the following words in Coriolanus's face:

> You speak o'the people,
> As if you were a god to punish, not
> A man of their infirmity. (III, 1)

These two views are only superficially contradictory. Coriolanus despises the world, because the world is mean. He wants to destroy the world, including Rome, because the world and Rome do not deserve to exist:

> I offer'd to awaken his regard
> For's private friends: his answer to me was,
> He could not stay to pick them in a pile
> Of noisome musty chaff: he said 'twas folly,
> For one poor grain or two, to leave unburnt,
> And still to nose the offence. (V, 1)

Coriolanus opposes the world with his own absurd system of values. His defeat originated the moment he agreed, in spite of himself, to go to the Forum, show his scars and ask for votes. This was demanded of him not only by his mother, by Menenius Agrippa and the patricians, but also by the people and their tribunes. Shakespeare's dramatic irony shows itself in the fact that both parties – conflicting and hating each other though they were – demanded from Coriolanus a gesture of compromise. In the sudden reversal of values, brought about in the ending of the tragedy, Coriolanus is the only one who rejects compromise and gestures, or at least tries to reject them:

> Like a dull actor now,
> I have forgot my part . . . (V, 3)

The world has again proved stronger than Coriolanus. Brutus was right: Coriolanus is only a man, full of weaknesses, like all other men. Coriolanus wants to destroy the world, because the world contradicts the laws of nature. But in the name of the same laws of nature Coriolanus has been condemned by his mother, wife and son. He has to condemn himself. Coriolanus feels he has been caught, fallen into a trap set for him by the ruthless and all too real world. He falls victim to his own mythology, to a mad dialectic of the laws of nature.[1]

> But out, affection!
> All bond and privilege of nature, break!
> Let it be virtuous to be obstinate.
>
> . . . .
>
> I melt, and am not
> Of stronger earth than others. – My mother bows;
> As if Olympus to a molehill should
> In supplication nod: and my young boy
> Hath an aspect of intercession, which
> Great nature cries 'Deny not'.   (V, 3)

Coriolanus has realized that he has been cheated in the distribution of parts. He wanted to play the role of an avenging deity, while in the scenario of history he was given only the role of a traitor. All that is left him is self-destruction. He will spare Rome to confirm his own nobility, to get out of the part imposed on him. But in saving Rome he has to commit another treason. As a perjurer he will be killed by the Volscians. Coriolanus's death is at the same time tragic and ironic. It is tragic in the world created by Coriolanus; tragic according to his mad and absolute system of values. It is ironic in the real world. Coriolanus's bravery and nobility will be praised by the man who has killed him, the Volscian leader, Aufidius. He will pay the final tribute to Coriolanus, just as Augustus Caesar will to Anthony, or Fortinbras to Hamlet. There is joy in Rome, and peace is celebrated. For the first time in this grim drama, full of clattering swords and howling crowds, there is music, and the

[1] See H. Heuer, *From Plutarch to Shakespeare. A Study of 'Coriolanus'*, 'Shakespeare Survey', No. 10, 1957.

sun rises.[1] *Coriolanus* ends in the same way as Dürrenmatt's *Visit*. Alfred Ill has been murdered; the people of Güllen enjoy their new affluence, and joyously celebrate the feast of justice.

> The trumpets, sackbuts, psalteries, and fifes,
> Tabors, and cymbals, and the shouting Romans,
> Make the sun dance. Hark you! (V, 4)

Here lies the thorn in the flesh of this drama which for a long time has been the reason for its unpopularity. The image of the world is flawed and lacks cohesion. Contradictions have not been resolved, and there is no common system of values for the *polis* and for the individual. 'He loves your people; but tie him not to be their bedfellow,' says Menenius Agrippa to Brutus, referring to Coriolanus. This is not true. Coriolanus did not love the people. But this does not mean that Coriolanus should be condemned. In that sentence there is contained in a nutshell the bitter drama of renaissance humanism; of any humanism, in fact.

[1] See G. Wilson Knight, *The Sovereign Flower*, London, 1958.

PART II: COMEDIES

Titania and the Ass's Head

> May all to Athens back again repair
> And think no more on this night's accidents,
> But as the fierce vexation of a dream.
> > (*Midsummer Night's Dream*, IV, 1)

I

The philologists have long ago discovered the devilish origin of Puck. Puck has simply been one the names for the devil. His name was invoked to frighten women and children together with the ogre and the incubus. Authors of commentaries on Shakespeare have for a long time pointed also to the similarities between Puck and Ariel, to certain repetitive situations, even lines of dialogue. Puck and Ariel lead wanderers astray, turn themselves into an *ignis fatuus* on the swamps:

> Mislead night-wanderers, laughing at their harm.   (II, 1)

This has always been a favourite occupation of devils in popular folklore. Both Puck and Ariel have devoted themselves to it with great satisfaction. Ariel turns into a chimera and a harpy; it is he who bites Caliban, pricks and tickles him unbearably. George Lamming says: 'Ariel is Prospero's source of information; the archetypal spy, the embodiment – when and if made flesh – of the perfect and unspeakable secret police.'

Shakespeare introduced such monsters in only two of his plays: in *Midsummer Night's Dream* and *The Tempest*. The *Dream* is a comedy; *The Tempest* had also for a long time been regarded as a comedy. The *Dream* forecasts *The Tempest*, although written in a different key. Just as *As You Like It* seems to forecast *King Lear*. Sometimes one has the impression that Shakespeare has in fact written three or four plays and kept repeating the same themes in different registers and keys, until he broke with all harmony in the *musique concrète* of *King Lear*. The storm came upon Lear and made him go mad in the same forest of Arden where, not so long ago, in *As You Like It*, another exiled prince, another exiled brother, and a pair of lovers, had deluded themselves that they would find freedom, security and happiness. Exiled princes are accompanied by clowns; or rather, by one and the same clown. Touchstone knows very well that the idyll of the Forest of Arden is only an illusion, that there is no escape from the world's cruelty, and that sooner or later we shall have to pass through 'this cold night [that] will turn us all to fools and madmen'. (*King Lear*, III, 4.)

The affinities between Puck and Ariel are important not only for a literary interpretation of the *Dream* and *The Tempest*. Even more important are they, perhaps, for theatre productions of the two plays. If Ariel, the 'airy spirit', is a devil, Prospero becomes an embodiment of Faust: like Faust, he masters the powers of nature and, like Faust, he loses in the end. This realization may enable one to enliven dramatically the character of Prospero, who almost invariably appears dull on the stage. Ariel, who is all thought, intelligence, and the devil, will never more appear as a ballet dancer in tights, with little gauze wings, who floats over the stage with the help of stage machinery.

But the conception of Puck must be changed, if he is to embody in him something of the future Ariel. He must not be just a playful dwarf from a German fairy tale, or even a poetic gremlin in the fashion of a romantic *féerie*. Only then, perhaps, will the theatre at last be able to show his twofold nature: that of the Robin Goodfellow, and of the menacing devil Hobgoblin. 'Those that Hobgoblin call you, and sweet Puck,' *Dream*. (II, 1.) The little fairy is afraid of him, wants to tame him, addresses him in endearing terms. Puck, the household brownie, suddenly takes the form of the Evil one:

> Sometime a horse I'll be, sometime a hound,
> A hog, a headless bear, sometime a fire;
> And neigh, and bark, and grunt, and roar, and burn,
> Like horse, hound, hog, bear, fire, at every turn.   (III, 1)

In the 1963 production of *The Tempest* at Stratford-upon-Avon, Ariel was represented as a silent boy with a concentrated expression. He never smiled. In the 1959 production of *The Tempest* at the People's Theatre, Nowa Huta, Ariel had a double. In the latest Stratford production he was accompanied by four dumb doubles. The devil is always able to multiply himself. The doubles were masks which copied the face of the original Ariel.

> Their sense thus weak, lost with their fears thus strong,
> Made senseless things begin to do them wrong;
> For briers and thorns at their apparel snatch.
>
> (*The Tempest,* III, 2)

This is not Ariel haunting the royal murderers on Prospero's isle. It is the good-natured Robin Goodfellow chasing the worthy Master Quince's troupe which has not done anybody any harm. Puck is a devil, and can multiply himself too. One can easily visualize a performance where Puck will be accompanied by devilish doubles, looking like his reflections in a mirror. Puck, like Ariel, is quick as thought:

> I'll put a girdle round about the earth
> In forty minutes.   (*Dream*, II, 1)

Shakespeare was not far wrong. The first Russian sputnik encircled the earth in forty-seven minutes. For Puck, just as for Ariel, time and space do not exist. Puck is a quick-change artist and a prestidigitator, something of a *commedia dell'arte* Harlequin. The Harlequin as shown a few years ago by the unforgettable Marcello Moretti in *The Servant of Two Masters* at the Piccolo Teatro of Milan. He had in him something of an animal and a faun. A black leather mask, with openings for eyes and mouth, endowed his face with a feline and foxy expression. But above all, he was a devil; like Puck. He multiplied himself, doubled and trebled, seemed to be exempt from the laws of gravity; he changed and pupated himself, could be in several places at once. All characters have a limited repertory of gestures. Harlequin knows all the gestures. He has the intelligence of a devil.

What, a play toward! I'll be an auditor;
An actor too perhaps, if I see cause.   (*Dream*, III, 1)

Puck is not a clown. He is not even an actor. It is he who, like Harlequin, pulls all the characters on strings. He liberates instincts and puts the mechanism of this world in motion. He puts it in motion and mocks it at the same time. Harlequin is the stage manager and producer; just as Puck and Ariel are the stage managers and producers of the respective spectacles devised by Oberon and Prospero.

Puck has sprinkled the eyes of the lovers with berry juice. When at last will the theatre show us a Puck who is a faun, a devil, and Harlequin, all combined?

II

According to Shakespeare's latest biographer, A. L. Rowse,[1] the original performance of *Midsummer Night's Dream* took place in the old London palace of the Southampton family at the corner of Chancery Lane and Holborn. It was a spacious house in the late Gothic style, with larger and smaller galleries running on various levels round an open rectangular court which adjoined a garden well suited for walks. It is difficult to imagine more suitable scenery for the real action of *Midsummer Night's Dream*. It is late at night and the entertainment is over. All the toasts have been drunk, dancing has stopped. Servants are still holding lamps in the courtyard. But the adjoining garden is dark. Tightly embracing couples are slowly filtering through the gate. Spanish wine is heavy; the lovers have remained. Someone has passed by; the boy is waking up. He does not see the girl asleep by his side. He has forgotten everything, even that he left the dance with her. Another girl is near; to reach her it is enough for him to stretch his arm. He has stretched his arm, he runs after her. He hates now with an intensity equal to that with which an hour ago he desired.

[1] A. L. Rowse, *William Shakespeare, A Biography*, London, 1963.

> Content with Hermia. No; I do repent
> The tedious minutes I with her have spent.
> Not Hermia but Helena I love.   (II, 2)

A feature peculiar to Shakespeare is the suddenness of love. There is mutual fascination and infatuation from the very first glance, the first touch of hands. Love falls down like a hawk; the world has ceased to exist; the lovers see only each other. Love in Shakespeare fills the entire being with rapture and desire. All that is left in the *Dream* of these amorous passions is the suddenness of desire:

> *Lysander.* I had no judgement when to her I swore.
> *Helena.* Nor none, in my mind, now you give her o'er.
> *Lysander.* Demetrius loves her, and he loves not you.
> *Demetrius (awaking).* O Helen, goddess, nymph, perfect, divine!
> To what, my love, shall I compare thine eyne!
> Crystal is muddy.   (III, 2)

The *Dream* is the most erotic of Shakespeare's plays. In no other tragedy or comedy of his, except *Troilus and Cressida*, is the eroticism expressed so brutally. Theatrical tradition is in the case of the *Dream* particularly intolerable, just as much in its classicist version, with tunic-clad lovers and marble stairs in the background, as in its other, operatic variation, with flowing transparent muslin, and rope-dancers. For a long time theatres have been content to present the *Dream* as a brothers Grimm fable, completely obliterating the pungency of the dialogue, and the brutality of the situations.

> *Lysander.* Hang off, thou cat, thou burr! vile thing, let loose.
> Or I will shake thee from me like a serpent!
> *Hermia.* Why are you grown so rude? what change is this,
> Sweet love?
> *Lysander.* Thy love! out, tawny Tartar, out!
> Out, loathed medicine! hated potion, hence!   (III, 2)

Commentators have long since noticed that the lovers in this love quartet are hardly at all distinguishable from one another. The girls differ only in height and in the colour of their hair. Perhaps only Hermia has one or two individual traits, which let one trace in her an earlier version of Rosaline from *Love's*

Labour's Lost, and the later Rosalind from *As You Like It*. The boys differ only in names. All four lack the distinctness and uniqueness of so many other, even earlier, Shakespearian characters.

The lovers are exchangeable. Perhaps that was his purpose? The entire action of this hot night, everything that has happened at this drunken party, is based on complete exchangeability of love partners. I always have the impression that Shakespeare leaves nothing to chance. Puck wanders round the garden at night and encounters couples who exchange partners with one another. It is Puck who makes the observation:

> This is the woman, but not this the man.   (III, 2)

Helena loves Demetrius, Demetrius loves Hermia, Hermia loves Lysander. Later Lysander runs after Helena, Helena runs after Demetrius, Demetrius runs after Hermia. This mechanical reversal of the objects of desire, and the interchangeability of lovers is not just the basis of the plot. The reduction of characters to love partners seems to me to be the most peculiar characteristic of this cruel dream; and perhaps its most modern quality. The partner is now nameless and faceless. He or she just happens to be the nearest. As in some plays by Genet, there are no unambiguous characters, there are just situations. Everything has become ambivalent.

> *Hermia.* . . . wherefore? O me! what news, my love?
> Am not I Hermia? are not you Lysander?
> I am as fair now as I was erewhile.   (III, 2)

Hermia is wrong. For in truth there is no Hermia, just as there is no Lysander. Or rather there are two different Hermias and two different Lysanders. The Hermia who slept with Lysander and the Hermia with whom Lysander does not want to sleep. The Lysander who sleeps with Hermia and the Lysander who is running away from Hermia.

Midsummer Night's Dream was staged for the first time as a topical, almost 'private' comedy, a part of a wedding celebration. Most probably it was – Rowse's arguments sound quite convincing here – the wedding of the Earl of Southampton's illustrious mother. If so, then the young Earl must have taken part in the preparation of the performance and possibly even acted in it, accompanied by his admirers. All his male and female lovers and friends, all that splendid circle in which a few years before Shakespeare found himself together with Marlowe, must have come to his mother's wedding. I would have wished the 'Dark Lady' of the Sonnets to have been present as well among the original spectators.

> I do but beg a little changeling boy
> To be my henchman.   (*Dream*, II, 1)

If *Love's Labour's Lost*, the transparent comedy about young men who determined to do without women, is rightly considered to have been a play with a secret meaning to the initiated, how much more must this be true of the *Dream*? The stage and auditorium were full of people who knew one another. Every allusion was deciphered at once. Fair ladies laughed behind their fans, men elbowed each other, homosexuals giggled softly.

> Give me that boy, and I will go with thee.   (II, 1)

Shakespeare does not show the boy whom Titania, to spite Oberon, has stolen from the Indian king. But he mentions the boy several times and stresses the point. For the plot the boy is quite unnecessary. One could easily invent a hundred other reasons for the conflict between the royal couple. Apparently the introduction of the boy was essential to Shakespeare for other, non-dramatic purposes. It is not only that Eastern pageboy that is disturbing. The behaviour of all the characters, not only commoners but also royal and princely personages, is promiscuous:

> . . . the bouncing Amazon,
> Your buskin'd mistress and your warrior love.   (II, 1)

The Greek queen of the Amazons has only recently been the mistress of the king of the fairies, while Theseus has just ended his liaison with Titania. These facts have no bearing on the plot, nothing results from them. They even blur a little the virtuous and somewhat pathetic image of the betrothed couple drawn in the First and Fifth Acts. But these details undoubtedly represent allusions to contemporary persons and events.

I do not think it is possible to decipher all the allusions contained in the *Dream*. Nor is it essential. I do not suppose, either, it matters a great deal that we discover for whose marriage Shakespeare hastily completed and adapted his *Midsummer Night's Dream*. It is only necessary for an actor, designer and producer to be aware of the fact that the *Dream* was a contemporary play about love. Both 'contemporary' and 'love' are significant words here. The *Dream* was also a most truthful, brutal and violent play. Coming after *Romeo and Juliet*, as it did, the *Dream* was, as it were, a *nouvelle vague* in the theatre of the time.

The fairies' wings and Greek tunics are simply costumes; not even poetic but carnival costumes. How easily one can imagine the great entertainment that must have been given at the wedding of the brilliant countess, the Earl of Southampton's mother, or at another, equally magnificent wedding. The ball is given with stylish and fantastic costumes. In the Italian courts, and later in England until the Puritan reaction, masked balls were a favourite form of entertainment, and were called 'impromptu masking'.

But all the rooms are empty now. The splendid cavalier dressed up as a northern Oberon, accompanied by a retinue of boys in rough leather jackets and fur caps with stags' antlers, has departed. They went to go on drinking in a tavern on the other bank of the Thames. The boys and girls in Greek tunics left even earlier. The last to leave was Titania, whose earrings made of pink pearls the size of peas roused general admiration. The halberdiers are gone, torches burnt out. Early in the morning, refreshed by a short sleep, the host goes out into the garden. On the soft grass, the entwined couples are still asleep:

> Good morrow, friends. Saint Valentine is past:
> Begin these wood-birds but to couple now? (IV, 1)

Hermia was the first to rise, though she had gone to sleep last. For her it was the craziest night. Twice did she change her lovers. She is tired and can hardly stand on her feet.

> Never so weary, never so in woe;
> Bedabbled with the dew, and torn with briers;
> I can no further crawl, no further go;   (III, 2)

She is ashamed. She does not quite yet realize that day has come. She is still partly overwhelmed by night. She has drunk too much.

> Methinks I see these things with parted eye,
> When every thing seems double.   (IV, 1)

The entire scene of the lovers' awakening in the morning a-bounds in that brutal and bitter poetry that every stylized theatre production is bound to annihilate and destroy.

III

The metaphors of love, eroticism and sex undergo in *Midsummer Night's Dream* some essential changes. They are completely traditional to start with: sword and wound; rose and rain; Cupid's bow and golden arrow. The clash of two kinds of imagery occurs in Helena's soliloquy which forms a coda to act one, scene one. This soliloquy is above her intellectual capacities and for a while singles her out from the action of the play. It is really the author's monologue, a kind of Brechtian 'song' in which, for the first time, the philosophical theme of the *Dream* is stated; the subject being Eros and Thanatos.

> Things base and vile, holding no quantity,
> Love can transpose to form and dignity.
> Love looks not with the eyes, but with the mind,
> And therefore is wing'd Cupid painted blind.   (I, 1)

The last couplet is the most difficult to interpret and it is disturbing in its ambiguity. The imagery here shows a striking similarity to the formulas of the Florentine neo-platonists, particularly Marsilio Ficini and Pico della Mirandola. On the basis of the orphic doctrine they promulgated a peculiar *mystique* of Eros. Particularly famous was a paradox of Mirandola's, contained in his *Opera*: 'Ideo amor ab Orpheo sine oculis dicitur, quia est supra intellectum.' Love is blind, because it is above intellect. The blindness gives fulfilment and ecstasy. Plato's *Feast*, understood either mystically, or concretely, was also among the favourite books of Elizabethan neo-platonists. But, following the Florentine example, neo-platonism as practised in Southampton's circle had a distinctly epicurean flavour.

'Mind' in this context seems to mean imagination and desire. Shakespeare usually breaks through stereotypes. For the neoplatonic dialectics of Love born through Beauty and culminating in sensual pleasure ('Amor igitur in Voluptatem a pulchritudine dessinit'), Shakespeare substitutes the Eros of ugliness, born through desire and culminating in folly.[1]

Cupid, the boy who shoots his arrows blindfolded, has been evoked in this soliloquy, but only for a little while, because the imagery here is far more abstract and enters a quite different sphere of meanings:

> Wings, and no eyes, figure unheedy haste.   (I, 1)

In Helena's soliloquy the blindfolded Cupid has been transformed into a blind driving force, a Nike of instinct.

Schopenhauer obviously borrowed this image from the *Dream*. But the blind Nike of desire is also a moth. Starting with Helena's soliloquy, Shakespeare introduces more and more obtrusively the animal erotic symbolism. He does it consistently, stubbornly, almost obsessively. The changes in imagery are in this case just an outward expression of a violent departure from the Petrarchian idealization of love.

It is this passing through animality that seems to us the midsummer night's dream, or at least this aspect of the *Dream* is the most modern and revealing. This is the main theme joining together all the three separate plots running parallel in the play. Titania and Bottom will pass through animal eroticism in

---

[1] Compare Edgar Wind, *Pagan Mysteries in the Renaissance*, London, 1958.

a quite literal, even visual sense. But even the quartet of lovers enter the dark sphere of animal love-making:

> *Helena.* I am your spaniel; and, Demetrius,
>   The more you beat me, I will fawn on you:
>   Use me but as your spaniel, spurn me, strike me . . . (II, 1)

And again:

>   What worser place can I beg in your love . . .
>   Than to be used as you use your dog?   (II, 1)

Pointers, kept on short leashes, eager to chase, or fawning upon their masters, appear frequently on Flemish tapestries representing hunting scenes. They were a favourite adornment on the walls of royal and princely palaces. But here a girl calls herself a dog fawning on her master. The metaphors are brutal, almost masochistic.

It is worth having a closer look at the 'bestiary' evoked by Shakespeare in the *Dream*. As a result of the romantic tradition, unfortunately preserved in the theatre through Mendelssohn's music, the forest in the *Dream* still seems to be another version of Arcadia. But in actual fact, it is rather a forest inhabited by devils and lamias, in which witches and sorceresses can easily find everything required for their practices.

>   You spotted snakes with double tongue,
>   Thorny hedgehogs, be not seen;
>   Newts, and blind-worms, do no wrong,
>   Come not near our fairy queen.   (II, 2)

Titania lies down to sleep in a meadow among wild thyme, oxlips, musk-roses, violets and eglantine, but the lullaby sung by the fairies in her train seems somewhat frightening. After the creatures just quoted they go on to mention long-legged poisonous spiders, black beetles, worms and snails. The lullaby does not forecast pleasant dreams.

The bestiary of the *Dream* is not a haphazard one. The dried skin of a viper, pulverized spiders and bats' gristle appear in every medieval or renaissance prescription book as drugs to cure impotence and women's afflictions of one kind or another.

All those are slimy, hairy, sticky creatures, unpleasant to touch and often rousing violent aversion. It is the sort of aversion that is described by psychoanalytic textbooks as sexual neuroses. Snakes, snails, bats and spiders form also a favourite bestiary of Freud's theory of dreams. Oberon orders Puck to make the lovers sleep that kind of sleep when he says:

> . . . lead them thus
> Till o'er their brows death-counterfeiting sleep
> With leaden legs and batty wings doth creep.   (III, 2)

Titania's fairies are called; Pease-Blossom, Cobweb, Moth, Mustard-Seed. In the theatre Titania's retinue is almost invariably represented as winged goblins, jumping and springing in the air, or as a little ballet of German dwarfs. This sort of visual interpretation is so strongly suggestive that even commentators of the text find it difficult to free themselves from it. However, one has only to speculate on the selection of these names to realize that they belong to the same love pharmacy of the witches.

I imagine Titania's court as consisting of old men and women, toothless and shaking, their mouths wet with saliva, who sniggeringly procure a monster for their mistress.

> The next thing then she waking looks upon.
> Be it on lion, bear, or wolf, or bull,
> On meddling monkey or on busy ape,
> She shall pursue it with the soul of love.   (II, 1)

Oberon openly announces that as a punishment Titania will sleep with a beast. Again the selection of these animals is most characteristic, particularly in the next series of Oberon's threats:

> Be it ounce, or cat, or bear,
> Pard or boar with bristled hair . . .   (II, 2)

All these animals represent abundant sexual potency, and some of them play an important part in sexual demonology. Bottom is eventually transformed into an ass. But in this nightmarish summer night, the ass does not symbolize stupidity. Since antiquity and up to the Renaissance the ass was credited with the strongest sexual potency and among all the quadrupeds is supposed to have the longest and hardest phallus.

I visualize Titania as a very tall, flat and fair girl, with long arms and legs, resembling the white Scandinavian girls I used to see in rue de Harpe or rue Huchette, walking and clinging tightly to Negroes with faces grey or so black that they were almost undistinguishable from the night.

> Thou art as wise as thou art beautiful. (III, 1)

The scenes between Titania and Bottom transformed into an ass are often played for laughs in the theatre. But I think that if one can see humour in this scene, it is the English kind of humour, 'humeur noir', cruel and scatological, as it often is in Swift.

The slender, tender and lyrical Titania longs for animal love. Puck and Oberon call the transformed Bottom a monster. The frail and sweet Titania drags the monster to bed, almost by force. This is the lover she wanted and dreamed off; only she never wanted to admit it, even to herself. Sleep frees her from inhibitions. The monstrous ass is being raped by the poetic Titania, while she still keeps on chattering about flowers:

> *Titania.* The moon methinks looks with a watery eye;
> And when she weeps, weeps every little flower,
> Lamenting some enforced chastity.
> Tie up my love's tongue, bring him silently. (III, 1)

Of all the characters in the play Titania enters to the fullest extent the dark sphere of sex where there is no more beauty and ugliness; there is only infatuation and liberation. In the coda of the first scene of the *Dream* Helena had already forecast:

> Things base and vile, holding no quantity,
> Love can transpose to form and dignity. (I, 1)

The love scenes between Titania and the ass must seem at the same time real and unreal, fascinating and repulsive. They are to rouse rapture and disgust, terror and abhorrence. They should seem at once strange and fearful.

> Come, sit thee down upon this flowery bed,
> While I thy amiable cheeks do coy,
> And stick musk-roses in thy sleek smooth head,
> And kiss thy fair large ears, my gentle joy.   (IV. 1)

Chagall has depicted Titania caressing the ass. On that picture the ass is sad, white and affectionate. To my mind, Shakespeare's Titania, caressing the monster with the head of an ass, ought to be closer to the fearful visions of Bosch and to the grotesque of the surrealists. I think also that modern theatre, which has passed through the poetics of surrealism, of the absurd, and through Genet's brutal poetry, can depict this scene truly for the first time. The choice of visual inspiration is particularly important in this context. Of all the painters, Goya is, perhaps, the only one whose fantasies penetrated the dark sphere of bestiality even farther than those of Shakespeare. I am thinking of the *Caprichos*.

IV

All the men are ugly, mouse- or rabbit-like, dwarfish or hump-backed. They spy on, or rather sniff at, tall girls in black shawls thrown over their shoulders; their dresses have high waists, but are long and reach down to their ankles. Sometimes the girls lift up their dresses to adjust their garters or stockings, but even in that vulgar gesture they remain inwardly absent. For the most part they sit stiffly up in high chairs contemptuous and aloof. As if on exhibition, they show themselves and their assets; they fasten the garters of their black stockings, stick out their buttocks, and expose their round breasts from under their tight bodices. Misshapen men with prominent wide noses sneak around their legs and posteriors. Sluts in black mantillas, with finely dressed hair on to which tortoise-shell combs are fastened, sit there deep in their thoughts, looking haughtily straight ahead from behind their black fans. Beside them old women sit or walk, wearing the same sort of black shawls and tortoise-shell combs. The old hags are toothless and that is perhaps why their mouths are wide open in a silent smile. The sluts and the hags show a considerable likeness to each other. On examining these drawings closely one realizes that the likeness is not a chance one; that Goya deliberately and with a certain satisfaction, as it were, gives the same faces to splendid young women, and to repulsive old hags. All the repellent elements in the features of these haughty girls are revealed fully when repeated in old age. Only then those elements become beastly, vulgar, ugly. All the drawings have been done with the same soft line which makes even the black spots seem warm, grey, mouse-like. For in reality, it is not only the men and the old hags that give the appearance of rats, but also all those young women, contemptuous and immovable, regal and whorish, carnal and absent at the same time.

The women are slim and tall; the men small and looking as if they were only able to spy on and sniff at the women; as if they had to stand up on their toes if they wanted to look them in the face. Goya must have inspired the drawings of Bruno Schulz.

I still remember these drawings: small, black men with heads large like those of children ill with dropsy, watching intently the slippers, or the little feet of giantesses. Schulz's drawings have the same soft line, the same warm mouse-like greyness that Goya's drawings had. Those large-headed men in bowler hats and coats too big for them, misshapen, humbacked, crippled, yet excited almost to the point of orgasm by a little falling slipper of a giantess, are like mice.

Todos Caeran. A small withered tree with human hens in black three-cornered hats. Bird-like hen-whores with little wings stick out their round breasts and jig on their thin hen's legs. Clumsy cocks with their hackles up, also jigging ridiculously on similar thin little legs, jump on them. While other hen-whores and cocks with repulsive wrinkled old faces perch on the little withered tree.

At the bottom there are three women. Two young ones, with

breasts sticking out of their bodices, in ample skirts, and one very old, with hands folded as if in prayer, somehow also bird-like, in spite of a big snout in place of nose and chin. The young women, excited and fluttering, drive an awl into the buttocks of a hen, with an old head on a long neck. One of them holds him by the wings, the other holds the awl in his rump. The old woman is praying, the young ones laugh; it is an animal and sexual sort of laughter that deforms their faces and, as in the other drawings, gives them the same vulgar grimace.

Ya van desplumados. Four women, two young ones and two old hags, beat with brooms and chase away little bird-like men with hen's legs and the sad faces of hunchbacks. Again we find in these sluts in mantillas the same evil glow in the eyes, the same vicious smile, a trace, or rather forecast, of future deformation in the way their mouths open, their cheeks swell.

The asses. Whole herds of asses. In white nightcaps, ugly, without any traces of good nature, inflated and conceited, they teach a young ass, his muzzle wide open, the alphabet. Their stupidity is human, not asinine. A big ass, naked, with hairy hooves, self-satisfied and blissful, is seated comfortably in an easy chair. A hairy ape, or perhaps a man with an ape's head, plays a mandolin, while two servants hiding behind the chair laugh and clap their hands. A good-looking ass in a loose coat and long trousers, from under which hooves are visible, is reading a book about asses. An ass-doctor, benign and smooth-faced, takes a patient's pulse. An astonishing huge, white ass, calm and understanding, is standing in front of a large black-board, on which a hairy ape is drawing something. Tired and stooping peasants are carrying big, white, heavy, hideous asses on their shoulders. But the peasants are hideous too, hideous and ugly. They are even uglier than the asses they carry. A tall slut, her expression, as always in Goya's drawings, contemptuous and absent, is straddling on a black ass with a huge muzzle. The girl's thighs are bare, and a large black comb is pinned in her hair.

Goya, or animal eroticism. Everything here is hairy, everything part of the same night. Everything has to do with squeezing, handling, sucking, sticking. Bats have the bellies and genitals of men, or women, and sometimes the flabby breasts of old women. They throw themselves on girls with protruding buttocks, they hang around old toothless hags, with noses eaten away by syphilis. She-bats, with wide-open fox-like muzzles and hairy female genitals, fly over a sleeping youth's head. In the second part of the series everything becomes even more animal, hairy and nightmarish. Sometimes it is even difficult to name those half-animal, half-human, cat-like, rat-like and fox-like beings. In the last drawings the bats become an obsession: they turn into succubae and incubi, fly with their mouths always wide open; they have the heads of imbeciles, or crawl on little, thin, hairy legs.

In the early part of the series the animals are still symbols of stupidity, cunning, force or debauchery, as in a medieval or early Renaissance apologue. But gradually the animals become independent, as it were, of this summary symbolism; they cease to symbolize men, and are only animal variations of the human form. Goya discovers the dark sphere, in which all forms – asinine, bovine, ovine, rat's, bat's, mouse's, cat's, male, female, young and old – have all penetrated one another and go on infecting one another with hairiness, snoutiness, with muzzles and noses, with protruding ears, with the black openings of female genitals and toothless mouths. Only occasionally, among those he- and she-bats with cat's whiskers, fox-like muzzles and naked bellies, there appear the absent, contemptuous, carnal sluts in black mantillas, with ingeniously dressed hair and long black skirts.

One of them is dancing. She has lifted her black-stockinged leg high in the air, and holds her hands above her head. Her eyes are closed. She does not see the bats sniffing at her. One of them, with the head of an old baldish cat, has already caught at her hair. Another, with the low-hanging big head of a dwarf, is already looking under her black skirt. The girl is dancing. A third bat, with a naked belly, male uncovered genitals and the head of a starved yet sexy cat, has already landed on her breasts.

The girl does not defend herself, does not see them; but she is dancing for them.

Titania has embraced the ass's head and traces his hairy hooves with her fingers. She is strikingly white. She has thrown her shawl on the grass, taken the tortoise-shell comb out of her fine coiffure and let her hair loose. The ass's hooves are entwining her more and more strongly. He has put his head on her breasts. The ass's head is heavy and hairy.

> For she his hairy temples then had rounded
> With coronet of fresh and fragrant flowers.   (IV. 1)

Titania has closed her eyes: she is dreaming about pure animality.

V

The night is drawing to a close and the dawn is breaking. The lovers have already passed through the dark sphere of animal love. Puck will sing an ironic song at the end of Act Three. It is at the same time a coda, and a 'song' to summarize the night's experiences.

> Jack shall have Jill;
> Nought shall go ill;
> The man shall have his mare again, and all shall be well. (III, 2)

Titania wakes up and sees a boor with an ass's head by her side. She slept with him that night. But now it is daylight. She does not remember ever having desired him. She remembers nothing. She does not want to remember anything.

Titania. My Oberon! what visions have I seen!
    Methought I was enamour'd of an ass.
Oberon. There lies your love.
Titania. How came these things to pass?
    O, how mine eyes do loathe his visage now!   (IV, 1)

All are ashamed in the morning: Demetrius and Hermia, Lysander and Helena. Even Bottom. Even he does not want to admit his dream:

Methought I was – there is no man can tell what. Methought I was, and methought I had, – but man is but a
patched fool, if he will offer to say what methought I had.

(IV, 1)

In the violent contrast between the erotic madness liberated by
night, and the censorship of day, which orders everything to be
forgotten, Shakespeare seems most ahead of his time. The
notion that 'life's a dream' has, in this context, nothing of
baroque mysticism. Night is the key to day.

We are such stuff
As dreams are made on . . .

(*The Tempest*, IV, 1)

Not only Ariel is an abstract Puck with a sad and thoughtful
face. The philosophical theme of the *Dream* will be repeated in
The Tempest, doubtless a more mature play. But the answers
given by Shakespeare in *A Midsummer Night's Dream* seem
more unambiguous, perhaps one can even say more materialistic, less bitter.

The lunatic, the lover, and the poet
Are of imagination all compact.   (*Dream*, V, 1)

The madness lasted throughout the June night. The lovers are
ashamed of that night and do not want to talk about it, just as
one does not want to talk of bad dreams. But that night
liberated them from themselves. They were their real selves in
their dreams.

And sleep, that sometimes shuts up sorrow's eye,
Steal me awhile from mine own company.   (III, 2)

The forest in Shakespeare always represents Nature. The
escape to the Forest of Arden is an escape from the cruel world
in which the way to the crown leads through murder, a brother
robs a brother of his inheritance, and a father asks for his
daughter's death is she chooses a husband against his will. But
it is not only the forest that happens to be Nature. Our instincts
are also Nature. And they are as mad as the world.

Lovers and madmen have such seething brains.   (I, 1)

The theme of love will return once more in the old tragedy of Pyramus and Thysbe, performed at the end of the *Dream* by Master Quince's troupe. The lovers are divided by a wall, cannot touch each other and only see each other through a crack. They will never be joined together. A hungry lion comes to the rendezvous and Thysbe flees in panic. Pyramus finds her bloodstained mantle and stabs himself. Thysbe returns, finds Pyramus's body and stabs herself with the same dagger. The world is cruel for true lovers.

The world is mad and love is mad. In this universal madness of Nature and History, brief are the moments of happiness:

> Swift as a shadow, short as any dream;
> Brief as the lightning in the collied night. (I, 1)

Shakespeare's Bitter Arcadia

Viola. What country, friends, is this?
Captain. This is Illyria, lady.   (*Twelfth Night*, I, 2)

I

The Sonnets can be interpreted as a drama. They have action
and heroes. The action consists of lyrical sequences which
slowly mount to a tragedy. There are three characters: a man, a
youth and a woman. This trio exhaust every form of love and
go through all its stages. They exhaust all the variants and
forms of faithlessness, every kind of relationship, including
love, friendship, jealousy. They go through the heaven and hell
of love. The diction of the Sonnets, however, is not Petrarchan,
and another epithet would be more apt here: the characters go
through Eden and through Sodom.

The fourth character of the drama is time. Time which
destroys and devours everything. Greedy time which has been
compared to gaping jaws. It devours the fruits of human
labour and man himself.

> O time, swift despoiler of created things! How many kings, how
> many peoples hast thou brought low! How many changes of
> state and circumstance have followed since the wondrous form of
> this fish died here in this hollow, winding recess? Now destroyed
> by time, patiently thou liest within this narrow space, and with thy
> bones despoiled and bare art become an armour and support to the
> mountain which lies above thee.[1]

This Shakespearian quotation is taken from the writings of the
young Leonardo da Vinci. The theme of 'Time, the wrecker of
all' occurs again and again as a refrain in the poetry of the late
Renaissance and Baroque periods. But for Leonardo, as for

[1] Leonardo da Vinci's *Notebooks*, trans. by E. McCurdy, New York, 1935, p. 136.

Shakespeare, the wrecking force of time is not just a stylistic figure, or even an obsession. Time is the foremost actor in any tragedy.

> When time is old and hath forgot itself,
> When waterdrops have worn the stones of Troy,
> And blind oblivion swallow'd cities up,
> And mighty states characterless are grated
> To dusty nothing.   (*Troilus and Cressida*, III, 2)

That was Cressida. No Shakespearian play is so close to the Sonnets, with its bitter images of the inevitable end of love.[1]

> Injurious time now, with a robber's haste,
> Crams his rich thievery up, he knows not how.   (IV, 4)

That was Troilus. In the Sonnets, as in *Troilus and Cressida*, time, the 'great-siz'd monster of ingratitudes' (III, 3), 'injurious Time', is against the lovers. It destroys cities and kingdoms as well as love and beauty, breaks the oaths of princes and lovers' vows.

> . . . Time, whose million'd accidents
> Creep in 'twixt vows, and change decrees of kings.
>   (Sonnet. CXV)

Let us invoke Leonardo once more. He speaks of the same voracious time:

> O Time, thou that consumest all things! O envious age, thou destroyest all things and devourest all things with the hard teeth of the years, little by little, in slow death! Helen, when she looked in her mirror and saw the withered wrinkles which old age had made in her face, wept, and wondered to herself why ever she had twice been carried away. O Time, thou that consumest all things! O envious age, whereby all things are consumed![2]

Three Leonardian images contain three kinds of time. Geological time: the time of the earth, of oceans and mountain erosion; archaeological time, for all history becomes archaeology in the

[1] A detailed list of the images of time in the *Sonnets* and in *Troilus and Cressida* was made by Caroline Spurgeon in *Shakespeare's Imagery*, Cambridge, 1935.
[2] Op. cit. p. 52.

end: of the pyramids, destroyed cities, kingdoms of which only the names have remained; and, finally, human time in which grave stands next to cradle and all faces are mortal.

> Against my love shall be, as I am now,
> With Time's injurious hand crush'd and o'erworn;
> When hours have drain'd his blood and fill'd his brow
> With lines and wrinkles . . .   (LXIII)

The three Leonardian kinds of time can always be found in Shakespeare. When the earth is covered with blood, human time becomes again the inhuman time of nature. It is then that blind Gloster takes leave of the deranged Lear:

> O ruin'd piece of nature! This great world
> Shall so wear out to nought.   (*King Lear*, IV, 6)

The three kinds of time, inter-linked one with another, are continually invoked in the Sonnets. That is why the Sonnets are a great prologue.

> . . . where, alack,
> Shall Time's best jewel from Time's chest lie hid?
> Or what strong hand can hold his swift foot back?
> Or who his spoil of beauty can forbid?   (LXV)

The first theme of the Sonnets is the attempt to preserve beauty and love from the destructive action of time. A son is not only the heir of the family, not only a continuation, but above all a repetition of the same face and the same features; literally the way of making time stand still:

> Now is the time that face should form another.   (III)

Love takes place in time, but is directed against time. It tries to save something, to leave a trace behind it, no matter what the cost.

> And nothing 'gainst Time's scythe can make defence
> Save breed, to brave him when he takes thee hence.   (XII)

In Shakespeare's Sonnets love is a mortal combat in which the only real adversary is decay:

> When I perhaps compounded am with clay,
> Do not so much as my poor name rehearse,
> But let your love even with my life decay.   (LXXI)

To defy physical death is to prolong life in one's offspring.
Negation of doom and oblivion consists in the concept of fame,
inherited from antiquity. A poem will last. With his Sonnets
Shakespeare writes his *monumentum aere perennius*:

> And thou in this shalt find thy monument,
> When tyrants' crests and tombs of brass are spent.
>
>   (CVII)

This combination, in one line, of brass and tyranny is typical of
the Renaissance. Black lines of verse, letters written on paper,
fragile stanzas are to defy the entire force and authority of
time. They are to ensure immortality.

> Against confounding age's cruel knife.   (LXIII)

Shakespeare's *exegi monumentum* was probably written for a
young man with slightly slanting eyes and golden, finely curled
hair falling on to his left shoulder. Not only did that face have a
feminine perfection of beauty, but also clear signs of cruelty in
the line of the mouth and contempt in the cold, almost absent,
gaze.

> And tongues to be your being shall rehearse.
>
>   (LXXXI)

The Sonnets were almost certainly addressed to the Earl of
Southampton, who was ten years Shakespeare's junior. His
face, as can be judged from the portraits, was an almost exact
repetition of his mother's features.[1] Shakespeare had a perfect
right to say:

> Thou art thy mother's glass, and she in thee
> Calls back the lovely April of her prime.   (III)

Shakespeare's most amazing characteristic is always the inter-

[1] See A. L. Rowse, *William Shakespeare: A Biography*, London, 1963. The
author's arguments relating to the chronology and addressee of the Sonnets
seem convincing.

mingling of chance and rule, of the concrete and the universal.

A man, a youth, and a woman. But the love game in the Sonnets is not performed by abstract characters, as in a game of chess. Shakespeare's *aere perennius* was written for a youth who happened to be the heir to a great family and a great fortune. The relationship of love and friendship is woven into a complicated pattern of a beginner poet and actor's dependence on a rich noble patron.

> . . . men as plants increase
> Cheered and check'd even by the self-same sky.   (XV)

The Sonnets have two frames of reference. Like the poems of the English metaphysical poets, Donne and Herbert, they are a pure existentialist drama and, at the same time, are filled with concrete historical matter. There are in them heavens deaf to human calls, the four elements, and the slowly trotting horse on which the older man goes away from his faithless lover.

Shakespeare's *monumentum* is not only to save the boy's effeminate beauty from oblivion. The handful of rhymes are to secure immortality as well as the young gentleman's patronage. It is easier to secure immortality. The character of a rival poet, possibly Marlowe, can be discerned between the lines of the Sonnets. The favours of the young nobleman have been sought by many.

This intermingling of great with small, of one particular epoch with all epochs, is almost tangible in the Sonnets. The time on Shakespeare's clock is Elizabethan, but it strikes the hours not only for the fair youth and the Dark Lady, but for all lovers.

II

Shakespeare's Sonnets have their own poetic diction, their erotic quality and their metaphysics. One hundred and twenty-six are addressed to the youth; in the remainder Shakespeare addresses the Dark Lady. The dramatic action consists in the double treachery of the youth and the woman. The two unite.

The man does not know by whom he has been betrayed more completely, of whom he ought to be more jealous, who has taken revenge on whom. He begs, persuades, threatens, tries to convince. The last couplets of each sonnet are directed straight at the addressee. They are almost spoken; they are lines in a play.

The Sonnets are a prologue in yet another sense. They are the prologue to Shakespeare's erotic poetry, or at least to the erotic aspects of the comedies of his early period. The real theme of the Sonnets is the choice, or rather the impossibility of choice between the youth and the woman, the fragile boundary between friendship and love, the fascination with all beauty, the universality of desire which cannot be contained in or limited to one sex. The same theme, treated in a variety of moods, from *buffo* to a most serious approach, from ambiguous and spoilt idyll to mockery and derision, will return in *The Two Gentlemen of Verona*, in *Love's Labour's Lost*, in *As You Like It* and in *Twelfth Night*, in the undercurrent of *The Merchant of Venice*, in the loving friendship and brutal rejection of Falstaff by Henry V.

Ambiguity in the Sonnets is at the same time a poetic and an erotic principle. Compared with Shakespeare's Sonnets, the sonnets of Petrarch seem transparent and pure as crystal, but cold, artificial, contrived. Beauty and goodness are permanent values in them, never to be questioned; the conflict is between the body and the mind. In Shakespeare's Sonnets this rigid division into physical and spiritual is blurred. Good intermingles with evil, beauty with ugliness, desire with revulsion, passion with shame. There are other divisions, too, at once more baroque and more modern. Passion looks at itself; indecision is the food of pleasure; insight does not kill passion but inflames it even more. Eroticism here is exact and precise, sharpened by observation, aggravated by self-analysis.

> . . . although to-day thou fill
> Thy hungry eyes even till they wink with fulness,
> To-morrow see again, and do not kill
> The spirit of love with a perpetual dulness.

Let this sad interim like the ocean be
Which parts the shore, where two contracted new
Come daily to the banks . . .   (LVI)

The erotic partner here is real and fictitious at the same time;
the eye wages a struggle with the heart, day with night, touch
with sight. The partner is bodily present and yet created by
imagination and desire. Eroticism is the pupil of Renaissance
painting, and itself becomes in turn the school of a new sensibility.

Since I left you, mine eye is in my mind;
And that which governs me to go about
Doth part his function, and is partly blind,
Seems seeing, but effectually is out;
For it no form delivers to the heart
Of bird, of flower, or shape, which it doth latch;
Of his quick objects hath the mind no part,
Nor his own vision holds what it doth catch;
For if it see the rud'st or gentlest sight,
The most sweet favour or deformed'st creature,
The mountain or the sea, the day or night,
The crow or dove, it shapes them to your feature.   (CXIII)

Botticelli is said to have maintained that it is a waste of time to
imitate views of nature, since it is enough to throw a sponge
soaked in paint against a wall to be able to discern the most
lovely landscapes in the stains that thus appear. Leonardo
consciously used this method as a means of stimulating the
inventiveness of the intellect and a painter's imagination. He
did not even have to throw a sponge. He wrote:

Look at walls splashed with a number of stains, or stones of
various mixed colours. If you have to invent some scene, you can
see there resemblances to a number of landscapes, adorned with
mountains, rivers, rocks, trees, great plains, valleys and hills, in
various ways. Also you can see various battles, and lively postures
of strange figures, expressions on faces, costumes and an infinite
number of things, which you can reduce to good integrated form.
This happens on such walls and varicoloured stones, [which act]

like the sound of bells, in whose pealing you can find every name and word that you can imagine.[1]

Shakespeare went through a similar school of imagination. And he knew both its applications: the lyrical and the mocking. In the Sonnets it was lyrical. In *Hamlet* the same school of imagination turned into a sharp lesson of political opportunism:

> *Hamlet.* Do you see yonder cloud that's almost in shape of a camel?
> *Polonius.* By th'mass, and 'tis like a camel, indeed.
> *Hamlet.* Methinks it is like a weasel.
> *Polonius.* It is back'd like a weasel.
> *Hamlet.* Or like a whale?
> *Polonius.* Very like a whale.   (III, 2)

We can now end the quotation from Leonardo:

> I have seen in the clouds and on walls stains which have stimulated me to make beautiful discoveries of various things, and which, though in themselves completely devoid of perfection in the representation of any particular detail, did not lack perfection in movement and other activity.[2]

This is not the first of the amazing convergences in the thought of Leonardo and Shakespeare, which are the more strange in that they were not based on any direct tradition or transmission, except for the strong influence of Italian quatrocento culture on Elizabethan England. That influence was very marked at the royal court, even more at the colleges of Cambridge and Oxford where the humanities flourished, and among the circles of young aristocrats with university links. From Italy came painting, music and architecture, models of language and style, new theories of action which had effectiveness as their criterion; a new ideal of personality whose criterion was harmony; new philosophy and new customs. Marlowe told everybody that only fools were unable to appreciate boys and tobacco. In the circles of Southampton and his friends customs became not unlike those in the Florence of the Medici.

---

[1] *Notebooks of Leonardo da Vinci*, trans. by J. Richter, Oxford University Press 1952, p. 182.
[2] Trans. by the present translator.

Savonarola's violent anti-sodomite invectives are well known. Botticelli, Leonardo, Michelangelo were accused of pederasty. Leonardo's notes about his disciples and apprentices are ambiguous, particularly those relating to the young Jacomo, whom he called 'Salai' – little devil – and to whom he was astonishingly generous and indulgent:

In the first year, a cloak: two lire; six shirts: four lire; three doublets: six lire; four pairs of hose: seven lire eight soldi; garment with lining: five lire; twenty-four pairs of footwear: six lire five soldi; a beret: one lira; belts, laces: one lira.[1]

Leonardo's propensity for boys was most certainly suppressed. Among his notes we find the following: 'Whoso curbs not lustful desires puts himself on a level with beasts.'[2] And again: 'Intellectual passion drives out sensuality.'[3] He knew a great deal about eroticism. He wrote: 'Our body is subject to heaven, and heaven is subject to the spirit.'[4] But at the same time he wrote: 'If you kept your body in accordance with virtue your desires would not be of this world.' The most disturbing, almost obsessive, drawings of Leonardo are those representing an old or middle-aged man looking at a youth with curled hair and a Greek profile.

Not only was *Eros socraticus* a more or less tolerated practice; it was above all a philosophy of love, an aesthetic and metaphysical sanction for widely differing forms of friendship between an adult man and a youth. The Florentine Humanist Academy declared pure love directed at youths as the highest form of the affinity of souls. Pico della Mirandola and Ficino composed treatises on spiritual pederasty in which it was sometimes difficult to distinguish the community of souls from the community of bodies. Mirandola's young friend was buried in the same crypt at St Mark's monastery where the remains of his

[1] Trans. by the present translator.
[2] Leonardo da Vinci's *Notebooks*, McCurdy, p. 63.
[3] Op. cit., p. 63.
[4] Op. cit., p. 47.
[5] Op. cit., p. 64.

master reposed. Ficino, in his sophisticated commentaries on Plato's *Symposium*, identified Phaedrus with his friend, whose youthful beauty was praised by those present at the feast. The apologies of pure love for boys differed in the degree of their sincerity, but their metaphysics was always the same.

> Each of us, then, is but a tally of a man, since every one shows like a flat-fish the traces of having been sliced in two; and each is ever searching for the tally that will fit him. All the men who are sections of that composite sex that at first was called man-woman are woman-courters; our adulterers are mostly descended from that sex, whence likewise are derived our man-courting women and adulteresses. All the women who are sections of the woman have no great fancy for men; they are inclined rather to women, and of this stock are the she-minions. Men who are sections of the male pursue the masculine . . . Some say they are shameless creatures, but falsely: for their behaviour is due not to shamelessness but to daring, manliness, and virility, since they are quick to welcome their like . . . They are quite contented to live together unwedded all their days. A man of this sort is at any rate born to be a lover of boys or the willin mate of a man, eagerly greeting his own kind.[1]

The philosophical foundation of Socratic eroticism was Plato's *Symposium*, or, more exactly, the old myth of the first men contained in it. They were double men; they had four arms and legs, two faces and two sexual organs. They were proud and blasphemed against the gods. To punish them Zeus cut them in two. The split halves have longed for reunion ever since. Shakespeare's Sonnet XXXIX closes with the amazingly Platonic coda:

> And that thou teachest how to make one twain,
> By praising him here who doth hence remain.

Ficino wrote that the philosophical family of Platonists can be recognized 'by the passionate fondness for the physical and spiritual beauty of human beings'. Leonardo spent the last years of his life at the castle of Cloux near Amboise. Tradition

[1] Plato, *Symposium*, trans. by W. R. M. Lamb, London, Heinemann, 1946, p. 141.

has it that he used to be visited there by François I. The young King, on his way back from the hunt, used to leave his hounds in the courtyard and go to Leonardo to talk about Plato. Ficino's writings were known to his contemporaries in France and discussed at the Sorbonne. Neo-platonist schools came into being at Oxford and Cambridge towards the end of the sixteenth century. Shakespeare's aristocratic friends may not have read Ficino but certainly knew Plato's *Symposium*.

> Well, when one of them – whether he be a boy-lover or a lover of any other sort – happens on his own particular half, the two of them are wondrously thrilled with affection and intimacy and love, and are hardly to be induced to leave each other's side for a single moment. These are they who continue together throughout life, though they could not even say what they would have of one another. No one could imagine this to be the mere amorous connexion, or that such alone could be the reason why each rejoices in the other's company with so eager a zest: obviously the soul of each is wishing for something else that it cannot express, only divining and darkly hinting what it wishes.[1]

Shakespeare's Sonnets have often been compared with the poems of Michelangelo which, too, are centred on two persons: a youth and a woman. The drama of choice was a similar one. But the tone of Michelangelo's poems is a darker one, and the transitions from pure animality to mysticism, from exultation over the youth's beauty – compared with the sun in whose brightness the Divine beauty is reflected – to absolute asceticism and resignation, more violent. Michelangelo tried also to combine platonism with Christianity. Feelings inspired by the youth are free from original sin; there is in them a longing for lost purity. The sonnet 'Non è sempre di colpa aspra e mortale' (Love is not always a harsh and deadly sin) ends with the following triplets:

> The love of that whereof I speak, ascends:
> woman is different far; the love of her
> but ill befits a heart all manly wise.

[1] Op. cit., p. 143.

> The one love soars, the other downward tends;
> the soul lights this, while that the senses stir,
> and still his arrow at base quarry flies.[1]

Shakespeare was far more down to earth, but the choice
between angelic and diabolic, between the sphere of light and
the sphere of shadow, is the same for him as for Michelangelo:

> Two loves I have of comfort and despair,
> Which like two spirits do suggest me still:
> The better angel is a man right fair,
> The worser spirit a woman colour'd ill.
> To win me soon to hell, my female evil
> Tempteth my better angel from my side,
> And would corrupt my saint to be a devil,
> Wooing his purity with her foul pride.   (CXLIV)

Erotic customs and disguises were related to a peculiarly interpreted Platonic metaphysics. *Eros socraticus* carried with it a
certain pattern of beauty and the model of an act. It was the act
of a youth, of course, for which the Florence of the Medici
became famous. Verrocchio was the first to create the model of
the 'girl-youth' which was to be used to depict angels. Angels
were sexless, though they were regarded by the more sophisticated theologians as androgynous beings. Verrocchio's 'youth-
girl', a sad ephebe with a disturbing, ambiguous beauty,
combined the charms of both sexes. As in Shakespeare's Sonnet XX:

> A woman's face, with Nature's own hand painted,
> Hast thou, the master-mistress of my passion.

Girls in their turn became like boys. Botticelli's she-angels sur-
rounding the Virgin, or his nymphs in Primavera's train, had
narrow hips, high waists, small breasts. Flora looks like a tall,
fair-haired boy who has been disguised for a carnival procession,
dressed in a transparent veil with flowers, his hair combed and
curled. He has a sad triangular face, still almost Gothic. He
seems to be ashamed of his participation in this masquerade. He

[1] *The Sonnets of Michelangelo*, trans. by J. A. Symonds, Vision Press, London,
1950, p. 129.

turns his head back at the sight of girls, tempting and tempted, present and absent. He smiles with the corner of his mouth, but the smile is like a grimace. In Signorelli's fresco at Orvieto depicting the resurrection of the dead it is no longer possible to distinguish boys from girls. They all have long, loose hair, slender figures, features not yet set, still promising, slim legs of overgrown boys, slightly rounded shoulders, and the small hands of women. These master-mistresses, youth-girls, are sad and embrace each other affectionately.

The three Florentine Davids, those of Donatello, Verrocchio and Michelangelo, represent the changes in the idea of male beauty and the model of an ephebe. They get progressively smaller, more strained, more girlish. The latest of them, Michelangelo's David, leans backwards, bows his head, slightly raises his right foot. His left arm is bent at the elbow, his hand on the nape of his neck. He smooths down his hair. It is at once a coquettish and a defensive gesture, but not the gesture of a youth. His eyes are half closed, his mouth slightly open, as if he were just waking, as if the world were only just beginning to exist for him. When one looks at him from behind, or even sideways, he appears like a young girl, with legs some- what too heavy, a girl not yet transformed into a woman. The biblical David turned into Apollo.[1] Shakespeare shows the same model of an ephebe in his Sonnets:

> That I might see what the old world could say
> To this composed wonder of your frame;
> Whether we are mended, or whe'r better they,
> Or whether revolution be the same.
>   O, sure I am, the wits of former days
>   To subjects worse have given admiring praise.   (LIX)

Even in the figures of Michelangelo's titans and giants, the elements of the sexes are always mixed. Those athletic torsos have a touch of feminity in them. Titans have small heads with refined features; huge bodies are accompanied by narrow

---

[1] On the connection between Neo-platonism and Florentine painting and sculpture, cf. A. Chastel, *Art et humanisme à Florence au temps de Laurent le Magnifique*, Paris, 1959. See particularly the excellent chapter *Eros Socraticus*.

female arms, or long slender legs; as if the substance of human bodies were not wholly organized and could arbitrarily combine male and female elements. The Florentine David-Apollo is a 'youth-girl', but in Michelangelo we find also a combination of feminity in full bloom with mature masculinity. Bodies of youths and girls, of men, women and old people blend with one another. Dawn and Night in the Medici Chapel have their breasts widely apart. But it is enough to step back a little, to cast one's eye on their heads or feet, to cover with one's hands fragments of their torsos and abdomens, for Dawn and Night to turn into statues of sad masculinity, their faces alike contracted with pain, their profiles Greek, their noses straight. Dying slaves have the gentle and flowing contours of women, their fetters look like veils to cover their almost developed breasts. Masculinity and femininity, pain and pleasure, death and orgasm have blended into one, have become one body, contorted in one spasm.

In the Medici Chapel sculptures the elements of sex have been combined by suffering; in the Sistine Chapel the sexes have been blended in exaltation, rapture and joy. The huge figures of patriarchs are framed by the *putti* and *ignudi* in place of medallions. They invariably have almond eyes, curled locks and headbands over their foreheads. They cuddle together, embrace each other and play. They are represented always in pairs, but the social attributes given to them seem to depend on the artist's whim. The muscular cherubs of Michelangelo are little fauns, in whom everything is roundness and promise. New contradictions have been blended here: shame and pleasure, innocence and awareness. These children are erotically mature and conscious of their caresses.

Michelangelo's Florentine Bacchus is even more ambiguous: in the full bloom of youth, boasting of his androgynous beauty, sensuous and inviting to sensual pleasure; evading attentions and yet offering himself.

Shakespeare was influenced by the same classical tradition. On a number of occasions he consciously evoked it in the Sonnets:

On Helen's cheek all art of beauty set,
And you in Grecian tires are painted new.   (LIII)

Sometimes it seems that Leonardo kept painting the same few
faces again and again. Most frequently he painted his own face
as a young man. He gave it to the archangel Michael. St Anne,
St John the Baptist, Leda and Bacchus have the same kind of
face: mouths with upturned corners, high foreheads, thick eye-
lids, straight, long noses. All have the same expression of
serenity and sadness, even the same smile. Except that with St
Anne the smile is hardly perceptible, with Leda contemptuous,
with St John – ambiguous.

> *Pour que sourie encore une fois Jean-Baptiste*
> *Sire je danserais mieux que les séraphins . . .*

Apollinaire was more disturbed by St John's smile than by that
of Mona Lisa. St John is not an ephebe. His shoulders are full,
his breasts clearly outlined. Leonardo's St John is a man; but in
all the copies, both contemporary and later, at the Palazzo
Rosso in Genoa, in Paris and at Basle, he imperceptibly changes
into a woman with the tired face of an old courtesan who
coquettishly holds up a corner of her robe with her left hand to
cover her nipple. He has become like Leda. He anticipates
Bacchus, whose androgyny, taken over from antiquity, is
intentional and complete.

> What is your substance, whereof are you made,
> That millions of strange shadows on you tend?
> Since every one hath, every one, one shade,
> And you, but one, can every shadow lend.   (LIII)

The Sonnets are a dramatic prologue for a third reason. The
Dark Lady will be transformed in turn into Julia of *The Two
Gentlemen of Verona* and into Rosaline of *Love's Labour's Lost*;
later she will serve as a model of the harsh and sensuous
Hermia in *A Midsummer Night's Dream*. We shall find her in
Cressida: pure and faithless, affectionate and mocking. Perhaps
it is to her that Rosalind in *As You Like It* is indebted for her
audacity, and Viola in *Twelfth Night* for her determination in
amorous exaltation.

Julia, Rosalind and Viola have disguised themselves as boys. Viola has become Cesario, Rosalind has turned into Ganymede. The Dark Lady of the Sonnets has unexpectedly become the fair 'master-mistress'. Her charm is irresistible. She seduces men and women alike: the former as a girl, the latter as a boy. She is an almost perfect androgyny. This is how Viola of *Twelfth Night* describes herself:

> I am all the daughters of my father's house,
> And all the brothers too . . .   (II, 4)

III

Twelfth Night opens with a lyrical fugue accompanied by an orchestra:

> If music be the food of love, play on;
> Give me excess of it, that, surfeiting,
> The appetite may sicken, and so die. –
> That strain again! – it had a dying fall.   (I, 1)

The exposition gives one the impression of a broken string; broken by itself, or by someone. It is like an overture in which the instruments get mixed up. From the first scene, music and lyrical elements sound in disharmony. The orchestra has stopped, then begins again. In vain:

> Enough; no more;
> 'Tis not so sweet now as it was before.   (I, 1)

The passions are hungry, but choke with their own appetite. The Duke's monologue is spoken in the style and poetic diction we know from the Sonnets. The style is refined, the diction authentic. There is tension and anxiety in it. Love is an entry into the sphere of risk and uncertainty; everything in it is possible.

> O spirit of love, how quick and fresh art thou!
> . . . .
> . . . so full of shapes is fancy,
> That it alone is high-fantastical.   (I, 1)

This hurrying of images we know also from the Sonnets. The lyrical fugue breaks just as suddenly as the music. The dialogue becomes brutal and quick:

> *Curio.* Will you go hunt, my lord?
> *Duke.* What, Curio?
> *Curio.* The hart. (I, 1)

From the very first lines everything in *Twelfth Night* is ambiguous. The hunt is for Olivia. But the hunter has been hunted down himself. The Duke is both Actaeon and stag. Again the phrasing reminds one of the Sonnets:

> And my desires, like fell and cruel hounds,
> E'er since pursue me. (I, 1)

Viola with the Captain will presently be shipwrecked on the shore of the very same country of Illyria. Shakespeare deals with the plot of a sister losing her twin-brother in a storm at sea in just a couple of lines. The plot is a pretext. The theme of the play is disguise. Viola, in order to serve the Duke, has to pretend she is a boy. Girls have dressed up as boys in fairy tales, stories and legends, in the folklore of all peoples, in lyric and epic poetry from Homer to the present time.[1] They hide their sex under armour in order to fight in war; under a monk's hood to enter a monastery; they put on students' clothes to enter an Alma Mater. The Middle Ages knew heroic disguise and hagiographic disguise. The Renaissance took a liking to amorous disguise. We find it in Italian comedy, as well as in the volumes of tales from which Shakespeare derived the plots and ideas for his comedies. Disguise had its justification in prevailing customs. Girls could not travel alone; they were not even supposed to walk alone in the evenings in the streets of Italian cities. Disguise had its theatrical justification, too: it created at the outset the possibility of mistaken identity which facilitated the development of the plot, and was a ready-made farcical situation.

> I'll serve this duke:
> Thou shalt present me as an eunuch to him. (I, 2)

[1] The motif of the 'change of sexes' is listed (ATh 514) in the international catalogue of popular fairy tales. On this motif in legends, stories and fairy tales, cf. J. Krzyżanowski, *Dziewczyna chłopcem* (Girl turned boy), *Slavia Orientalis*, vol. XII (1963), no. 2.

Disguise was not anything out of the ordinary. But in this first scene between Viola and the Captain we observe a striking brutality in the dialogue. In the first version of the comedy, say the experts, Viola was to sing the songs later given to the Clown and that is why the Captain introduces her to the Duke as an Italian *castrato*. But even with this emendation there is something shocking in this proposition. A young girl is to turn into a eunuch. It is as if a chill went down our spines. As with everything in Shakespeare, this is intended. The same word will be repeated, only more strongly:

> Be you his eunuch, and your mute I'll be:
> When my tongue blabs, then let mine eyes not see.	(I, 2)

Disguise was nothing out of the ordinary, but in *Twelfth Night* there is something disturbing in it. A girl disguises herself as a boy, but first a boy has disguised himself as a girl. On the Elizabethan stage female parts were acted by boy actors. That was a limitation, as theatre historians well know. Female parts in Shakespeare are decidedly shorter than male parts. Shakespeare was well aware of the limitations of boy actors. They could play girls; with some difficulty they could play old women. But how could a boy act a mature woman? In all Shakespeare's plays, in the whole Elizabethan drama even, there are very few such parts. Lady Macbeth and Cleopatra are sexually mature. Their parts, however, are curtailed to suit a boy actor's scope. This is a fact known to all actresses who have played Cleopatra or Lady Macbeth. There is little substance in those parts, as if whole pages have been torn out of them. Shakespeare was afraid to show Cleopatra in love scenes, he preferred to relate them. He described her physical charms, but did not want to show them. Between Macbeth and his wife matters of sex are never clearly explained. Either the conjugal bed was burnt-out land for them, or in this marriage the woman had the role of the man. In *Macbeth*, or in *Anthony and Cleopatra*, one can see how Shakespeare grappled with the limitations of his actors. But on at least two occasions Shakespeare used this limitation as the theme and theatrical instrument of comedy. *Twelfth Night* and *As You Like It* were written for a stage on which boys played the parts of girls. The disguise is a double one, played on two levels as it were: a boy dresses up as a girl who disguises herself as a boy.

> 'Tis beauty truly blent, whose red and white
> Nature's own sweet and cunning hand laid on:
> Lady, you are the cruell'st she alive,
> If you will lead these graces to the grave,
> And leave the world no copy. (I, 5)

This passage has been compared with the Sonnets. Their style and diction is repeated in *Twelfth Night* once more. Even the actual words are similar:

> She carv'd thee for her seal, and meant thereby
> Thou should'st print more, not let that copy die. (XI)

That appeal was addressed by a man to a youth who was his lover and patron at the same time. In *Twelfth Night* the lines are spoken by the Duke's page to Countess Olivia; by a girl disguised as a boy, to a boy disguised as a girl. But the girl disguised as a boy is a boy disguised as a girl.

> What country, friends, is this?
> This is Illyria, lady. (I, 2)

We are still in Illyria. In that country ambiguity is the principle of love as well as of comedy. For, in fact, Viola is neither a boy nor a girl. Viola-Cesario is the 'master-mistress' of the Sonnets. The music of *Twelfth Night* has been written for that particular instrument. Viola is an ephebe and an androgyny.

> Dear lad, believe it;
> For they shall yet belie thy happy years
> That say thou art a man: Diana's lip
> Is not more smooth and rubious; thy small pipe
> Is as the maiden's organ, shrill and sound;
> And all is semblative a woman's part. (I, 4)

Duke Orsino, Viola and Olivia are not fully drawn characters. They are blank, and the only element that fills them is love. They cannot be dissociated from one another. They have no

independent being. They exist only in and through mutual
relationships. They are infected, and they infect, with love.
Orsino is in love with Olivia, Olivia is in love with Cesario,
Cesario is in love with Orsino. That is how things look on the
surface of the dialogue, on the upper level of the Shakespearian disguise. A man, a youth, a woman: love has three
faces, as in the Sonnets. This is the Illyria theme. Duke Orsino
is the First Person here. He personifies the *Eros socraticus*:

> There is no woman's sides
> Can bide the beating of so strong a passion
> As love doth give my heart; no woman's heart
> So big, to hold so much; they lack retention.
> Alas, their love may be call'd appetite, –
> No motion of the liver, but the palate.   (II, 4)

And a little later, in the same outburst:

> . . . make no compare
> Between that love a woman can bear me
> And that I owe Olivia.   (II, 4)

Everyone in Illyria speaks about love in verse. It is a refined,
occasionally too contrived verse. Authentic drama takes place
under the surface of that court rhetoric. Only sometimes the
rhythm is broken and a cry reaches out to the surface. Thus
Olivia cries after Cesario's first departure:

> Even so quickly may one catch the plague?   (I, 5)

This cry might have been uttered by Orsino or by Viola. Every
character here has something of the fair youth and the Dark
Lady. Every character has been endowed with a bitter knowledge about love. Love in Illyria is violent and impatient; it
cannot be gratified or reciprocated.

> As I am man,
> My state is desperate for my master's love;
> As I am woman, – now, alas the day! –
> What thriftless sighs shall poor Olivia breathe!   (II, 2)

As in the Sonnets, the three characters exhaust all the forms of
love. Olivia loves Cesario, Cesario loves Orsino, Orsino loves

Olivia. But Cesario is Viola. On the middle level of Shake-
pearian disguise Olivia loves Viola, Viola loves Orsino,
Orsino loves Olivia. Shakespeare's triangle has been modified:
there are now two women and one man, or rather a man, a girl
and a woman.

> How will this fadge? my master loves her dearly;
> And I, poor monster, fond as much on him;
> And she, mistaken, seems to dote on me.   (II, 2)

Viola seems to Olivia a girlish youth and to Orsino a boyish
girl. A Shakespearian androgyne acts a youth for Olivia and a
girl for Orsino. This triangle is now commuted for the third
time. Olivia and Orsino are now simultaneously in love with
Cesario-Viola, with the youth-girl. Illyria is a country of
erotic madness. Shakespearian names and places often have
hidden associations. The circle has been closed, but it is a
circulus vitiosus. In all metamorphoses, on all levels of Shakespearian disguise, these three – Olivia, Viola and Orsino – chase
one another, unable to join. Like wooden horses in a merry-go-
round, to use Sartre's expression. Viola-Cesario incessantly
circles round between Olivia and Orsino.

The appearance of Sebastian does not really make any
difference. Sebastian is a character in the plot of the play, but
does not participate in the real love drama. He was taken over
by Shakespeare lock, stock and barrel from the Italian story to
provide the solution proper for a comedy. But even in the adventures of this conventional character Shakespeare does not
abandon ambiguity. In Illyria the aura of inversion embraces
everybody:

> I could not stay behind you: my desire,
> More sharp than filed steel, did spur me forth.   (III, 3)

Antonio, the other captain of the ship, is in love with Sebastian.
He has saved him from shipwreck and now accompanies him on
his adventures, following him round Illyria. He is faithful and
brave, but also ridiculous and common. He should be big and
fat, very ugly, should have an uncouth beard and look amazingly like the first Captain who accompanied Viola. Shakespeare

frequently repeats in the *buffo* tone a theme previously dealt with seriously or lyrically. Sebastian is Viola's twin and double. If Viola is boyish, Sebastian must be girlish. A bearded giant now chases a girlish youth round Illyria. This is the last but one of *Twelfth Night's* metamorphoses.

The appearance of Sebastian does not dispel the basic ambiguity of erotic situations in Illyria, but, on the contrary, seems to aggravate it even more. Who has been deceived? Olivia or Orsino? Who has been deluded by appearance? Is desire part of the order of nature, or of love? Love is mad. But what about nature? Can nature be mad and irrational? Olivia fell in love with Cesario; Cesario turned out to be Viola. But Viola changed again into Sebastian:

> you have been mistook:
> But nature to her bias drew in that.   (V. 1)

A youth fell in love with the Duke; the youth was a disguised girl. Nothing stands in the way of another marriage to be concluded:

> Your master quits you; and, for your service done him,
> So much against the mettle of your sex
>
> . . . .
>   . . . you shall from this time be
> Your master's mistress.   (V, 1)

The comedy is over. *Twelfth Night; or, What You Will.* What will you have: a boy, or a girl? The actors take off their costumes: first the Duke, then Viola and Olivia. The last metamorphosis of the amorous triangle has been accomplished. What remains is a man and two youths. 'But nature to her bias drew in that.' A boy acted a girl who acted a boy; then the boy changed again into a girl who again turned into a boy. Viola transformed herself into Cesario, then Cesario became Viola, who turned into Sebastian. Ultimately then, in this comedy of errors, what was just an appearance? There is only one answer: sex. Love and desire pass from a youth to a girl and from a girl to a youth. Cesario is Viola, Viola is Sebastian. The court model of ideal love has been ironically analysed to the end. Or rather, presented more realistically.

> . . . So full of shapes is fancy
> That it alone is high-fantastical. (I, 1)

Genet's play *The Maids* begins with a scene in which the mistress punishes the maid, scolding and slapping her on the face. After a dozen lines or so we begin to realize that this is a game, that on the stage there is no mistress or maid, but two sisters of whom one pretends to be the mistress and the other – her own sister. They play a comedy of rebellion and humiliation. In *The Maids* there are three female parts: the mistress and two sisters, but in a commentary to the play Genet asks that all the parts be acted by men. Passion is one; it only has different faces: of man and woman; of revulsion and adoration; of hate and desire.

There have been productions of *Twelfth Night* in which Sebastian and Viola were acted by one and the same person. This seems the only solution, even if its consistent treatment requires the epilogue to be dealt with in a thoroughly conventional manner. But it is not enough for Cesario-Viola-Sebastian to be acted by one person. That person must be a man. Only then will the real theme of Illyria, erotic delirium or the metamorphoses of sex, be shown in the theatre.

IV

The disguise is a masquerade. A masquerade, too, has its eroticism and its metaphysics. Eroticism is the easiest to represent. It has frequently been attested to in literature and manners. In Aretino's *Dialogues of Courtesans*, teachers of the profession on numerous occasions advised their adepts to disguise themselves and pretend to be boys, the most effective means to rouse passion. Male attire was to protect a girl when on a journey, but the disguise made her even more attractive, and that in three ways: men who were fond of women could discern a female shape under the disguise; men who were fond of youths could see in the disguised girl the girlish youth they desired; and

women, deceived by the garments, were roused to violent
affection by the smooth and charming youth:

> Then in a female garb her friend array'd,
> That all who saw might know her for a maid:
> And more – she hop'd the cause of her distress
> From error nourish'd by the manlike dress;
> The dress once chang'd, her fond desire might cease,
> And all her bosom he compos'd to peace.
> Ah! how unlike that night the couch they press'd!
> One fondly lock'd in all-composing rest:
> One waking sigh'd, or if she clos'd her eyes,
> In broken slumbers flattering visions rise.
> She fancies, at her prayer, indulgent Heaven
> To Bradamant a better sex had given.
> As worn with tedious watch the patient dreams
> (Long parch'd with feverish thirst) of limpid streams,
> And cooling draughts; so she in sleep enjoys
> What all in vain her waking thought employs.
> Sudden she starts, extending round the bed
> Her longing hands; but finds the blessing fled.[1]

Such were the experiences of Bradamanta in Ariosto's *Orlando
Furioso*, when she dressed up as a knight and deluded the
Spanish princess. In a manner no less poetically refined,
Shakespeare's contemporary, John Donne, depicted the
dangers of disguise in *Elegy XVI, On His Mistress*, where he
tried to dissuade her from setting out on a journey in man's
attire:

> Dissemble nothing, not a boy, nor change
> Thy body's habit, nor mind's; be not strange
> To thyself only; all will spy in thy face
> A blushing womanly discovering grace.
>
> . . . .
>
> Th' indifferent Italian, as we pass
> His warm land, well content to think thee Page,
> Will hunt thee with such lust, and hideous rage,
> As Lot's fair guests were vexed.[2]

[1] *Orlando Furioso*: trans. from the Italian of Ludovico Ariosto, with notes, by
John Hoole, London, 1799, book 25, 11, 291–308, vol. III, p. 227.
[2] John Donne, *Poems*, London, Dent, 1947. pp. 81-2.

Masquerade was a favourite kind of entertainment adopted by the English royal court and by aristocratic households after the Italian fashion. The exact manner of a masquerade depended, of course, on the taste of the host. One such masquerade was shown by Marlowe in *Edward II*. He described it with relish and great skill, also with so much precision that its character could be established beyond doubt:

> Therefore I'll have Italian masques by night,
> Sweet speeches, comedies, and pleasing shows;
> And in the day, when he shall walk abroad,
> Like sylvan nymphs my pages shall be clad;
> My men, like satyrs grazing on the lawns,
> Shall with their goat-feet dance an antic hay.
> Sometime a lovely boy in Dian's shape
> With hair that gilds the water as it glides,
> Crownets of pearl about his naked arms,
> And in his sportful hands an olive-tree,
> To hide those parts which men delight to see,
> Shall bathe him in a spring; and there, hard by,
> One like Actaeon peeping through the grove,
> Shall by the angry goddess be transformed,
> And running in the likeness of an hart
> By yelping hounds pulled down shall seem to die.
>
> (*Edward II*, I, 1)

Twelfth Night could begin with just such a scene, represented as a masque. This extract from Marlowe's play shows a striking similarity to it in its poetic diction and a near identity of tropes and symbols. We have left Actaeon in Illyria. The fair-haired boy bathing in a stream is no other than the fair master-mistress of the Sonnets. He plays with an olive branch, pearls adorn his bare arms, he covers his sex with his hand. Again we find ourselves in the circle of Florentine painting and sculpture. This 'boy in Dian's shape' recalls the two Bacchuses: that of Leonardo and that of Michelangelo.

The anatomical counterpart of disguise is the hermaphrodite; its metaphorical counterpart is the androgyne. The androgyne is an archetype; a concept and image of the union of the male and female elements. In antiquity a child with signs of bisexuality used to be killed by its own parents. The anatomical hermaphrodite was regarded as a freak of nature or a sign of the anger of the gods. Only gods were androgynous; particularly those from whom everything originated. In every theogony the creation of the world had been preceded by births of androgynous deities. The Magna Mater of antiquity was a bisexual being; so were nearly all the oriental deities and the Hebrew Isis. In Hesiod's theogony, androgynous Chaos gave birth to androgynous Erebus and female Night. Earth gave birth of itself to Heaven and the stars. In Kariá a statue of Zeus with six nipples arranged in a triangle was found. In Cyprus there was a cult of a bearded Aphrodite. Elsewhere a bald Venus was worshipped. The early Roman head of Janus was originally represented with a male and a female face.

Dionysus was one of the oldest bisexual deities. He used to be represented with the accessories of both sexes. In a discovered fragment of an unknown tragedy of Æschylus someone exclaims at the sight of Dionysus: 'Whence art thou coming, man-woman, and where is thy country? What means thine apparel?' In the hellenistic period Dionysus was represented as a youth with the shape of a girl. Ovid and Seneca gave him 'the face of a virgin'.[1] These ideas were inherited by the Renaissance. The feast of Dionysus included a liturgical dressing-up of boys as girls and girls as boys. Girls carried phallic statuettes. The tradition of the Dionysia and Saturnalia remained particularly vivid in the Italian carnival.

The decline of the Renaissance, and later of the Cinquecento, the period of Mannerism and Baroque, brought with it a revival of ancient myths in art, philosophy and religious mysticism. These myths became more and more syncretic. They expressed the discrepancy between Epicureanism and spiritualism, as well as the new links between the Orphic tradition, and platonism and Christianity. They filled in all the gaps left by the philosophy of nature which no longer sufficed for the understanding of the world that was becoming more and more bitter.

[1] Cf. Marie Delcourt, *Hermaphrodite*, Paris, 1958.

All the androgynous myths, with their images of bisexual deities and symbols of Bacchus-Dionysus, Hermes, Diana-Aphrodite, had a wide and active circulation in that period. They were useful for all kinds of speculations and entered into complex involvements with metaphysics and alchemy. Most frequently, however, they appeared in close proximity with socratic eroticism. Here belongs the myth of Actaeon who, for spying on Diana in her bath, was turned into a stag and torn to pieces by hounds, and the myth of Narcissus, who became enamoured of his own reflection when looking at it in a lake. He saw there the image of a naked youth.

Here belongs also the myth of Ganymede. Michelangelo gave his youthful friend – the very same for whom he had written his love sonnets – a series of drawings among which there was one representing the capture of Ganymede by Jupiter in the shape of an eagle. In the Florence of the Medici the myth of Ganymede had, of course, a double meaning. It symbolized a mystical love which brought with it communion with the deity and its direct contemplation. But it remained above all, as it had been in antiquity, the symbol of pederasty.

> For never doted Jove on Ganymede
> So much as he on cursed Gaveston.
>> (Marlowe, *Edward II*, I, 4)

Rosalind assumed the name of Ganymede when she escaped to the Forest of Arden. Shakespeare adopted this from Lodge's story which served him as material for the plot of *As You Like It*. The choice and assumption of this name was not a matter of chance.

> I'll have no worse a name than Jove's own page;
> And therefore look you call me Ganymede.
>> (*As You Like It*, I, 3)

Rosalind, disguised as a boy, meets Orlando in the Forest of Arden. Orlando is in love with her and she is in love with him. But Orlando does not recognize Rosalind in the shape of Ganymede. Rosalind woos him with intensity, but she does so as a boy, or rather as a boy who in this relationship wants to be a girl for his lover. Rosalind plays Ganymede who in turn plays Rosalind:

> *Orlando.* I would not be cured, youth.
> *Rosalind.* I would cure you, if you would but call me Rosalind, and come every day to my cote and woo me.
>
> . . . .
>
> *Orlando.* With all my heart, good youth.
> *Rosalind.* Nay, you must call me Rosalind.   (III, 2)

This is just the beginning. These scenes belong to the finest and most refined among Shakespeare's love dialogues and, but for the fact that the term 'mannerism' has a certain traditional pejorative flavour, they should be recognized as a masterpiece of mannerism. On the surface of the dialogue, on the higher level of a disguise, identical with that of *Twelfth Night*, two youths, Ganymede and Orlando, play a love game. On the intermediate level we have Rosalind and Orlando in love with each other. But the real Rosalind happens to be a disguised boy.

The border-lines between illusion and reality, between an object and its reflection, are gradually lost. Once more one has to recall the theatrical aesthetics of Genet. The theatre represents in itself all human relationships, but not because it is their more or less successful imitation. The theatre is the image of all human relationships just because it is based on falseness; original falseness, rather like original sin. The actor plays a character he is not. He is who he is not. He is not who he is. To be oneself means only to play one's own reflection in the eyes of strangers.

There are no whites and blacks existing separately. Negroes are black only for white men, just as white men are white only for Negroes. The 'real' Negroes are white men who play blacks; just as 'real' whites are blacks who play whites. But Negroes and white men exist together, and so they infect each other with their images, just as mirrors placed at certain angles repeat the reflection of each object an infinite number of times. The 'real' girl is a disguised boy.

In the love scenes of the Forest of Arden, just as in those of

Illyria, the theatrical form and the theme completely corre-
spond with and inter-penetrate each other; on condition, that
is, that female parts are played, as they were on the Elizabethan
stage, by boys. An actor disguised as a girl plays a girl disguised as a boy. Everything is real and unreal, false and
genuine at the same time. And we cannot tell on which side of
the looking glass we have found ourselves. As if everything
were mere reflection.

> *Ganymede.* And I am your Rosalind.
> *Celia.* It pleases him to call you so; but he hath a Rosalind of a
>   better leer than you.
> *Ganymede.* Come, woo me, woo me; for now I am in a holiday
>   humour, and like enough to consent. – What would you say to
>   me now, an I were your very very Rosalind?   (IV, 1)

Rosalind plays Ganymede who plays Rosalind. She plays herself being married to Orlando. At that wedding ceremony
Celia will play the priest. The amazing poetics of these scenes
have not yet been demonstrated. As if our contemporary
theatre had no proper instrument. And yet these scenes contain
Genet's theatre to the same degree that Beckett's theatre is contained in *King Lear*; except that they are sur-Genet, just as the
quartet of madmen, real and feigned, in the third act of *Lear*, is
sur-Beckett.

The love scenes in the Forest of Arden have the logic of
dreams. Plans, persons, tenses – past, present, future – are
intermingled; so is parody with poetry.

> *Ganymede.* Come, sister, you shall be the priest, and marry us. –
>   Give me your hand, Orlando. – What do you say, sister?
> *Orlando.* Pray thee, marry us.
> *Celia.* I cannot say the words.
> *Ganymede.* You must begin, – 'Will you, Orlando,' –
> *Celia.* Go to. – Will you, Orlando, have to wife this Rosalind?
> *Orlando.* I will.
> *Ganymede.* Ay, but when?
> *Orlando.* Why now; as fast as she can marry us.
> *Ganymede.* Then you must say, – 'I take thee, Rosalind, for wife.'
> *Orlando.* I take thee, Rosalind, for wife.

Ganymede. I might ask you for your commission; but, – I do take
   thee, Orlando, for my husband: – there's a girl goes before
   the priest.   (IV, 1)

Disguise is a dangerous game. It is a game in which one dis-
cards one's own shape and assumes, or at least borrows, a
strange one. The Harlequin is a transformist, but he comes
from the devil. An evil spirit leads people astray because it
continually assumes different shapes; the shape of a man, an
animal, or even of an inkstand.

> Disguise, I see, thou art a wickedness,
> Wherein the pregnant enemy does much.
> *(Twelfth Night*, II, 2)

The most dangerous disguise of all is the one where sex is
changed. Transvestism has two directions: sacral and sexual;
liturgical and orgiastic. An orgy can also be part of a liturgical
feast. In the Saturnalia boys and girls used to exchange their
clothes. Laws and rules were suspended. Boys behaved like
girls, girls behaved like boys. Values and judgements were
mixed up. For one night everything was permitted. But in a
liturgical disguise, laws and rules were only suspended, never
revoked. Disguise was, as it were, a return to Chaos from
which Law had emerged and in which there had as yet been no
division into the male and the female.[1]

Every disguise involves not only an invitation to Cythera, a
call to orgy, but is a diabolic invention in a much deeper sense.
It is the realization of man's eternal dream of overcoming the
boundaries of his own body and of his sex. It is a dream of
erotic experience in which one is one's own partner, in which
one sees and experiences sensual pleasure, as it were, from the
other side. One is oneself and at the same time someone else,
someone like oneself and yet different.

Disguise has its metaphysical plane, a remnant perhaps from
the periods when it was part of liturgy. That metaphysical
plane could at any rate still be traced in it at the time of the

---

[1] On liturgical disguise and the mythology connected with it cf. Mircae
Éliade, *Méphistophélès et l'Androgyne*, Paris, 1962.

Renaissance. Not only was it an attempt at eroticism free from the limitations of the body. It was also a dream of love free from the limitations of sex; of love pervading the bodies of boys and girls, men and women, in the way light penetrates through glass.

In the closing scenes of *As You Like It* one can discern this double significance of disguise: the spiritual and the physical; the intellectual and the sensual. Everything has been mixed up: the bodies of boys and girls; desire and love. Sylvius loves Phebe, the shepherdess; Phebe loves Ganymede; Ganymede loves Orlando; Orlando loves Rosalind. Ganymede is Rosalind, but it is Rosalind that is Ganymede, because Rosalind is a boy, just as Phebe is a boy. Love is an absolute value, and at the same time absolutely a matter of chance. Eroticism goes through bodies like an electric current and makes them tremble. Every Rosalind is Ganymede and every Ganymede is Rosalind.

> *Ganymede.* . . . Look, here comes a lover of mine, and a lover of
>   hers.
>
> .   .   .   .
>
> *Phebe.* Good shepherd, tell this youth what 'tis to love.
> *Silvius.* It is to be all made of sighs and tears; –
>   And so am I for Phebe.
> *Phebe.* And I for Ganymede.
> *Orlando.* And I for Rosalind.
> *Ganymede.* And I for no woman.
> *Silvius.* It is to be made all of faith and service; –
>   And so am I for Phebe.
> *Phebe.* And I for Ganymede.
> *Orlando.* And I for Rosalind.
> *Ganymede.* And I for no woman.
> *Silvius.* It is to be all made of fantasy,
>   All made of passion, and all made of wishes;
>   All adoration, duty, and observance,
>   All humbleness, all patience, and impatience,
>   All purity, all trial, all deservings; –
>   And so am I for Phebe.
> *Phebe.* And so am I for Ganymede.
> *Orlando.* And so am I for Rosalind.
> *Ganymede.* And so am I for no woman.   (V, 2)

The love scenes in *As You Like It* take place in the Forest of Arden. This forest is like all Shakespeare's forests, except that it is possibly more amazing; as if it contained, repeated or foretold them all. Shakespearian forests are real and enchanted; tragic and grotesque; pathetic and lyrical scenes are being performed in them. In Shakespeare's forest, life is speeded up, becomes more intense, violent and at the same time, as it were, clearer. Everything acquires a double significance: the literal and the metaphorical. Everything exists for itself and is also its own reflection, generalization, archetype.

In a Shakespearian forest, the lovers in the course of a summer night went through the dark sphere of animal eroticism. They came to know the urgency of desire and possession. They exchanged partners. In another of Shakespeare's forests, four characters from *As You Like It* will pass through tempest and hurricane: the prince who has renounced his crown; the exiled minister; the exiled brother and the clown. They will be reduced to bare existence which must suffice for itself and in itself find reasons for being, as there can be no appeal from it, whether to the empty heavens, to bloody history, or to nonrational nature. In the last of the Shakespearian forests, on Prospero's island, the history of the world will be performed in quick motion, in three hours.

First, the Forest of Arden means escape; escape from the cruel kingdom where, as always in Shakespeare, two themes obsessively repeat themselves: the exile of a lawful prince and the depriving a younger brother of his inheritance. For Shakespeare this is rudimentary social history in a nutshell. In *As You Like It* the daughter of the dethroned prince will also be exiled. The opening of the play has nothing of the calm and light-heartedness that, following the nineteenth-century pattern, critics still try to detect in *As You Like It* and *Twelfth Night*. It even seems singularly dark:

> O, what a world is this, when what is comely
> Envenoms him that bears it!   (II, 2)

A tyrant has ascended the throne, a brother persecutes his

brother, love and friendship have been destroyed by ambition, the world is ruled by sheer force and money. From the duke's feast wrestlers are being carried away, with broken ribs. The opening of *As You Like It* has the atmosphere of the Histories; the air is stuffy and everyone is afraid. The new prince is distrustful, suspicious, jealous of everything and everybody, unsure of his position, sensing the enemy in everyone. As in the Histories, the only hope of salvation is in escape; escape at any price and as fast as one can.

> This is no place; this house is but a butchery. (II, 3)

The opening of the play is violent and brutal; the close – naïve and idyllic, written in a few lines, deliberately devoid of motivation. The bad duke meets a hermit and is converted. Brother restores brother to his inheritance.

> Thou offer'st fairly to thy brothers' wedding:
> To one, his lands withheld; and to the other,
> A land itself at large, a potent dukedom. (V, 4)

Between the dark prologue and the fairy-tale epilogue there is the Forest of Arden: the most English of all Shakespearian forests. It is like the one in Warwickshire, near Stratford. Tall oaks grow in it, there are many glades and clearings, streams flow down mossy stones. People wander among briers and thorns. In this forest birds sing, does, hares and deer ('poor dappled fools') run about. It is here that the exiled duke has taken refuge:

> They say he is already in the forest of Arden, and a many merry men with him; and there they live like the old Robin Hood of England: they say many young gentlemen flock to him every day, and fleet the time carelessly, as they did in the golden world. (I, 1)

In this Forest of Arden good gentlemen play at free men and noble brigands; the priest is to marry the clown to the milkmaid; sheep are herded by peasants who declaim about love; girls dress up as boys; a melancholy courtier mocks himself and everyone around.

It is a strange kind of forest in which almost all the characters

of Shakespeare's world meet. It is a real forest, as well as a
feudal utopia and a sneering comment on that utopia. A lioness
with her cub has wandered into the forest, and snakes crawl on
the moss.

> Now go we in content,
> To liberty, and not to banishment.   (I, 3)

This is the coda of the first act. It is spoken by Celia to Rosalind
before their escape into the forest. The kingdom of liberty is at
the same time the kingdom of nature; idyllic, poeticized nature,
reminding one of Theocritus:

> And this our life, exempt from public haunt,
> Finds tongues in trees, books in the running brooks,
> Sermons in stones, and good in every thing:
> I would not change it.   (II, 1)

The kingdom of liberty and nature is contrasted with life at
court; harmony and freedom – with captivity of mind, bon-
dage of heart, insecurity of life.

> Are not these woods
> More free from peril than the envious court?   (II, 1)

But from the very first scene the idyll is blurred. As in *Twelfth
Night*, the instruments are in discord. The music of the Forest
of Arden is all in disharmony.

> And yet it irks me the poor dappled fools,
> Being native burghers of this desert city,
> Should in their own confines with forked heads
> Have their round haunches gored.   (II, 1)

To all appearances we seem to remain in the same poetic key.
Hunting scenes traditionally include sentimental lamentations
over a wounded stag deserted by its fellows. But here the tone
is different. The kingdom of nature is equally ruthless and
egotistic as the world of civilization. There is no return to primeval harmony. It is the dispossessed who dispossess here, and
they kill who have themselves escaped with their lives.

> . . . you do more usurp
> Than doth your brother that hath banish'd you.   (II, 1)

In Arcadia all are equal. Unknown is the power of money and the advantage of superior birth. Law does not yield to force, and the only people who are unhappy are those whose love is un-requited. Rosalind had hardly arrived in the Forest of Arden than she overheard two shepherds talking, the younger com-plaining to the elder that his love was not requited. Rosalind is hungry and sleepy. Like Homeric heroes, Shakespearian heroes every now and then feel hunger and the need for sleep, even when they are unhappy in love, or engaged in a con-spiracy.

Rosalind and Celia are looking for shelter and food. They will, of course, pay with gold. The romantic Rosalind is sober enough. Just as Shakespeare was. The Forest of Arden, where the golden age was to come anew, is ruled by the capitalist laws of hire.

> But I am shepherd to another man
> And do not shear the fleeces that I graze:
> My master is of churlish disposition. (II, 4)

And even more to the point:

> Besides, his cote, his flocks, and bounds of feed,
> Are now on sale. (II, 4)

Rosalind the Arcadian, Rosalind the heroine of romance, Rosalind the character of pastoral court comedy, buys the cottage, land and sheep:

> I pray thee, if it stand with honesty,
> Buy thou the cottage, pasture, and the flock,
> And thou shalt have to pay for it of us. (II, 4)

Arcadia has been turned into real estate, into landed property. Says the shepherd:

> . . . if you like upon report,
> The soil, the profit and this kind of life,
> I will your very faithful feeder be,
> And buy it with your gold right suddenly. (II, 4)

A lovely enumeration, and a lovely order: 'the soil, the profit, and this kind of life'. Lovely, and very English. Very

Shakespearian, for that matter, because of all we know about Shakespeare, one thing only is certain: he was a competent judge of houses and land, and knew how to buy them.

Historians of literature make a careful distinction between writers who imitated Shakespeare and those who followed the Ariosto fashion. And rightly so. The kind of fantasy, or of mockery, prevalent in northern Europe, differed from that characteristic for the South, though it happened occasionally that an author invoked in one work the spirits both of Shakespeare and Ariosto. Not only Slowacki comes to mind in this respect, but also, perhaps, de Musset. But even more interesting than the most preposterous attempts at investigating literary influences would be to envisage Shakespeare in Ariosto's sphere, in the 'green world', as Northrop Frye used to call the enchanted Shakespearian forests. In that 'green sphere' Orlando Furioso fights the infidels, meets the hippogriffs, goes mad for love and tries to obtain from magicians the secrets of a love philtre. It is in this 'green sphere' that Ariosto wages his peculiar combat with the feudal madness which must be ridiculed and mocked, but without which life would lose all its beauty and poetry. The same kind of combat against feudal madness, only more bitter, will be waged later by Cervantes.

Of all Shakespeare's works, *As You Like It* and *Twelfth Night* are conceived most in the spirit of Ariosto. There is a similar combination of pathos and irony, mockery and lyricism. This mixture of techniques and literary genres is something very modern, and the theatre is wrong to draw back from it. Even more modern, closer to our own time, is the ambiguous attitude to madness; or rather, to the escape into madness, into mythology and into disguise. It is not only Rosalind that disguises herself as Ganymede. Elizabethan outlaws disguise themselves as noble brigands of Robin Hood's time. They are rather like Don Quixote who put on some old armour he had found in the attic. Shakespeare has no illusions; not even the illusion that one can live without illusions.

He takes us into the Forest of Arden in order to show that one must try to escape, although there is no escape; that the

Forest of Arden does not exist, but those who do not run away will be murdered. Without her escape to the non-existent forest, Rosalind will not marry Orlando, and Orlando will not regain his paternal inheritance.

Two pairs of shepherds, real and invented, derived from English pastures and from pastoral Arcadia, serve as the system of mirrors which enables Shakespeare to discredit and ridicule courtly refinement with its code of honour, its charms of the 'natural state' and it conventions of pastoral romance.

> *Corin.* And would you have us kiss tar? The courtier's hands are perfumed with civet.
> *Touchstone.* Most shallow man. . . . civet is of a baser birth than tar – the very uncleanly flux of a cat. (III, 2)

A very similar device was to be used later by Jonathan Swift. The juxtaposition of the great and the small can be a system of mirrors too. It is enough to reduce man a hundred times in size for dynastic wars and endeavours to obtain court preferment to become a flea circus. It is enough to magnify him a hundred times for a kiss to become a monstrosity. Says Touchstone to Corin:

> That is another simple sin in you; to bring the ewes and the rams together, and to offer to get your living by the copulation of cattle; to be bawd to a bell-wether; and to betray a she-lamb of a twelvemonth to a crooked-pated, old, cuckoldy ram, out of all reasonable match. (III, 2)

It is not just the mechanism of ridicule that is Swiftian here. Shakespeare is the forerunner of Swift in his slowly and consistently growing disgust at nature. His hatred of nature, directed above all at the sphere of reproduction and sexual instinct, found its apogee in *King Lear* and *Othello*. But already here, in the calm landscape of the forest, the word 'natural' begins to acquire the meaning we give it when referring to 'natural functions'.

> . . . 'tis such fools as you
> That makes the world full of ill-favour'd children . . .
> (III, 5)

It might have been a line spoken by the Fool in *King Lear*. In *As You Like It* it is not spoken by Touchstone. This is the sweet, tender, passionate Rosalind mocking Sylvius who is in love with Phebe. Rosalind, Phebe and Audrey are also the successive mirrors in which love sees itself. Idyllic shepherds and shepherdesses had always been beautiful. In *As You Like It* only Ganymede-Rosalind, the youth-girl, has the right to beauty. In the mocked-at Arcadia shepherdesses are plain.

> I see no more in you than in the ordinary
> Of nature's sale-work . . .   (III, 5)

says Rosalind of Phebe. And goes on:

> He's fall'n in love with her foulness.   (III, 5)

Phebe is plain to Rosalind and beautiful to Silvius. Phebe is plain only in one of the mirrors. Audrey is plain in all of them. Audrey is meant to be plain and stupid. She is natural. The clown wants to marry a girl who is plain and stupid, so as not to have any illusions. The marriage ceremony is to be performed by Sir Oliver Martext whose parish is, of course, also to be found in the Forest of Arden. But the clown chases the priest away. They are joined according to the laws of nature; natural nature, that is.

Phebe is poetic and behaves in a Petrarchan manner. She wears pastoral costume. But in Shakespeare even shepherdesses from a fictional Arcadia suddenly become real. Phebe had dressed herself up as a shepherdess, so let her have the red hands of a swineherd. Shakespeare leaves nothing of the over-sweetened and over-aestheticized pastoral idyll.

> Come, come, you are a fool,
> And turn'd into the extremity of love.
> I saw her hand: she has a leathern hand,
> A freestone-colour'd hand; I verily did think
> That her old gloves were on, but 'twas her hands:
> She has a housewife's hand.   (IV, 3)

In *Twelfth Night* one notes a similar contrast between sophisticated poetry used in the declarations of love, and the brutal drawing of comic scenes. Here again, as in the Forest of Arden, the mixture of techniques and styles matches the confused image of the world. At all times, however, it is a real world, always the same, bitter, cruel and fascinating; the world which one cannot accept, but from which there is no escape; a world for which there is no justification except that it is the only one that exists.

The critics distinguish in *Twelfth Night* two contrasting levels, two plots and themes: the idealized image of love, and the flesh-and-blood company of Messrs Toby Belch and Andrew Aguecheek; make-believe and reality. *Twelfth Night* and *As You Like It* are generally considered the most romantic of the Comedies. But of all the 'contemporary reactions' to Shakespeare, from Elizabethan times to ours, the romantic was the most false and the one that left behind it the most fatal theatrical tradition. Surely, one must be absolutely deaf to hear in Viola's endless rounds between Olivia and Orsino nothing but the romantic music of love.

Twelfth Night is only superficially a play in Italian costume, set in a fictitious Illyria. *Twelfth Night* was a contemporary play to the same extent as *A Midsummer Night's Dream*, *Love's Labour's Lost* and *As You Like It*. With all its appearances of gaiety, it is a very bitter comedy about the Elizabethan *dolce vita*, or at any rate about the *dolce vita* at every level and in every wing of the Southampton residence. On this *dolce vita* the figure of Malvolio casts his shadow. He is the English Tartuffe, but perhaps even more a hater of men than a Puritan. He has a chain with a silver spoon round his neck, and wears ridiculous yellow stockings and crossed garters. But the shadow he casts is black.

It has been rightly observed that the Clown in *Twelfth Night* is the link between both themes of the comedy. He is the only character to visit both wings of the palace, to wander up and down all its floors. He accompanies the Duke's lute players on his tambourine and he drinks in the merry company of Sir Toby and Sir Andrew. He sings and scoffs in both places, and frequents the state rooms of the palace as well as the servants' quarters. The gay comedy ends with his melancholy song, whose refrain will be taken up by the Fool in *King Lear*. This song is the last dissonance in the play's music.

The clowns in *As You Like It* and *Twelfth Night* are Shakespeare's most original addition to the inherited plots. If wisdom becomes clowning, then clowning becomes wisdom. If the world has come to stand on its head, one can adopt the right attitude to it only by turning somersaults. These are the presuppositions of clownish logic. The world makes clowns of everybody, except clowns. They are the only ones to have escaped general buffoonery by hiding under their fools' caps. Feste and Touchstone are not clowns any more; their jokes have ceased to be funny. They are disagreeable. Disintegration is their function. They live in a bare world, bereft of myths, reduced to knowledge without illusions.

The clownish echo in the Forest of Arden is a double one. Not only Touchstone echoes the characters of the play. The other critical echo is provided by Jaques:

> If he, compact of jars, grow musical,
> We shall have shortly discord in the spheres.   (II, 7)

As You Like It and *Twelfth Night* are already close in time to *Hamlet*. In the figure of Jaques Shakespearian scholars long ago perceived the first outline of the Prince of Denmark. Before Jaques turns into Hamlet he must first go through the school of clowning. Feste and Touchstone are philosophical clowns already. But they are only clowns. When they have taken off their fools' caps, they cease to exist. Before a philosophical clown can become Hamlet, he must find personal reasons for his bitterness. He must first be a man.

> . . . the sundry contemplation of my travels, which by often rumination, wraps me in a most humorous sadness.   (IV, 1)

And earlier on, he speaks even more like Hamlet:

> Why, 'tis good to be sad and say nothing.   (IV, 1)

At the beginning Jaques is a repentant libertine; or at least this is how the Duke describes him. He is a melancholiac pure and simple, the essence of melancholy; as if he were filled with bile, according to the Elizabethan classification of humours. He is even sentimental at first, sorry for a wounded stag. But he soon fastens his look upon the clown:

> O noble fool!
> A worthy fool! Motley's the only wear.   (II, 7)

Like King Lear in his wanderings to the far end of the cold night, Jaques undergoes in the Forest of Arden a lesson of clownish education. Soon he envies the clown his freedom:

> I must have liberty
> Withal, as large a charter as the wind,
> To blow on whom I please; for so fools have.   (II, 7)

The Forest of Arden is a return to the golden age, the only place in the feudal world where alienation has ceased to operate. And in this Forest of Arden, it is Jaques who feels his alienation most fully and is, to use our terminology, most thoroughly frustrated.

> Invest me in my motley; give me leave
> To speak my mind, and I will through and through
> Cleanse the foul body of th' infected world,
> If they will patiently receive my medicine.   (II, 7)

Jaques has learned from the Fool not only his philosophy, but also his language; the language Hamlet will speak. At the end of the play everyone will leave the Forest of Arden; except Jaques. He is the only one who has no reason to leave the forest because he has never believed in it, has never entered Arcadia.

In the Renaissance period the first pastoral romance entitled Arcadia was written by Sannazaro. He was a Neapolitan, and imitated Vergil. He found Arcadia, the real and the poetic, the pastoral and the philosophic, in Greece. Lorenzo the Magnificent used to cultivate poetry in his spare time; he wrote sylvan and bucolic poems. Poets whose patron he was, the sweet Angelo Politiano and his numerous followers, sang praises of the Tuscan landscape, with its calm, flat hill-tops and silent olive groves. The philosophers Ficino and Mirandola composed philosophical treatises in praise of the purification that rustic landscape gives to the soul. In the Florentine circle the Arcadian myth found, however, much more prominent reflection in painting than in literature. In Signorelli's great canvas, painted for Lorenzo around 1490 and called *The Concert of Pan*, art historians have found the fullest expression of the intellectual climate prevalent in the Medici house and of the cultural mythology associated with it. Chastel writes in his excellent book on Florentine art:

> What adds a significant tone to this scene is a nymph sitting on the left bank, in the classical attitude of melancholy. In a sense she provides the psychological key to the composition where, surrounding the dreamy god, there is expressed a tangle of desires and illusions whose substance and effects have again and again been analysed in Lorenzo's poetry. Pan is a Saturnian god of nature, desire and their unending cycles. The youth playing on a flute and the sage standing on the pedestal of the throne represent two spiritual powers, proper for the definition of the cosmos: music and philosophy. They form parts of a complete 'pastoral' work, and the meaning given to the god's companions widens the scope of the composition to the dimensions of an Arcadia worth visiting. . . . Signorelli painted the *summa* of all that Lorenzo himself associated with the Medici deity. The dull sadness of the scene, its melancholy atmosphere, heightened by the reddish tones of dusk, long falling shadows which underline the immobility of the figures, all this gives a poignant accent to this literary evocation. The poetry of this masterpiece is not limited to Lorenzo himself, but for the first time expresses the sentimental foundation of the humanist 'pastoral category' which was to find its fuller expression and development in Sannazaro's *Arcadia*.[1]

It is easy to see how well this description fits in with the inner atmosphere of *As You Like It*. A modern art historian will find in Signorelli the same inner contradiction between a dream and its realization, between the need for harmony and its inevitable disruption.

With Sannazaro began the literary career of pastoral works

[1] A. Chastel, op. cit., p. 232, trans. by the present translator.

which for two centuries, the sixteenth and the seventeenth, enjoyed great popularity. Pastoral romances, poems and comedies were written in Italy, France and Spain. To this genre belong Tasso's *Aminta*, Honoré d'Urfé's *Astrée*, Montemayor's *Diana*, written in Castilian and Cervantes' *Galatea*. Lope de Vega wrote his *Arcadia*, too. Sir Philip Sidney transferred Arcadia to Elizabethan England.

There are many different Arcadias. They can be pastoral or knightly; philosophical or abounding in supernatural events. But every one of them is populated by shepherds and shepherdesses looking like ephebes. They talk about love and friendship. Frequently girls dress themselves up as boys, particularly in works by Italian and Spanish writers. Spenser, in his commentaries to *The Shepheard's Calendar*, which was published in 1579 and originated the pastoral fashion in England, praised the mutual love of young shepherds; love philosophical and tender, pure and faithful; love exercised in the Greek manner.

The Arcadian myth and the myth of androgyny are almost invariably connected with each other. What do they mean, what purpose do they serve? Arcadia is the image of the lost paradise. It is a paradise derived both from antiquity and from the Bible. It is the golden age of humanity, and the garden of Eden from which the first parents of humanity were banished.

> Here feel we but the penalty of Adam,
> The seasons' difference.   (II, 1)

Shakespeare's imagination is always wonderfully realistic. The opening scenes in the Forest of Arden might start with the frostbitten companions of the exiled Duke trying to warm themselves by rubbing their hands, stamping their feet, beating their shoulders with their fists.

> . . . the icy fang
> And churlish chiding of the winter's wind,
> . . . bites and blows upon my body,
> Even till I shrink with cold . . .   (II, 1)

Round that Arcadia there wanders a girl-boy. The myth of

androgyny is also an invocation of the image of a lost paradise where primeval Harmony or Chaos prevailed; Harmony or Chaos are different terms for a situation in which all contradictions coexist, to be ultimately reconciled. (There is also a third, modern term to describe the myth of reconciled contradictions; the term has a rather scientific sound: entropy. It is a kind of eschatology for physicists and cyberneticists, the last of the eschatologies.) For the Gnostics Logos was a means of reconciling contradictions. That very term, *coincidentia oppositorum*, was recognized by Nicholas de Cusa as the least imperfect definition of the nature of God. Man was created in the image and likeness of God. However, it was not man or woman that was created in the image and likeness of God, but androgyny. Mankind takes its origin from androgyny.[1]

On Michelangelo's Sistine Chapel frescoes representing the Creation, Adam has the sad head of a woman. Leo the Hebrew in his *Dialoghi d'Amore* connected with biblical tradition the platonic myth of the remaining halves of the first men cut in two by Zeus. Adam was an androgyny. Only after the expulsion from Paradise did God divide the sexes. The arguments of Leo the Hebrew were widely known in humanist circles and even reached Poland. Jan Kochanowski (1530–84) writes in his *Wzór pań mężnych* (Model of gallant ladies):

> Eve, the mother of all kinds, rightly takes the first place in these tales. And that not because she was the most ancient and preceded every other person, but through her strange origin and the uncommon way she had been created. What is there that the fair sex can boast of as compared to the male? Eve was not, as Adam was, modelled of clay, but, according to Moses, was taken out of his side and carved from the very bone. If any man wants to find more about our original parents' creation than is given in the simple words of Moses, let him, amongst other things, read the second dialogue of the learned Jew Leo, who argues that Plato took his androgyny from the very same place in Moses.

[1] Cf. M. Éliade, op. cit., particularly the section: *Le mythe de l'androgynes* pp. 128 ff. and G. R. Hocke, *Die Welt als Labyrinth, Manier und Manie in der europäischen Kunst.* Hamburg, 1957. Also Mario Praz, *The Romantic Agony*, Oxford, 1933, cf. R. Caillois, *L'Homme et le Sacr* Paris, 1958.

Leo the Hebrew only codified a three-fold tradition: gnostic, that of numerous Hebrew sects, and the Christian apocrypha which asserted that androgyny was at the beginning and would be at the end of the human race. After redemption from original sin men will return to their original nature and the sexes will be united again.

Androgyny is not only the archetype of the unity of the male and female elements, but occurs in various metaphysical speculations as the sign of reconciliation of all contradictions. We find the cosmic myth of androgyny in Paracelsus and in Jacob Boehme, who was Shakespeare's contemporary.

One of the names for the philosophers' stone was the Rebis. Rebis means 'double' or 'two bodies'. It was the androgynic symbol of the hermetics. In the famous treatise *Splendor Solis* of 1532, which was the bible of the alchemists, we find a fascinating hermaphroditic *Discordia Concors*. It symbolized not only man and woman, but also sun and moon, earth and water, sulphur and mercury, beginning and end. These opposites were not just visualized in the person of a hermaphrodite, but were also contained in an 'egg' held in his-her hand. This 'egg' of the world' constituted a symbol of transcendental harmony.

What was the ultimate function of these myths? In the Florentine circle of the court of the Medici, the arcadian myth and the Platonic myths were perhaps an attempt to find a metaphysical and moral sanction, drawing its authority from antiquity and biblical tradition, for the type of culture that was being created; they were a search for the principle that would enable men to find unity in politics, art and custom. At that time these myths had probably lost their sacral character, but they continued to fire the imagination.

In the sixteenth and seventeenth centuries hope for the political and religious unity of the world was destroyed. Hope for the establishment of a humanist republic of scholars and artists also failed. Great philosophical systems competed with one another but had already lost their universal character. Experience went far beyond the possibilities of generalization, and could no longer be contained in abstract and rigid theories. This applied not only to scientific experiments, but to the experience of sailors and bankers, soldiers and lawyers, doctors and craftsmen. They were richer and more varied than the teaching of the law of nations and the origin of power, than Aristotelian logic and the theory of elements, than all the philosophies and all metaphysics. For a long time earth had been like a crystal ball in which the Cosmos was reflected. Now only pieces of broken glass remained, and every one of them refracted the world and light in a different way. The historical imagination saw in the story of mankind a polarization between the golden age and apocalyptic doom. In the era of the Baroque and Mannerism all inherited myths acquired a much more violent and dramatic character.

The Forest of Arden mocks Arcadia and constitutes a new Arcadia. Love is the escape from cruel history to an invented forest. Shakespeare is like a Bible; he creates his own myths. The Forest of Arden is a place in which all dreams meet; it is a dream and the awakening from a dream.

Coincidentia oppositorum! The unification of all opposites! In the Forest of Arden love is both earthly, and platonically sublimated. Rosalind is Ganymede and the most girlish of girls. Constant-fickle, calm-violent, fair-dark, shy-impudent, prudent-madcap, tender-mocking, childish-grownup, cowardly-courageous, bashful-passionate. As in Leonardo, she is an almost perfect androgyny and personifies the same longing for the lost Paradise where there had as yet been no division into the male and female elements.

> All this the world well knows; yet none knows well
> To shun the heaven that leads men to this hell.
>
> (Sonnet, CXXIX)

Prospero's Staff

> . . . Not a soul
> But felt a fever of the mad, and play'd
> Some tricks of desperation.   (*The Tempest*, I, 2)

I

The performance is drawing to a close. For the last time
Prospero has called Ariel and drawn a magic circle. The elements have been tamed, the tempest is over, Prospero returns
among men and renounces his magic powers.

> But this rough magic
> I here abjure; and, when I have required
> Some heavenly music . . .
> . . . .
> I'll break my staff,
> Bury it certain fadoms in the earth . . .   (V, 1)

On the surface the ending of *The Tempest* seems happier than
that of any other great Shakespearian drama. Prospero wins
back the throne of Milan. Alonso, the King of Naples, has
regained his son and regrets his former treachery. Liberated
Ariel has vanished into thin air. Caliban has realized that he had
mistaken a drunkard for a god. The young lovers, Miranda and
Ferdinand, play chess 'for a score of kingdoms'. The ship has
been saved and awaits them in a quiet bay. Trespasses and
crimes have been forgiven. Even the two treacherous brothers
are invited to supper at Prospero's cell. It is evening, a brief
peaceful moment after tempest. The world which had left its
orbit – as in *Hamlet's* 'The time is out of joint' – has now been
restored to moral order.

> In one voyage . . .
> . . . found . . .
> Prospero, his dukedom
> In a poor isle; and all of us, ourselves
> When no man was his own.   (V, 1)

'When no man was his own . . .' The morality play has been performed, the spell is over, and so is madness. In all Shakespeare's dramas there are brief moments of peace and quiet. But almost always they occur before the storm. In this instance, the storm has already happened. In the morning both princes and all the *dramatis personae* are to embark for Naples. The action of *The Tempest* returns to its prologue and all the characters resume their former places. History has turned full circle. Will it repeat itself once more?

The Shakespeare Histories are histories of reigns. The agony of the old monarch and the coronation of the new one form their prologues and epilogues at the same time. The *dramatis personae* are always changing. In *The Tempest* the same ruler regains his dukedom. It is as if nothing has changed, as if everything – the desert island included – were just a theatre performance staged by Prospero, a performance in which he has played the leading part. A similar performance to that devised and staged by Hamlet at the castle of Elsinore.

The ending of *The Tempest* is more disturbing than that of any other Shakespearian drama. This may be the reason why none of the commentators has noticed that the action returns to the point of departure. Perhaps this seemed too obvious. Or it may have disturbed the previous romantic and idyllic interpretation of *The Tempest* as a play of forgiveness and reconciliation with the world. And yet, an analysis of the dramatic structure of *The Tempest* has to be, if not the key, then at least the beginning of any interpretation. History has returned to the point of departure and begins anew. But what history? And what does that strange morality play mean whose action takes place within less than four hours, that is to say, not much longer than it takes to perform the play on the stage?

Shakespeare, who usually plays with time freely, condensing months in one scene, or – as in *The Winter's Tale* – letting sixteen years pass between two acts, counts the time of *The Tempest* up to a minute. It is after two when Alonso's ship catches fire from thunderbolts and is wrecked on the rocks. It is 6 p.m. when the characters go to supper. Prospero has regained his dukedom,

Alonso has found his son, Ferdinand has won Miranda. Shakespeare's clock, the dramatic clock which can count years in a minute, behaves on this occasion in the manner of all clocks. In Shakespeare's day, performances usually began at three and ended at six. Prospero's magic started operating between two and three, and was completed by six. One can hardly fail to notice a conscious design in this.

The characters of the play go through the tempest, and through a trial. The spectators witness the tempest with them, at exactly the same time. The characters go to supper; at the same time the actors and the spectators will go to supper. The tempest is over, the magic is over, and so is the performance. Life begins again, in the same way as before the tempest, before the performance, for characters and audience alike. Has nothing changed? But before they leave, the spectators will have to listen to the epilogue. Prospero, or rather the actor playing Prospero, comes forward and speaks the epilogue. This, Prospero's final soliloquy, is one of the most beautiful written by Shakespeare, and also one of the most tragic and puzzling. Prospero speaks directly to the audience:

> . . . my project . . .
> . . . was to please: now I want
> Spirits to enforce, art to enchant;
> And my ending is despair.   (V, 1)

In Spanish plays – those of Calderon, and even more those of Lope de Vega – it was customary for an actor to appeal to the audience at the end and ask their indulgence for the shortcomings of the performance. But in Shakespeare a tragic epilogue of this sort, directed straight at the audience, is found only in *The Tempest*. It is written in quite a different key, it is a great lyric fugue, and one has, indeed, to be blind not to see in it moving personal accents. *The Tempest* is the last of Shakespeare's great works. Having completed it, he probably wrote only a few scenes for Fletcher's tragedy *Henry VIII*. *The Tempest* is Shakespeare's crowning work. No wonder that many generations of students and critics have seen in it a poetic

testament, a farewell to the theatre, a philosophical and artistic
autobiography. Under the guise of Prospero Shakespeare is
said to have represented himself.

There have been learned Shakespearian scholars who tried to
interpret *The Tempest* as a direct autobiography, or as an allegorical political drama. Chambers, for whom *The Tempest* contained Shakespeare's optimistic creed, connected the play with
the turning point in his life which occurred after 1607 and was
marked by a departure from the black philosophy of *Hamlet*.
J. D. Wilson saw in *The Tempest* a reflection of the idyllic atmosphere of Stratford and the peaceful old age the poet spent with
his daughter and granddaughter. Robert Graves saw in *The
Tempest* – as well as in the sonnets – a veiled autobiography.
The witch Sycorax was to be synonymous with the 'Dark
Lady'; Ariel's captivity meant surrender to love's passion,
while Trinculo was supposed to represent Ben Jonson himself.
Ariel was meant to be the martyred king Henry IV of France.[1]
All these interpretations are ridiculous and childish. No less
childish are the theories which see in Ariel and Caliban rigid,
complete and clear philosophical allegories, or the exposition of
an esoteric mystic system.

A great magician, whom the elements obey, at whose command graves and the dead rise, who knows how to eclipse the
sun at noon and to hush the winds, rejects the magic wand and
renounces power over human fate. He is now an ordinary
mortal, defenceless as everybody else:

> Now my charms are all o'erthrown,
> And what strength I have's mine own, –
> Which is most faint.   (V, 1)

This interpretation is, indeed, tempting. But one easily
realizes that it consists of one metaphor only: that of a poet-
magician, poet-creator, and a silence which is the price of
return to the world of human beings. One notices just as easily
how romantic that metaphor is, in its style, as well as in its
philosophy and aesthetics; in the conception of the poet as a

[1] L. Gillet, *Shakespeare*, Paris, 1931.

demiurge; in the conflict between the poet and the world, between Ariel and Caliban, between pure spirituality and pure bestiality. All this symbolism is closer to Victor Hugo and Lamartine, and even more to the German *Romantische Schule*, than to the Shakespearian theatre, which invariably depicts cruel nature, cruel history, and man who struggles in vain trying to get the better of his fate.

The theatre tradition of the Shakespearian *Tempest* was lost very early. From the Restoration until the middle of the nine-teenth century *The Tempest* was performed in England in Dryden's adaptation. It was a meaningless court fairy tale. The romantic era brought with it a symbolic interpretation, and an illusionist *Tempest*, performed by means of all the available mechanics and optics. These two bad traditions – the fairy tale one and the allegorical – were then united and brooded over interpretations of *The Tempest* almost until the present day. Poetizing was substituted for great poetry; an allegorical spec-tacle replaced serious morality. The dramatic qualities of *The Tempest* were lost in dubious aesthetics. The play's philosophic bitterness was also lost. *The Tempest* became more and more of a romantic and operatic fairy story, with the main part given to a ballet dancer, dressed in bright tights, waving her silver gauze wings and floating in the air by means of a mechanical device. Even Leon Schiller did not fully free himself from this tradition when in 1947 he tried to counter the romantic notion of *The Tempest* with an optimistic tale of the philosopher-king and the unlimited power of reason; a tale taken out of the Age of Enlightenment, as it were.

The true *Tempest* is serious and severe, lyrical and grotesque. Like all great Shakespearian dramas, it is a passionate reckoning with the real world. For this reading of *The Tempest* one has to go back to Shakespeare's text, and to Shakespeare's theatre. One has to see in it a drama of the men of the Renaissance, and of the last generation of humanists. In this sense, but in this sense only, can one find in *The Tempest* the philosophical auto-biography of Shakespeare and the summa of his theatre. *The Tempest* will then become a drama of lost illusions, of bitter

wisdom, and a fragile – though stubborn – hope. The great
themes of the Renaissance will then be restored to *The Tempest*:
those concerned with the philosophical utopia; with the limits
of experience; with man's efforts to conquer the physical
world; with dangers threatening the moral order; with nature,
which is and is not the measure of man. We shall then find in
The Tempest the world Shakespeare lived in – the times abounding in great voyages, newly discovered continents and mysterious isles, dreams of man floating in the air like a bird, and of
machines that would enable him to capture the strongest
fortresses. It was an era which saw a revolution in astronomy,
in the melting of metals and in anatomy; an era of the commonwealth of scholars, philosophers and artists; an era of science,
which for the first time became universal; of philosophy, which
discovered the relativity of all human judgements; an era of the
most magnificent architectural exploits, and of astrological
horoscopes, commissioned by the Pope and the princes; an
era of religious wars and of stakes set up by the Inquisition; of
an unparalleled splendour of civilization, and of plagues
which decimated cities. It was a wonderful, cruel and dramatic
world, which suddenly exposed both the power, and the
misery, of man; a world in which nature and history, royal
power, and morality, have for the first time been deprived of
theological meaning.

The Elizabethan theatre represented the world. Over the
Shakespearian stage at the Globe hung a huge canopy with
golden signs of the zodiac symbolizing the Heavens. It was,
after the fashion of the Middle Ages, a Theatrum Mundi. But a
Theatrum Mundi after an earthquake.

II

The Tempest has two endings: a quiet evening on the island,
when Prospero forgives his enemies and the story returns to
the point of departure; and Prospero's tragic monologue,
spoken directly to the audience, a monologue out of time. But
The Tempest also possesses two prologues. The first of these is

the dramatic one; it takes place on the ship, which is set on fire by lightning and tossed on the rocks by the wind. The other prologue consists of Prospero's account of how he had lost his dukedom and came to live on the uninhabited island; it narrates the previous history of the *dramatis personae*.

On the surface, the first prologue – like Prospero's closing monologue – seems unnecessary. It takes place out of the island and only provides, as it were, a frame. But it serves a double dramatic purpose. It shows a real tempest, as distinguished from the inner storm, from the madness which will overcome the characters in view of the audience. It is only after the physical and material tempest has been depicted that the morality will be performed. All that happens on the island will be a play within a play, a performance produced by Prospero.

But this dramatic prologue has one other purpose. It is a direct exposition of one of the great Shakespearian theses, a violent confrontation of nature with the social order. The ship carries a king. What is royal might and majesty when confronted with raging elements? Nothing. Shakespeare repeats Panurge's famous invocation from the fourth book of *Gargantua and Pantagruel*, but how much more sharply and strongly he does it.

Gonzalo. Nay, good, be patient.
Boatswain. When the sea is. Hence! What cares these roarers for the name of king? To cabin: silence! Trouble us not.
Gonzalo. Good, yet remember whom thou hast aboard.
Boatswain. None that I more love than myself. You are a counsellor; if you can command these elements to silence, and work the peace of the present, we will not hand a rope more; use your authority: if you cannot, give thanks you have lived so long . . .

(I, 1)

This in a nutshell, and in a condensed form, is the theme of *King Lear*.

In the prologue to *The Tempest*, the deprivation of majesty's sacred character – so characteristic of the Renaissance – is realized once more. Faced with the roaring sea, a boatswain means more than a king.

Now for Prospero's account, which is the other prologue to
The Tempest. It is a long account and seems to include some
undigested elements of an old play from which Shakespeare has
probably taken the plot. It is of no importance. Prospero's
story takes up one of the main, basic – almost obsessional –
Shakespearian themes: that of a good and a bad ruler, of the
usurper who deprives the legal prince of his throne. This is
Shakespeare's view of history, eternal history, its perpetual,
unchanging mechanism. It is repeated in the Histories and in
the Tragedies – in *Hamlet* and *Macbeth* – even in the comedies,
for this theme is present in *Measure for Measure* and in *As You
Like It*. Only in the Roman tragedies, although the mechanism
of history and of the struggle for power remains the same, are
the *dramatis personae* different; they include the senate and the
people, the patricians, tribunes and army generals.

In Prospero's narrative the framework of feudal history is
bare, purged of all allegory and chance, almost deprived of
names and character; it is abstract like a formula. Prospero's
account is a summary of Machiavelli's treatise, *The Prince*.

> . . . the liberal arts . . .
> . . . being all my study,
> The government I cast upon my brother,
> And to my state grew stranger . . .
> . . . Thy false uncle –
>
> . . . .
>
> Being once perfected how to grant suits,
> How to deny them, who t'advance, and who
> To trash for over-topping, new created
> The creatures that were mine . . .
> . . . set all hearts i'the state
> To what tune pleas'd his ear; that now he was
> The ivy which had hid my princely trunk,
> And suck'd my verdure out on't . . .
>
> . . . .
>
> To have no screen between this part he play'd
> And him he play'd it for, he needs will be
> Absolute Milan.
>
> . . . .
>
> . . . confederates –

> ... with the King of Naples
> To give him annual tribute, do him homage ...
>
> . . . .
>
> ... one midnight ...
> ... did ... open
> The gates of Milan ... (I, 2)

Prospero's narrative is a description of a struggle for power, of violence and conspiracy. But it applies not only to the dukedom of Milan. The same theme will be repeated in the story of Ariel and Caliban. Shakespeare's theatre is the *Theatrum Mundi*. Violence, as the principle on which the world is based, will be shown in cosmic terms. The previous history of Ariel and Caliban is a repetition of Prospero's history, another illustration of the same theme. Shakespearian dramas are constructed not on the principle of unity of action, but on the principle of analogy, comprising a double, treble, or quadruple plot, which repeats the same basic theme; they are a system of mirrors, as it were, both concave and convex, which reflect, magnify and parody the same situation.[1] The same theme returns in various keys, in all the registers of Shakespeare's music; it is repeated lyrically and grotesquely, then pathetically and ironically. The same situation will be performed on the Shakespearian stage by kings, then repeated by lovers and aped by clowns. Or is it the kings who ape the clowns? Kings, lovers, clowns are all actors. Parts are written and situations given. So much the worse, if the actors are not suited for their parts and cannot play them properly. For they perform on a stage which depicts the real world, where no one chooses his or her part, or situation. Situations in Shakespearian theatre are always real, even when interpreted by ghosts and monsters.

Even before the sea currents took the raft, carrying Miranda and Prospero, to the island, the first act of violence and terror had already taken place. Ariel had been captured by the witch Sycorax and – for refusing to obey her abominable orders –

---

[1] Analogy as a principle of Shakespeare's dramatic writing has been referred to by F. Fergusson, *The Idea of the Theatre*; Moulton, *Shakespeare, the Dramatic Artist*; W. Empson, *Some Version of Pastoral*. Henry James uses the term 'the central reflector' in connection with *Hamlet*.

imprisoned in a cloven pine tree. He suffered, for until then he
had been free as air. 'Thou wast a spirit too delicate to act her
earthy and abhorr'd commands' – as Prospero will tell him
Prospero liberates Ariel, but only to make him serve, to make·
him obey his own power. Shakespeare is always in a hurry to
state the conflict and situations, abruptly and at once. No sooner
has Prospero ended his narrative, and Ariel given his account of
the shipwreck, than the conflict breaks out with full force. The
prologue is over; action has begun.

> *Ariel.* Let me remember thee what thou has promis'd,
>   Which is not yet perform'd me.
> *Prospero.* How now? moody?
>   What is't thou canst demand?
> *Ariel.* My liberty.
> *Prospero.* Before the time be out? no more!   (I, 2)

The theme of force has already been introduced twice. But on
the island there is another character of the drama: Caliban. The
same theme, the same situation will be repeated for the third
time. Only the parts will be reversed and Shakespeare will
introduce a new mirror. This time it will be a crooked mirror.
Caliban is the offspring of Sycorax's union with the devil. On
her death he assumed rule of the island. He was its rightful lord,
at least in the feudal sense. Caliban lost his realm, just as Prospero had lost his dukedom. Caliban was overthrown by Prospero, just as Prospero had been overthrown by Antonio. Even
before the morality proper is performed, and Prospero's enemies undergo the trial of madness, two acts of feudal history
have already been played out on the desert island.

> *Caliban.* This island's mine, by Sycorax my mother,
>   Which thou tak'st from me. When thou camest first,
>   Thou strok'dst me, and made much of me; wouldst give me
>   Water with berries in't . . .
>   . . . .
>   . . . I . . .
>   . . . first was mine own king . . .   (I, 2)

Caliban's first revolt still belongs to the antecedents of the drama. Caliban assaulted Miranda and tried to rape her. His attempt failed. Caliban was confined to a cave, forced to carry wood and water, and suffer torture consisting of cramps, aches, pricks. Shakespeare is a master of literality. Ariel's sufferings are abstract, and the liberty he seeks is abstract too. It is a rejection of all forms of dependence. Caliban's sufferings are concrete, physical, animal. Characters in Shakespearian dramas are never introduced by chance. The first scene in which Ariel appears brings a demand for liberty. The first appearance of Caliban marks a recollection of revolt. It is the entry of a slave. The cruelty of this scene is wholly deliberate; so is its brutal materialist quality.

> *Prospero.* Thou poisonous slave, got by the devil himself
>   Upon thy wicked dam, come forth!
> *Caliban.* As wicked dew as e'er my mother brush'd
>   With raven's feather from unwholesome fen,
>   Drop on you both! a south-west blow on ye,
>   And blister you all o'er! (I, 2)

The exposition is over. Such are the life-stories of the inhabitants of a desert island, on the rocky shores of which the ship carrying Prospero's old enemies has been wrecked.

For most commentators the island in *The Tempest* is a utopia, or a fairy isle. Let us look at it more closely, as it is going to be the scene of the drama proper. Where does this island lie, what does it signify, and how has Shakespeare described it?

From the itinerary of the sea-voyage undertaken by Alonso, King of Naples, who is returning from Tunis, and from the story of the witch Sycorax, who had come to the island from Algiers, it follows that Prospero's island should be situated in the Mediterranean. At the crossroads of both routes lies Malta. Other commentators place the island nearer to Sicily and think it is the rocky Pantelleria. Still others are of the opinion that the island lies near the shore of North Africa and take it to be Lampedusa. But Setebos, whom the witch Sycorax worshipped, was a god of the Patagonian Indians, while Ariel brings Prospero 'dew from the still-vex'd Bermoothes', or Bermuda.

In 1609 the Earl of Southampton sent a large fleet with the men and equipment necessary to colonize Virginia, the first English colony on the North American coast. The expedition raised hopes of fabulous fortunes and fired the imagination. For the first time not only astronomers, but also merchants, bankers and politicians realized that the earth is really round. The world inhabited by man was enlarged to twice its size in the course of a century, but at the same time dwindled in imagination; just as our galaxy dwindled after the first flights into the cosmos. The discovery of another hemisphere caused a shock that can only be compared to the landing of an earth-launched rocket on the moon and the photographing of its farther side. This planetary image of Earth originated in the era of the Renaissance. Thus Leonardo wrote about his works:

> My book attempts to prove that the Ocean, together with other seas, enables our world, through the medium of the Sun, to be luminous like the Moon and that, to the most distant, Earth seems a star; this is what I am arguing.   (C.A. 112. v)

Jean Fernel, one of the most eminent people of the new era, a humanist, mathematician and court physician to the King of France, wrote in his *Dialogue* in the year 1530: 'Our times have seen things not even dreamt of by the ancients . . . The Ocean has been crossed thanks to the bravey of our sailors, and new islands have been discovered . . . A new globe has been given us by the mariners of our times.' If new worlds, inhabited by intelligent creatures, have been discovered on earth, why should they not exist in the heavenly spheres as well? This is the conclusion reached by Giordano Bruno; a conclusion for which he was burnt at the stake in 1600, on the charge of heresy. At that time Shakespeare was beginning to write *Hamlet*. *The Tempest* was written eleven years later.

Recent commentators connect the origins of *The Tempest* with the accounts of the English fleet's expedition to Virginia in 1609. The expedition failed. The flag-ship *Sea Adventure*, caught in a storm, was wrecked and the sailors landed on an uninhabited island, forming part of Bermuda. They spent ten months there; then they built two new ships and eventually managed to reach Virginia. They called the islands on which they were thrown by the storm, Devil's Islands. At night they could hear mysterious howls and noises, which – according to contemporary accounts – they attributed to demons. It is from them that Shakespeare may have taken the Boatswain's story of:

> . . . strange and several noises
> Of roaring, shrieking, howling, jingling chains,
> And more diversity of sounds, all horrible. (V, 1)

These accounts made the colonists indignant, and the council of the colonists of Virginia published a pamphlet by William Barrett declaring that rumours of Bermuda being visited by devils and evil spirits were false, or at any rate exaggerated, and that in that 'tragical comedy there is nothing that could discourage the colonists'.[1] The settlers of Virginia interpreted Shakespeare more sensibly than some of his most recent commentators.

It has also been found that Prospero fed Caliban with a certain kind of inedible 'fresh-brook mussels', mentioned in accounts of the unfortunate expedition. In Ariel setting fire to the ship ('I'ld divide, and burn in many places; on the topmast, the yards, and bowsprit, would I flame distinctly') some Shakespearian scholars see the picture of the St Elmo fires, which so terrified those who were shipwrecked at the time of the Bermuda disaster.

Shakespeare's fantastic vision was always based on contemporary realities; thanks to them the world he showed in a condensed form on the stage became even more concrete. But it was always the whole world. It is useless, therefore, to look for the longitude and latitude of Prospero's island.

In *The Tempest* there is, doubtless, something of the atmosphere of long sea-voyages, mysterious desert islands; but there is also the anxiety and daring of the conclusions reached by Giordano Bruno. In any event, *The Tempest* is a long way removed from the naïve enthusiasm and childish pride of the first

[1] Quoted by L. Chambrun, *Shakespeare Retrouvé*, Paris, 1947.

witnesses of geographical discoveries. The questions raised by
The Tempest are philosophical and bitter.

The morality staged by Prospero will last less than four hours.
But the island itself is outside time. There is on it both winter
and summer. Prospero bids Ariel 'to run upon the sharp wind
of the north, to do . . . business in the veins o'the earth when
it is bak'd with frost'. The island has salt and sweet waters,
barren and fertile lands, lemon groves and quagmires. It
abounds in hazel-nuts, apples are ripe, there are truffles in the
forest. The island is inhabited by baboons, hedgehogs, vipers,
bats and toads. Jays have their nests here, sea-gulls perch
on the rocks. Berries grow here, there are sea-shells of various
kinds; feet are hurt by thorns; one hears mastiffs bark and cocks
crow.

Commentators on *The Tempest* find on this island the idyllic
atmosphere of an Arcadia. No doubt they interpret the play
only through bad theatre performances; those with a ballet-
dancer and a translucent screen. They see fairy tale and ballet
all the time. Well, one would rather trust those who undergo on
this island the trial of madness:

> All torment, trouble, wonder, and amazement,
> Inhabit here: some heavenly power guide us
> Out of this fearful country!   (V, 1)

That is why it is useless to look for Prospero's island even
among the white spaces of old maps, where the contours of the
land grow indistinct, the ocean blue turns pale and either
drawings of fantastic monsters appear, or the inscription: 'ubi
leones'. Even there the island does not exist. Prospero's island
is either the world, or the stage. To the Elizabethans it was
all the same; the stage was the world, and the world was the
stage.

On Prospero's island, Shakespeare's history of the world is
played out, in an abbreviated form. It consists of a struggle for
power, murder, revolt and violence. The first two acts of that
history had been played out even before the arrival of Alonso's
ship. Now Prospero will speed up the action. Twice more will

the same history be repeated; as a tragedy, and as a grotesque; then the performance will be over. Prospero's island has nothing in common with the happy isles of Renaissance utopias. It rather reminds us of the islands in the world of the late Gothic. Such worlds were painted by one of the greatest visionaries among painters, precursor of the Baroque and Surrealism, the mad Hieronymus Bosch. They rise out of a grey sea. They are brown or yellow. They take the form of a cone, reminding one of a volcano, with a flat top. On such hills tiny human figures swarm and writhe like ants. The scenes depict the seven deadly sins and the human passions, above all lechery and murder, drunkenness and gluttony. As well as people there are demons with beautiful, slender angelic female bodies and toads' or dogs' heads. Under the tables shaped like big tortoise-shells, old hags with flabby breasts and children's faces lie embracing half-men, half-insects with long hairy spider-like feet. Tables are set for a common feast, but the jugs and plates assume the shapes of insects, birds or frogs. This island is a garden of torment, or a picture of mankind's folly. It is even similar in its shape to the Elizabethan stage. Boats arrive at a quiet harbour at the foot of the mountain. This is the apron-stage. The main scenes take place in large caves and on terraces of the volcanic cone. The flat top of the mountain is empty. There are no actors on the upper stage. No one gives his blessing or sits in judgement over the follies depicted. The island is the scene of the world's cruel tortures. In that world Shakespeare was a witness. But there are no gods in it, and gods are not needed. Men will suffice:

> Our natures do pursue,
> Like rats that ravin down their proper bane,
> A thirsty evil; and when we drink we die.　　(I, 2)

This quotation from *Measure for Measure* could serve as an inscription to the large canvases by Bosch depicting 'The Temptation of St Anthony' or 'The Garden of Pleasure'. Such is Prospero's island. Ariel is its angel and its executioner. That is why when wishing to be seen he assumes in turn the form of a

nymph and a harpy. This is the sentence he pronounces on the
shipwrecked:

> Destiny, –
> That hath to instrument this lower world
> And what is in't, – the never-surfeited sea
> Hath caus'd to belch up you; and on this island,
> Where man doth not inhabit, – you 'mongst men
> Being most unfit to live. I have made you mad;
> And even with such-like valour men hang and drown
> Their proper selves.
>
> (III, 3)

On Prospero's orders Ariel pursues the shipwrecked, leads
them astray by his music, torments and scatters them. Alonso,
the King of Naples, and the loyal Gonzalo are tired. They fall
asleep with the entire retinue. Only the treacherous Antonio,
and the King's brother, Sebastian, are to keep watch. The story
of the plot aimed at seizing power will repeat itself. But Shakespeare uses a different mirror. The loss of the dukedom by
Prospero has been told concisely, with a dry precision, as if in
a history textbook; it has been unfolded like a formula, like a
mechanism. This time, action is slowed down and shown in a
typically Shakespearian close up. As in a film. Every second
counts, and we can observe every vibration of the soul, every
gesture. The King and Gonzalo are asleep. The moment is ripe.
It may never happen again:

> *Sebastian.* But, for your conscience, –
> *Antonio.* Ay, sir; where lies that? if 'twere a kibe,
> 'Twould put me to my slipper; but I feel not
> This deity in my bosom: twenty consciences,
> That stand 'twixt me and Milan, candied be they,
> And melt, ere they molest!
>
> (II, 1)

Antonio and Sebastian raise their swords. In a moment murder
will be committed. Shakespeare is, indeed, obsessed by this
theme. Only the mirrors change. And every one of these
mirrors is just another commentary on situations that remain
the same. Prospero's island, like Denmark, is a prison. Antonio's and Sebastian's plot repeats scenes from *King Lear*;

> If that the heavens do not their visible spirits
> Send quickly down to tame these vile offences,
> It will come,
> Humanity must perforce prey on itself,
> Like monsters of the deep.   (IV, 2)

Swords will be put back again, for Ariel is watching. He is both an agent-provocateur and the stage-manager of the performance produced by Prospero. Murder does not have to be commited. It is enough that it has been exposed. For it is only a morality that is being performed on the island. Prospero submits the castaways to a trial of madness. But what does this madness mean? Sebastian repeats Antonio's deed of twelve years ago. The island is a stage on which the history of the world is being acted and repeated. History itself is madness. As in *Richard III*:

> Welcome, destruction, blood and massacre!
> I see, as in a map, the end of all.   (II, 4)

Prospero conducts his characters through ultimate, eschatological situations. Sebastian repeats Antonio's attempt to assassinate his brother and gain power. But Antonio had made his attempt in Milan in order to become a real duke. Sebastian wants to murder his king and brother on a desert island. The ship has been tossed on the rocks, and only a handful of survivors are left stranded in a strange land. Sebastian's attempt is in fact a disinterested act, pure folly; like the theft of a sack of gold in a desert, among people condemned to die of thirst. Sebastian's gestures and motives are identical with Antonio's gestures and motives of twelve years ago, following the pattern of a real *coup d'état*. This is the essence of Shakespearian analogy and of the system of ever-changing mirrors. The history of mankind is madness, but in order to expose it, one has to act it out on a desert island.

The first tragic sequence of the scenario devised by Prospero is over. The *coup d'état* has been performed. But it has been performed by princes. The law of analogy has not yet been exhausted, and another great confrontation awaits us. Actors and their parts are changed again, but the situation remains the same. Shakespeare's world is a unity, and a conglomeration not only of styles. A *coup d'état* is not the privilege of princes only; and it is not just the princes who have a passion for power. A *coup d'état* has already been shown in *The Tempest* three times through tragic lenses; now it will be performed as a buffoonery. Characters in the Shakespearian theatre are divided into tragic and grotesque. But grotesque in the Shakespearian theatre is not just a gay interlude, intended to entertain the audience after the cruel scenes performed by kings and dukes. Tragic scenes in Shakespeare often have *buffo*, grotesque, or ironic undertones and the *buffo* scenes are often mixed with bitterness, lyricism and cruelty. In his theatre it is the clowns who tell the truth. And not just tell it; they re-enact situations usually reserved for princes. Stephano, the drunkard, and Trinculo, the clown, want power too. Together with Caliban they organize an attempt on Prospero's life. History again repeats itself. But this time it is only a farce. This farce, too, will prove itself tragic. But for the moment it is pure buffoonery:

> Monster, I will kill this man: his daughter and I will
> be king and queen, – save our graces! – and Trinculo
> and thyself shall be viceroys.   (III, 2)

Prospero's island is a scene symbolizing the real world, not a utopia. Shakespeare explains this clearly when speaking directly to the audience, almost over-emphatically. Gonzalo is the reasoner of the drama. He is loyal and honest, but simple-minded and ridiculous at the same time. The King has not yet fallen asleep. The assassination has not yet been attempted. Gonzalo begins to tell a story of a happy country. He must have read recently the famous chapter on cannibals from Montaigne's *Essays*. He is repeating Montaigne's words. In that happy country work and commerce are unknown, there are no offices and no power:

> *Gonzalo (ending)*. No sovereignty, – . . .

Antonio. The latter end of his commonwealth forgets the beginning.
Gongalo. All things in common nature should produce.

Without sweat or endeavour: treason, felony,
Sword, pike, knife, gun, or need of any engine,
Would I not have; but nature should bring forth,
Of it own kind, all foison, all abundance,
To feed my innocent people. (II, 1)

Human beings, beautiful and intelligent, live in a state of
nature, free from original sin and uncorrupted by civilization.
Nature is good and people are good. Such are the happy isles of
the anti-feudal utopias. They were being discovered in the
South Seas by the simple friars of the Order of St Francis who
found in them – long before Rousseau – good and noble
savages. These 'noble savages' had been written about by
Montaigne. But Shakespeare did not believe in 'good savages',
just as he did not believe in 'good kings'. When he did look for
a Utopia, he located it in the forest of Arden, where Robin
Hood had been with his company. But even this utopia had an
element of bitterness in it: Jaques did not find his place even
there. Shakespeare did not believe in the happy isles. They were
too close to the known continents.

A Midsummer Night's Dream is a comedy. *The Tempest* was
also regarded as a comedy by his contemporaries. The *Dream* is
a forerunner of *The Tempest* but written in a lighter vein. The
Duke is kind-hearted and understanding. Hermia's father forgives her. Hymen will join three happy couples. Such is the
situation in the epilogue. But in the prologue, the father demands the death penalty for his daughter, who has chosen her
lover against his will; the lovers flee to the forest. Hermia loves
Lysander. Demetrius is passionately in love with Hermia, Helena
with Demetrius. The world is cruel and irrational at the same
time; it makes a mockery of all feeling. But love itself is
irrational, too.

And nature? Nature is represented by the Athenian wood –
which is really the forest of Arden. Oberon and Titania live
there, but in fact it is the realm of Puck. Puck is not just a
country troll. He is also the *commedia dell'arte* Harlequin. But
the real Harlequin is the devil. To Shakespeare nature is just as

irrational as law and customs. It makes a mockery of feelings, order, conscious decisions.

Some berry juice has been put into a lover's eyes. He wakes, has no eyes for the girl asleep beside him; he runs after another, forgetting the one he has loved. Some more juice and he again forgets everything, even the fact that he has betrayed his girl. For he betrayed her during the night. Night and day have different laws.

Titania is slender, affectionate, lyrical. She wakes in the middle of the night and sees a fool with the head of an ass. That same night she will give everything up for him. She has dreamt about just such a lover, only she never wanted to admit it. In the morning she will want to forget it as soon as possible. Titania, embracing a monster with an ass's head, is close to Bosch's cruel visions. But at the same time there is in her something of the great grotesque of the surrealists. In these dream images of a summer night broken by day's sobriety there is a novel and precursory foretaste of depth-psychology and the subconscious. Madness lasts here throughout the June night. Then the dawn comes. Everybody wakes up thinking they have had strange and awful dreams. They do not want to remember their dreams. They are ashamed of the night. In the grand vision of love's madness Shakespeare is simultaneously a man of the Renaissance and a very modern writer. It is here that one should look for the truly modern Shakespeare: bitter, but very human.

On Prospero's island the laws of the real world apply to an even higher degree than in the forest of Arden. No sooner has Gonzalo finished telling his story and lain down to sleep beside the King than Antonio and Sebastian stand over him, bare swords in hand. A show commences, as cruel as the world; the same world that Hamlet looked upon:

> ... the whips and scorns of time,
> The oppressor's wrong, the proud man's contumely,
> The pangs of despised love, the law's delay,
> The insolence of office, and the spurns
> That patient merit of the unworthy takes... (*Hamlet*, III, 1)

Ariel has fulfilled Prospero's orders. His enemies have repeated gestures of twelve years ago. Gestures, not deeds. From the first to the final scene they were just a handful of shipwrecked men on a desert island. In such a situation they could only repeat gestures of hate. These gestures were madness itself, and this is the essence of the trial through which Prospero leads his actors. They have gone the whole way to the hell raging in their own souls. They have at last seen themselves 'naked like worms'. This expression taken from Sartre fits here most aptly. Alonso has realized the purpose of this trial:

> This is as strange a maze as e'er men trod;
> And there is in this business more than nature
> Was ever conduct of . . .   (V, 1)

The performance of *The Tempest* and the morality produced by Prospero is drawing to an end. It is almost six o'clock. The same clock has counted the inner time of the performance, and the time of the audience. For it is both the actors and spectators who – in the course of four hours – have gone through the same tempest. Everybody, in fact.

> Not a soul
> But felt a fever of the mad, and play'd
> Some tricks of desperation.   (I, 2)

On the island, which Shakespearian scholars took to be Arcadia, the history of the world has once more been performed and repeated.

III

Who is Prospero and what does his staff signify? Why does he combine knowledge with magic, and what is the ultimate sense of his confrontation with Caliban? For there is no doubt that Prospero and Caliban are the protagonists of *The Tempest*. Why does Prospero reject the magic wand and throw his books into the sea? Why does he return defenceless among men?

In none of the other Shakespearian masterpieces – except *Hamlet* – has the divergence between the greatness of the human

mind on the one hand, and the ruthlessness of history and the
frailty of the moral order on the other, been shown with equal
passion as in *The Tempest*. It was an antinomy deeply and
tragically experienced by the people of the Renaissance. Nine
immutable heavenly spheres, which according to medieval cosmogony floated concentrically above the earth, guaranteed
moral order. The heavenly hierarchy was paralleled by the
social hierarchy. And now the nine heavens had ceased to exist.
The earth had become just a little heap of dust in the starry
space, but at the same time the universe came nearer. The
heavenly bodies were moving according to laws discovered by
the human mind. The earth had become both very small and
very great. The natural order had been desanctified. History
had become just the history of man. One could dream that it
would change. But it did not change. Never before had people
felt so painfully the divergence between dreams and reality;
between human potentialities and the misery of man's lot.
Everything could change, and nothing did change. These are
the contradictions that Hamlet could not solve and which so
tormented him:

> What a piece of work is a man! how noble in reason! how infinite
> in faculty! in form and moving how express and admirable! in
> action how like an angel! in apprehension how like a god! the
> beauty ol the world! the paragon of animals! And yet, to me, what
> is this quintessence of dust? man delights not me; no, nor woman
> neither.　　　　　　　　　　　　　　　　　　　　(*Hamlet*, II, 2)

Hamlet had read Montaigne. In Montaigne the same contradictions are described with an even greater vehemence:

> Let us now but consider man alone without other help, armed but
> with his owne weapons [. . .] Let him with the utmost power of
> his discourse make me understand, upon what foundation, he
> hath built those great advantages and odds, he supposeth to have
> over other creatures. Who hath perswaded him, that this admirable
> moving of heavens vaults; that the horror-moving and continual
> motion of this infinite waste Ocean, were established, and con-
> tinue so many ages for his commoditie and service? Is it possible
> to imagine any thing so ridiculous, as this miserable and wretched

creature, which is not so much as master of himselfe, exposed and subject to offences of all things, and yet dareth call himselfe Master and Emperour of this universe? In whose power it is not to know the last part of it, much lesse to command the same.

And further on:

Of all creatures man is the most miserable and fraile, and there-withall the proudest and disdainfullest. Who perceiveth and seeth himselfe placed here, amidst their filth and mire of the world, fast tied and nailed to the worst, most senselesse, and drooping part of the world, in the vilest corner of the house, and farthest from heavens coape, with those creatures, that are the worst of the three conditions; and yet dareth imaginarily place himselfe above the circle of the Moone, and reduce heaven under his feet.

(*Essayes*, II, 2, trans. by John Florio)

A similar consciousness of the misery and greatness of man characterizes Prospero; only he is more tinged with bitterness. He is usually represented on the stage in a great black coat, studded with stars. In his hand he holds the magic wand. This costume immobilizes the actor, turns him into a Father Christmas, or a conjurer; it makes him pathetic and asks him to cele-brate his part. Prospero becomes solemn instead of being tragic and human. Prospero is the producer of the morality; but the morality has exposed the reasons of his failure; it repeats history, without being able to alter it. It is essential that Pros-pero's magic mantle be thrown off his shoulders, together with bad theatrical tradition.

Whenever I think of Prospero, I always see Leonardo da Vinci's head, drawn in his last self-portrait. His forehead is high and broad. Thin white hair comes down like remnants of a lion's mane and joins a long, God-the-Father-like beard. The beard comes up to his mouth. His mouth is tight, wry, with drooping corners. There is wisdom and bitterness in this face; there is no peace, and no surrender. This is the man, who on the margin of a large sheet filled with observations on the movement of bodies, wrote in the same clear, but even smaller, characters: 'Oh, Leonardo, wherefore toilest thou thus?'

Many critics writing on Prospero have recalled the figure of Leonardo; some writing on Leonardo have recalled *The Tempest*. Had Shakespeare heard of Leonardo? We do not know. He may have – from Ben Jonson, who was a highly erudite man, or from the Earl of Southampton, or from Essex and his noble friends. He may have come across the legend of Leonardo, who in the eyes of his contemporaries, and for a long time afterwards, was regarded as a man more advanced than anybody else in the knowledge of magic. White magic, of course, the natural magic, called empirical even then, as opposed to black or demoniac magic. Such magic was practised by Paracelsus, who regarded the air as a kind of spirit that escapes from fluids at boiling point. Air, 'an airy spirit', as Shakespeare called Ariel in his list of characters. White, natural magic was described by Pico della Mirandola, who took the view that a scientist 'unites heaven and earth and makes the lower world join the powers of the higher world'.

Not by chance, perhaps, Shakespeare gave Prospero the dukedom of Milan, where Leonardo had spent many years in the service of Lodovico Il Moro, and which he left in 1499 after the fall of the most mighty duke, going into exile which ended only with his death. All these are fantasies a historian of literature may amuse himself with in his leisure. Only one thing is important: that Shakespeare created in *The Tempest* a character that can be compared to Leonardo; and that through Leonardo's tragedy we shall understand better the tragedy of Prospero.

Leonardo was a master of mechanics and hydraulics. He devised plans of new spacious cities and a modern network of canals; he drew and projected new machines to be used in a siege, mortars with unprecedented explosive power, cannons with eleven barrels which could fire simultaneously, tank-like armoured vehicles, mechanically driven by means of a system of cog-wheels and levers. In his *Codice Atlantico* there are exact technical drawings of new rolling mills, movable canal excavators and quick-turning looms. There are observations on bird flight, on the way fish steer themselves, and numerous calculations of the size and weight of wings which could put man up in the air. There are plans and drawings of flying machines, as well as of a driver's apparel, complete with air cistern and breathing pipe, and even of submarines.

None of Leonardo's machines has ever been made. His tragedy was that the technical means available did not keep pace with his thought. The materials he had at his disposal were too heavy, and metalwork too primitive, for any of his machines to be able to move without an engine. Leonardo was painfully aware of the resistance of matter and the imperfection of instruments. But he could already perceive the emergence of a world in which man would wrench from nature her secrets and overcome her by his art and science:

> Do you not see then that the eye encompasses the beauty of the whole world? It is the master of ceremonies; it creates cosmography; it counsels and corrects all the arts of mankind; it takes man to various parts of the world; it is the prince of mathematics; the sciences based on it are the most accurate; it has measured the distances and sizes of stars; it has discovered the elements and their location; it has made possible forecasting future events from the courses of stars; it has given birth to architecture and to perspective, and to the divine art of painting . . .
>
> But why all these lofty and lengthy deliberations? What is there that has not been done thanks to the eye? It guides man from East to West; it has invented navigation. It surpasses nature in so far as simple creations of nature are finite, and the works commanded by the eye to the hands are infinite as can be witnessed by the painter when inventing innumerable shapes of animals and plants, trees and landscapes.

Prospero's great soliloquy in Act V of *The Tempest*, interpreted by the romantics as Shakespeare's farewell to the theatre and a confession of faith in the demiurgic power of poetry, is in fact closest to Leonardo's enthusiasm for power of the human mind, which has wrenched from nature her elemental forces. This soliloquy is a remote travesty of the famous passage in Ovid's *Metamorphoses*. The world is seen in movement and transformation; four elements are released: earth, water, fire and air. They do not obey the gods any more, but have been dominated by man who for the first time overthrows the natural order. Every age interprets this soliloquy through its own experience. To us it is an atomic soliloquy, and there is in it awe rather than enthusiasm. We interpret it much less symbolically and poetically, but more in a concrete and literal sense. To six generations of Shakespeare students – from Hazlitt to J. Dover Wilson – the durability of the world did not raise the smallest doubt. Perhaps that is why they saw in *The Tempest* an arcadian play. We hear in this soliquy an apocalyptic tone. It is not, however, the poetic Apocalypse of the romantics, but the Apocalypse of nuclear explosions and the atomic mushroom. Such a reading of Prospero's soliloquy, and the play, is certainly closer to the experience of men of the Renaissance and the violent contradictions they tried to reconcile. 'Leonardo's insatiable desire for knowledge'. Thus Leonardo entitled the following passage in his *Note-books*:

> Nor does the tempestuous sea make so loud a roaring when the northern blast beats it back in foaming waves between Scylla and Charybdis, nor Stromboli nor Mount Etna when the pent-up, sulphurous fires, bursting open and rending asunder the mighty mountain by their force, are hurling through the air rocks and earth mingled together in the issuing belching flames.
> Nor when Etna's burning caverns vomit forth and give out again the uncontrollable element, and thrust it back to its own region in fury, driving before it whatever obstacle withstands its impetuous rage ...
> And drawn on by my eager desire anxious to behold the might of the varied and strange forms created by the artificer nature, having wandered for some distance among the overhanging rocks, I came to the mouth of a huge cavern before which for a time I remained stupefied, not having been aware of its existence – my back bent to an arch, my left hand clutching my knee, while with the right I made a shade for my lowered and contracted eyebrows; bending continually first one way and then another in order to see whether I could discern anything inside, though this was rendered impossible by the intense darkness within; and after remaining there for a time, suddenly there were awakened within me two emotions – fear and desire – fear of the dark, threatening

cavern, desire to see whether there might be any marvellous thing therein.[1]

The world became great and small at the same time; for the first time the earth began to quake under their feet:

> Ye elves of hills, brooks, standing lakes, and groves;
> And ye that on the sands with printless foot
> Do chase the ebbing Neptune, and do fly him
> When he comes back; you demi-puppets that
> By moonshine do the green sour ringlets make,
> Whereof the ewe not bites; and you whose pastime
> Is to make midnight mushrumps, that rejoice
> To hear the solemn curfew; by whose aid –
> Weak masters though ye be – I have bedimm'd
> The noontide sun, call'd forth the mutinous winds,
> And 'twixt the green sea and the azur'd vault
> Set roaring war: to the dread-rattling thunder
> Have I given fire, and rifted Jove's stout oak
> With his own bolt: the strong-bas'd promontory
> Have I made shake; and by the spurs pluck'd up
> The pine and cedar: graves at my command
> Have wak'd their sleepers, oped, and let 'em forth
> By my so potent art.   (V, 1)

In the works of almost all the thinkers, poets, and philosophers of the Renaissance we find these sudden transitions from outbreaks of enthusiasm for conquering human thought to catastrophic visions of extermination. We find them in Michelangelo, and even more often in Leonardo, who is almost obsessed with the theme of universal destruction. His writings abound in detailed and violent descriptions of fires which consume whole cities, a new flood which will exterminate mankind, or a plague which will decimate it. Nature 'sends poisoned and pestilential air on to large centres of living beings, particularly men, who breed the most since other animals cannot devour them'. Even stylistically, it is a most Shakespearian phrase. Sometimes the analogies are really astonishing. In one of his unfinished letters Leonardo writes: 'The mouth kills more people than a dagger.'

[1] Leonardo da Vinci's *Note-Books*, arr. and trans. by E. McCurdy, Empire State Book Co., New York, 1935, p. 135.

('La bocca n'ha morti piú che 'l coltello.') Says Hamlet after the great scene with the players:

'I will speak daggers to her, but not use them.'

In Leonardo, as in Shakespeare, we often find the same kind of cruel and most modern reflections on human history, which, compared to earth's history is just a fleeting moment. Man is an animal like all other animals, only perhaps more cruel; but unlike all the other animals he is aware of his fate and wants to alter it. He is born and dies in an extra-human time, and he can never reconcile himself to that. Prospero's staff makes the history of the world repeat itself on a desert island. Actors can play that history in four hours. But Prospero's staff cannot change history. When the morality is over, Prospero's magic power must also end. Only bitter wisdom remains.

Another passage in Leonardo's writings seems to me to have a close bearing on *The Tempest*. Leonardo is writing about a stone which has rolled down from the mountain top. People tread over it, animals' hooves trample on it, cart-wheels ride over it. He ends: 'This is the fate of those who abandon life in solitude, life devoted to reflexion and contemplation, in order to live in cities among people full of sin.'

There is in this fragment the sad bitterness of Prospero's parting with the island:

> And thence retire me to my Milan, where
> Every third thought shall be my grave.   (V, 1)

This Leonardian divorce between thought and practice, between the realm of freedom, justice and reason on the one hand, and natural order and history on the other, was even more keenly experienced by the last Renaissance generation; the generation to which Shakespeare belonged. People at that time were conscious of a great era nearing its end. The present was repulsive, the future was assuming an even gloomier shape.

The great dreams of the humanists about a happy era had not been fulfilled; they turned out to be just a dream. Only the bitter consciousness of lost illusions remained. The new power of money made the old feudal power seem more cruel still. War, hunger, pestilence, terror of the princes and terror of the Church – this was the reality. Elizabeth ruled ruthlessly in England. Italy was turned over to the Spaniards. Giordano Bruno was handed to the Inquisition and burnt at Campo di Fiore.

At the turn of the sixteenth century it might have seemed that the Copernican system had finally prevailed. It was for the first time empirically confirmed thanks to the invention of the telescope and to the discovery of the satellites of Jupiter by Galileo. His treatise, *The Starry Harbinger*, published in 1610 – almost the year of *The Tempest* – meant a new triumph for science. The triumph was apparent rather than real. *Sidereus nuntius* tolled the knell of the great era. True, it fired the imagination of Campanella, but it was proclaimed heresy. The gloomy, dogmatic Aristotelians were winning again. In 1618 the Holy Office officially condemned the Copernican theory and so-called 'Pythagorean' views as contrary to the Bible. In 1633 Galileo's trial took place and he publicly recanted his heretical views:

> . . . I maintained and believed that the Sun is the centre of the world, and immovable, and that the Earth is not the centre, and moves. Therefore . . . I swear that I will never any more hereafter say or assert by speech or writing anything through which the like suspicion may be had of me; but if I shall know anyone heretical, or suspected of heresy, I will denounce him to this Holy Office, or to the Inquisitor, and Ordinary of the place in which I shall be.

Five years later the harassed old man wrote from his internment at home to one of his old comrades:

> Galileo, your dear friend and servant, has for a month now been altogether blind. This is irrevocable. Just think then, Your Grace, how sad I must be when I realize that the heavens, the sky and the universe, which by most strange observations and clear arguments I magnified a hundred, yea, a thousand times in comparison with what all scholars of former ages had seen, now are to me so small and narrow that they do not reach beyond the space occupied by my own person.

Prospero's staff did not change the course of history. It changed
nothing at all. The world remained as cruel as it had been, 'and
our little life is rounded with a sleep'. In Prospero's final
soliloquy I find the greatness, despair and bitterness of Galileo's
letter:

> now I want
> Spirits to enforce, art to enchant;
> And my ending is despair . . .   (V, 1)

Prospero is not Leonardo; still less is he Galileo. I am not concerned with analogies, suggestive though they might be. My
intention is to interpret *The Tempest* as a great Renaissance
tragedy of lost illusions.

Jean Paris, one of the most interesting among present-day
interpreters of *Hamlet*, has called it a drama on the 'end of
the era of terror'.[1] Old Hamlet had killed old Fortinbras;
Claudius had killed old Hamlet; young Hamlet ought to kill
Claudius; young Fortinbras ought to kill Hamlet. The path to
the throne leads through murder, and this chain is not to be
broken. But young Fortinbras does not kill Hamlet. When he
appears at Elsinore in his silver armour, steadfast and heroic,
the scene is empty. He will ascend the throne of Denmark
legally and without bloodshed. The 'end of the era of terror'
has been accomplished. The silvery Fortinbras has triumphed.
But will Denmark cease to be a prison? Hamlet's body has been
carried out by soldiers. No one will question the sense of feudal
history and the purpose of human life any more. Fortinbras
does not ask himself such questions. He does not even suspect
that such questions can be asked. History has been saved but at
what price?

Elizabethan writers on tragedy contemporary with Shakespeare saw in it an image of human life. According to them
tragedy could freely combine historical truth with fiction for a
didactic purpose. It was to warn the audience against giving
way to passion, and to show the consequences of transgression.
Puttenham formulated its aims thus:

[1] J. Paris, *Hamlet ou les personnages du fils,* Paris, 1957.

... when the posteritie stood no more in dread of them, their in-
famous life and tyrannies were layd open to all the world, their
wickedness reproached, their follies and extreme insolencies
derided, and their miserable ends pointed out in playes and
pageants, to shew the mutabilitie of fortune, and the iust punishment of God in revenge of a vicious and euill life.[1]

According to Sir Philip Sidney, the author of *Arcadia*, 'the poet
is indeed the right popular philosopher'. But Shakespeare was
no such popular philosopher, or – if he was – then only in the
same sense as Montaigne.

Shakespeare is far removed from the vulgar didacticism of
Puttenham or Sidney. A prince is to him always 'The Prince' of
Machiavelli who lives in the world where big fish devour small
fry. He devours, or is devoured. Shakespeare does not distinguish between a good king and a tyrant, just as he does not distinguish between a king and a clown. They are both mortals.
Terror and the struggle for power is not a privilege of princes;
it is a law of this world.

Shakespeare's view of history, pessimistic and cruel, is already
very near to the materialistic philosophy of Hobbes, as expressed in his *Leviathan*. Hobbes wrote during the Restoration.
To him kings had ceased to be God's anointed. They became
instead, History's anointed. Their absolute power and their
right to be ruthless was a result of the 'war of all against all'.
They were guarantors of social order against ever-threatening
anarchy.

Shakespeare viewed feudal history in the same way as
Hobbes, but he rebelled against its immutability. He was search-
ing for a solution to this tragic alternative of terror and
anarchy. He never crowned his Richards, Henrys or Macbeths
with the crown of 'historic inevitability'. He made kings equal
with commoners and showed that a horse can be worth more
than a kingdom.

On the desert island the history of the world has been performed. The performance is over; history begins once more.
Alonso will return to Naples, Prospero to Milan, Caliban will

[1] *The Art of English Poesie*, ch. XV, London, 1589.

become again the island's ruler. Prospero rejects his staff and will again be defenceless. If he had retained his staff, *The Tempest* would be no more than just a fairy tale. History is madness, but music heals human souls from madness. Only bitter wisdom can be opposed to history. One cannot escape history. Everyone has been through the tempest, and everyone is wiser. Even Caliban. He above all. One has to start again from the beginning; from the very beginning. Prospero agrees to return to Milan. In this alone lies the difficult and precarious optimism of *The Tempest*.

IV

Ariel is an angel and an executioner who acts on Prospero's orders. He has only two personal scenes: When he revolts in Act One, and when he asks Prospero to have pity on his enemies in Act Four. His dramatic conflict consists simply in his desire for freedom. Ariel has been regarded by various commentators as a symbol of the soul, thought, intelligence, poetry, air, electricity, and even – in Catholic interpretations – of Grace opposed to Nature. But on the stage Ariel is just an actor, or an actress, wearing costume or tights, sometimes a mask. Ariel dressed in period costume becomes part of a dated show, at best Prospero's page. Ariel in abstract costume can easily resemble a laboratory assistant working at an atomic reactor. Ariel in tights turns into a ballet dancer. Ariel in a mask, worn from the first act onwards, will not be part of the Shakespearian theatre. And then what sort of mask could Ariel have? Actors playing spirits must be human. Whenever I think of Ariel, I visualize him as a slim boy with a very sad face. His costume ought to be quite ordinary and inconspicuous. He can be dressed in dark trousers and white shirt, with a pullover. Ariel moves faster than thought. Let him appear and disappear from the stage imperceptibly. But he must not dance or run. He should move very slowly. He should stand still as often as possible. Only then can he become faster than thought.

Commentators on *The Tempest* concern themselves largely

with opposing Ariel to Caliban. To my mind this approach is philosophically flat and theatrically vacuous. In terms of dramatic action Ariel is not Caliban's opposite number. He is visible only to Prospero and the audience. To all the other characters he is just music or a voice.

Caliban is the main character next to Prospero. He is one of the greatest and most disturbing of Shakespearian creations. He is unlike anybody or anything. He has a full individuality. He lives in the play, but also outside it, like Hamlet, Falstaff and Iago. Unlike Ariel, he cannot be defined by one metaphor, or contained in one allegory. In the list of the *dramatis personae* he is described as 'a savage and deformed slave'. Prospero calls him 'devil', 'earth', 'tortoise', 'a freckled whelp', 'poisonous slave', and most frequently – monster. Trinculo calls him 'fish'. Caliban has legs like a man, but his arms are like fins. He chews something in his mouth all the time, snarls, walks on all fours. Dürer has painted a pig with two heads, a bearded child, a rhinoceros looking like a monstrous elephant. Leonardo, in his *Treatise on Painting*, gives the following recipe for a dragon: 'take the head of a mastiff, the eyes of a cat, the ears of a porcupine, the mouth of a hare, the brows of a lion, the temples of an old cock, and the neck of a tortoise'. Scholars have found engravings dating from the beginning of the seventeenth century representing Caliban-like monsters; they have concluded that Shakespeare's description most resembles a certain mammal of the whale family living mainly in the Malay area. So, Caliban would be a kind of huge cachalot.

But on the stage Caliban, like Ariel, is just an actor wearing costume. He can be represented like a fish, like an animal, or like a human. There has to be in him a kind of animal bestiality, and a reptile quality, otherwise the grotesque scenes with Stephano and Trinculo could not come off. But I would like to see him as human as possible. A metaphor of monstrosity expressed in words is something different from the concrete quality of gesture, mask and actor's make-up. Caliban is a man, not a monster. Caliban – as Allardyce Nicoll has rightly pointed out – speaks in verse. In Shakespeare's world prose is spoken only by grotesque and episodic characters; by those who are not part of the drama proper.

Caliban had been lord of the isle; after Prospero's departure he will again remain alone on it. Of all the characters in *The Tempest*, he is the most truly tragic. Perhaps he is the only one to change. All the other characters are drawn from the outside, as it were, shown in a few basic attitudes. This applies even to Prospero. Prospero's drama is purely intellectual. Ariel's drama, too, remains in the sphere of abstract concepts. Only to Caliban has Shakespeare given passion and a full life history.

Caliban had learned to speak. For let us remember that the island represents the history of the world. Caliban had been taught to speak by Miranda. She reproaches him when she reminds him of it. Language distinguishes men from animals. Caliban is a symbol of Montaigne's good cannibals, but he is not a noble savage. This is not the island of Utopia; here the history of the world will be stripped of all illusions. The use of language can become a curse and only aggravate slavery. Language is then limited to curses This is one of the most bitter scenes in the whole play:

> *Miranda.*[1] I pitied thee,
>   Took pains to make thee speak . . .
>   . . . when thou didst not, savage,
>   Know thine own meaning, but wouldst gabble like
>   A thing most brutish, I endow'd thy purposes
>   With words that made them known . . .
>
> *Caliban.* You taught me language; and my profit on't
>   Is, I know how to curse. The red plague rid you
>   For learning me your language!   (I, 2)

To Miranda Caliban is a man. When she sees Ferdinand for the first time, she will say: 'This is the third man that e'er I saw.' In the Shakespearian system of analogies and sudden confrontations Caliban is made Prospero's and Ferdinand's equal, and Shakespeare stresses this point very clearly. A little later the

[1] In the Cambridge edition, as well as in the 1623 Folio, these lines are spoken by Miranda and not by Prospero, as in other editions.

same theme is taken up again by Prospero. He speaks to Miranda, referring to Ferdinand:

> . . . foolish wench!
> To the most of men this is a Caliban,
> And they to him are angels. (I, 2)

Caliban is an unshapely monster, Ferdinand the handsomest of princes. But to Shakespeare beauty and ugliness is just a matter of what people look like to *other* people, in a place and part they have been asked to play.

The action develops on the island exactly as Prospero has planned it. The shipwrecked men have been scattered and brought to the point of madness. Fratricide, intercepted by Ariel at the last moment, has been meant as a warning and a trial. But the scenario devised by Prospero is spoilt by Caliban. Prospero has not foreseen his treason and the conspiracy plotted by Caliban together with Trinculo and Stephano. Caliban's treachery is a surprise to Prospero, and the only defeat he has suffered on the island. But it is the second defeat in Prospero's life. He had lost his dukedom as a result of his devotion to science and the arts; of the trust he had in his brother; in other words – because he had believed in the world's goodness. Caliban's treachery is a new failure as far as Prospero's educational methods are concerned. Again his staff has not proved all-powerful. Prospero wanted to perform on the island the history of the world to serve as warning to the shipwrecked, and to the audience. But the world's history turned out to be even more cruel than he had intended. It brought another bitter surprise, just at the moment when Prospero was solemnizing the betrothal of Ferdinand and Miranda, and evoking before their eyes a vision of the lost paradise.

> A devil . . .
> . . . on whom my pains,
> Humanely taken, all, all lost, quite lost;
> And as with age his body uglier grows,
> So his mind cankers. I will plague them all,
> Even to roaring. (IV, 1)

This is one of the crucial sentences in *The Tempest*, and perhaps the most difficult to interpret. It is the climax of Prospero's tragedy. Only after this scene will he break and reject his magic wand. The very words used by Prospero are also most interesting in themselves:

> . . . on whom my pains,
> Humanely taken, all, all lost, quite lost . . .

When Molière's Don Juan meets a beggar, he begins to sneer at heavenly justice. Then he offers him alms in return for a curse. But the beggar refuses. Don Juan eventually throws him a piece of gold saying: 'I give it to you for the love of humanity' ('Je te le donne pour l'amour de l'humanité'). No other phrase written by Molière has been the subject of so many interpretations. Some commentators see in this sentence – unfamiliar in seventeenth-century French – only an equivalent to the standard 'out of the goodness of my heart'. Others see in it a rationalist inversion, or even parody, of the traditional form 'pour l'amour de Dieu'. To others still, the word 'humanité' in Don Juan's mouth is used already in the full sense of the eighteenth-century's 'Humanity', and Don Juan is a precursor of enlightened humanitarianism.

Shakespeare's words 'humanely taken' are equally ambiguous. They can be understood in a very narrow sense and mean not much more than 'undertaken out of the goodness of my heart'. But we can also read in them the full sense of Renaissance 'humanitas'. To me, these two phrases: Molière's 'pour l'amour de l'humanité' and Shakespeare's 'humanely taken' show the same mark of genius.

If on Prospero's island the history of the world has been performed, then Caliban's history is a chapter from the history of mankind. With such a reading of *The Tempest*, three scenes acquire a special significance. The first of these occurs at the end of Act Two. Stephano has already made Caliban drunk. The plot has been laid down. The 'brave monster' will lead his new masters. It is then that Caliban sings for the first time. This drinking song ends with an unexpected refrain:

'Freedom, high-day! high-day, freedom! freedom, high-day, freedom!'

In the first scene of the play it was Ariel who asked for freedom. Shakespeare now repeats the same situation with a cruel irony. And not just once; twice. In Act Three, a drunkard, a clown and a poor monster are ready for the coup. They are on their way to assassinate Prospero. Caliban asks for a song. This time Stephano sings it:

> Flout 'em and scout 'em, and scout 'em and flout 'em;
> Thought is free.   (III, 2)

'Thought is free' – sings the drunkard. 'Thought is free' – repeats the fool. Only Caliban notices that the tune has suddenly changed. At this point Ariel appears with 'a tabor and pipe', and mixes up the tune. 'That's not the tune' – cries Caliban. Caliban has heard Ariel.

This in essence is the Shakespearian tragi-grotesque, which by its barbarity terrified the classicists, and which the romantics hailed as the principle of a new drama. But they were unable to repeat the Shakespearian tune. Instead of tragi-grotesque they wrote melodrama, like those of Victor Hugo. Grotesque and tragedy are mixed and intermingled in Shakespeare, like Stephano's and Trinculo's drunken song suddenly changing into Ariel's music.

Stephano and Trinculo are only grotesque characters, but Caliban is both grotesque and tragic. He is a ruler, a monster and a man. He is grotesque in his blind, dark and naïve revolt, in his desire for freedom, which to him still means just a quiet sleep and food. He is tragic, as he cannot be satisfied with his state, he does not want and cannot accept his fate – that of a fool and a slave. Renan saw Demos in Caliban; in his continuation of *The Tempest* he took him to Milan and made him attempt another, victorious coup against Prospero. Guéhenno wrote an apology for Caliban – People. Both these interpretations are flat and do not do justice to Shakespeare's Caliban.

In *The Tempest* there is Ariel's music and Caliban's music. There can be no performance of this play without a careful differentiation between them. But in *The Tempest* there is a moment when Caliban's music becomes close to Ariel's. That moment marks also a magnificent eruption of Shakespeare's poetry. Trinculo and Stephano are afraid of Ariel's music. Caliban hears it:

> Be not afeard; the isle is full of noises,
> Sounds, and sweet airs, that give delight, and hurt not.
> Sometimes a thousand twangling instruments
> Will hum about mine ears; and sometimes voices
> That, if I then had wak'd after long sleep,
> Will make me sleep again: and then, in dreaming,
> The clouds methought would open, and show riches
> Ready to drop upon me; that, when I wak'd
> I cried to dream again. (III, 2)

To me this passage is a Shakespearian book of Genesis. The history of mankind begins. The same that has been performed on the island. Caliban has been deceived again. He has been defeated, just as Prospero has been defeated. Caliban has no magic wand, and no wizard's staff will help him. He has mistaken a drunkard for God. But he has entered the path trodden by Prospero. He has undergone a trial and has lost his illusions. He has to make a fresh start once more. Just as Prospero has to make a fresh start when he returns to Milan to become duke once more. 'I'll be wise hereafter,' says Caliban at the end. And, when Prospero is gone, he will slowly, on all fours, climb up to the highest empty space at the top of Bosch's island, as Shakespeare presented it.

Only two characters are exempt from the law of repetition implicit in the play's construction. They are: Miranda and Ferdinand. They do not take part in the history of the world played on the island; or rather they participate in it in a different sense. Only for them everything really begins for the first time. In the course of four hours they will have discovered love, and each other. They are dazzled with each other. They represent the world's youth. But they do not see the world. From first to last they see only each other. They have not even noticed the struggle for power, the rebellion and plotting that have been going on around them. They are enchanted with each other.

Three scenes are decisive, as far as Miranda and Ferdinand are concerned. The first of these is the solemn betrothal, when Prospero, aided by Ariel, stages a show for their benefit. It is a typical Elizabethan masque. It may not have been wholly written by Shakespeare, or written only later, for a gala court performance of *The Tempest* on the occasion of marriage of James I's daughter to the Elector Palatine. The mask is allegorical; Greek deities appear in it and speak a pompous and stilted verse. But in spite of its artificiality the show is significant in so far as it revokes the golden age of humanity, when the earth had been free from sin and had borne its fruit without pain.

> Her peacocks fly amain.

On the island where the real history of the world has been performed, Prospero shows the young lovers the lost paradise.

> So rare a wonder'd father, and a wife,
> Makes this place Paradise.   (IV, 1)

And it is this very scene that is suddenly broken and ends on a jarring note. Real history breaks the idyll. Prospero learns of Caliban's treachery and for the first time gives way to anger. The allegorical mask disperses in confusion. Now follows the passage containing the best known sentence in *The Tempest*:

> We are such stuff
> As dreams are made on; and our little life
> Is rounded with a sleep.   (IV, 1)

The philosophical and poetic concept of 'life is a dream' is very common in the poetry of the Baroque; but the point of this Shakespearian phrase seems to me remote from Calderon's mysticism. There is in it rather the great anxiety of Hamlet's soliloquies, and one more warning to the young lovers on the frailty of all human endeavour. But, as is usual with Shakespeare, every metaphor and each image has a double meaning. The island is the world, the world is a stage, and all the people

in it are actors. Prospero has only staged a performance, brief
and fleeting like life itself.

> These our actors,
>> Are melted into air, into thin air:
>> And, like the baseless fabric of this vision,
>> The cloud-capp'd towers, the gorgeous palaces,
>> The solemn temples, the great globe itself,
>> Yea, all which it inherit, shall dissolve,
>> And, like this insubstantial pageant faded,
>> Leave not a rack behind.   (IV, 1)

At the end of the play, Prospero shows to the King of Naples
his son playing chess with Miranda. In Shakespeare's theatre
this scene was probably performed on the inner stage. Its walls
formed a natural frame, and the young couple looked like a
familiar Renaissance picture showing a lad and a girl playing
chess. What is the stake in this game?

> *Miranda.* Sweet lord, you play me false.
> *Ferdinand.* No, my dearest love,
>> I would not for the world.
> *Miranda.* Yes, for a score of kingdoms you should wrangle,
>> And I would call it fair play.   (V, 1)

Murder has nearly been committed twice within four hours in
order to gain one kingdom, and that on a desert island. Yet
Miranda and Ferdinand have not noticed anything. Everything
has happened beyond them. They play chess for a score of
kingdoms, they could just as well play for a hundred. To either
of them the kingdom does not exist. Ferdinand and Miranda
are outside history, outside the struggle for power and the
crown.

At last Miranda enters the stage proper. For the first time in
her life she sees so many people: the King, the King's brother
and the whole retinue. She exclaims in astonishment:

> O, wonder!
> How many goodly creatures are there here!
> How beauteous mankind is! O brave new world,
> That has such people in't!

This is the last of the great confrontations of *The Tempest*. Miranda is facing a gang of villains. One of them twelve years ago deprived her father of his throne. Another broke his word as an ally. Yet another had raised his sword against his brother, only a little while ago. Prospero has only a very brief reply to make. But how much bitter wisdom is there in this reply. Four words is all that Shakespeare needs here:

> 'Tis new to thee.   (V, 1)

V

In all his works Conrad mentions Shakespeare only twice. Once, when travestying Macbeth – he calls an unnamed Shakespearian drama a tale, like life, full of noise and winds meaning nothing. Macbeth says in one of his last scenes that life 'is a tale told by an idiot, full of sound and fury, signifying nothing'. In *Lord Jim* the narrator finds among Jim's possessions in Patusan a cheap one-volume edition of Shakespeare, and asks him if he has read it. 'Yes. Best thing to cheer up a fellow', replies Jim. Marlow adds: 'I was struck by this appreciation, but there was no time for Shakespearian talk.'

But among Conrad's most personal writings I find a passage which, to my mind, is very close to the 'bitter' interpretation of *The Tempest*, and to Prospero's mature wisdom. Conrad writes:

> The ethical view of the universe involves us at least in so many cruel and absurd contradictions, where the last vestiges of faith, hope and charity, and even of reason itself, seem ready to perish, that I have come to suspect that the aim of creation cannot be ethical at all. I would fondly believe that its object is purely spectacular: a spectacle for awe, love, adoration, or hate, if you like, but in this view – and this view alone – never for despair! Those visions, delicious or poignant, are a moral end in themselves. The rest is our affair. –   (J. Conrad, *A Personal Record*, ch. V)

In Prospero's final monologue we find the word 'despair'. –

K

'And my ending is despair.' But it is a despair which does not mean resignation. The key to the deepest understanding of *The Tempest* is found in another of Shakespeare's tragedies. It has the moving personal accents of Prospero's epilogue:

> My desolation does begin to make
> A better life.   (*Anthony and Cleopatra*, V, 2)

APPENDICES

APPENDICES

Shakespeare – Cruel and True[1]

If *Titus Andronicus* had six acts, Shakespeare would get at spectators sitting in the first row of the stalls and let them die in agony, because on the stage no one, except Lucius, remains alive. Even before the curtain rose on the first act, twenty-two sons of Titus had died already. And so it goes on all the time, until the general slaughter at the end of Act Five. Thirty-five people die in this play not counting soldiers, servants and characters of no importance. At least ten major murders are committed in view of the audience. And most ingenious murders they are. Titus has an arm chopped off; Lavinia has her tongue and hands cut off; a nurse gets strangled. On top of that we have rape, cannibalism and torture. Compared with this Renaissance drama, the 'black' American literature of our day may seem a sweet idyll.

Titus is by no means the most brutal of Shakespeare's plays. More people die in *Richard III*; *King Lear* is much more cruel. In the whole Shakespearian repertory I can find no scene as revolting as Cordelia's death. *King Lear* and *Richard III* are both masterpieces. In reading, the cruelties of *Titus* seem childish. I have recently re-read it, and found it ridiculous. I have seen it on the stage, and found it a moving experience. Why? Is it only because Sir Laurence Olivier is a tragedian of genius, and Mr Brook a great producer? I think there is more to it than just that.

When a contemporary play seems to us in reading flat and childish, while in the theatre it thrills and overpowers us, we say that it makes good theatre. But to say of Shakespeare that he makes good theatre is rather funny. And there is little doubt that *Titus Andronicus* is a play by Shakespeare, or rather a play

[1] The Shakespeare Memorial Theatre Company in *Titus Andronicus*. Produced by Peter Brook. Performed in Warsaw – June, 1957.

adapted by him. But so is *Hamlet* for that matter. The difference is that in *Titus* Shakespeare was just beginning to shape the dramatic material found in his model. He had already been forming great characters, but was unable as yet to make them fully articulate. They stammer, or – like Lavinia – have their tongues cut out. *Titus Andronicus* is already Shakespearian theatre; but a truly Shakespearian text is yet to come.

Brook and Olivier have both declared that they had been encouraged to produce *Titus* on realizing that this play already contained – though still in a rough shape – the seed of all the great Shakespearian tragedies. No doubt Titus's sufferings foretell the hell through which Lear will walk. As for Lucius, had he – instead of going to the camp of the Goths – gone to the university at Wittenberg, he would surely have returned as a Hamlet. Tamora, the queen of the Goths, would be akin to Lady Macbeth, had she wished to look inside her own soul. She lacks the awareness of crime, just as Lavinia lacks the awareness of suffering similar to that which plunged Ophelia into her madness. Watching *Titus Andronicus*, we come to understand– perhaps more than by looking at any other Shakespeare play – the nature of his genius: he gave an inner awareness to passion; cruelty ceased to be merely physical. Shakespeare discovered the moral hell. He discovered heaven as well. But he remained on earth.

Peter Brook saw all this in *Titus Andronicus*. But he was not the first to discover the play. It is true that for two centuries it had been regarded as an uncouth and imperfect work; a Gothic work, as classicists called it. But it had pleased the Elizabethan audience, being one of the most frequently performed plays. Mr Brook did not discover *Titus*. He discovered Shakespeare in *Titus*. Or rather – in this play he discovered the Shakespearian theatre, the theatre that had moved and thrilled audiences, had terrified and dazzled them.

If we were to ask the question who in our time was the first to show the true Shakespeare convincingly, there would be only one answer: Sir Laurence Olivier. The living Shakespeare of our time has been presented, first and foremost, in film. Film has discovered the Renaissance Shakespeare. In the production brought to us by the Shakespeare Company it is the return to the true Shakespeare in the theatre through the experiences of film that amazes us most. Above all I have in mind Olivier's films: *Henry V* and *Richard III*.

In what settings and costumes should Shakespeare be performed? I have seen Shakespeare played on a huge staircase and with a background of cubist prisms; among rachitic crooked trees (so popular with Polish stage designers), and in a wood so true to life that you could see every leaf rustle; in the so-called fantastic settings with fish scales, floating gauze and armour hired from the Opera; in décor striking for its pomp, or for its pseudo-noble functionalism.

Some were better than others, but all of them were bad. Only the film has shown that one way to transmit Shakespeare's vision could be the great paintings of the Renaissance and the Baroque; or tapestries, as in *Richard III*. Of course, this had to be a point of departure, not an imitation. A starting point for gesture, visual composition, costume. In Shakespearian tragedies, Romans should not be dressed in artificially contrived, stylized costumes that do not belong to any period; on the other hand, their costumes must not be accurate museum copies. They must be Romans as seen and painted by the Renaissance.

This is the way chosen by Mr Brook. Like a true artist, he does not copy, or impose an artificial unity. He has freely taken a full range of yellows from Titian, dressed his priests in the irritating greens of Veronese. The Moor, in his black-blue-and-gold costume, is derived from Rubens. The scene in the camp of the Goths where Aaron is tortured and tormented in a cage made up of big ladders also looks like Rubens.

It does not matter whether the colours have really been derived from the Venetians; or whether the dramatic visual compositions of characters are more indebted to El Greco or to Rubens. What matters is that it is painting as seen through film experience. There is nothing of the *tableau vivant* and of the opera about it. The scenes are composed like film shots and follow each other like film sequences.

Once Shakespeare's plays began to be filmed, action became as important as speech. All Shakespeare's plays are great spectacles abounding in the clatter of arms, marching armies, duels, feasts and drunken revels, wrestling contests, clowning, winds and storms, physical love, cruelty and suffering. The Elizabethan theatre was – like the Chinese opera – a theatre for the eyes. Everything in it was really happening. The audience believed that they were watching a tempest, a sinking ship, a king with his retinue setting out for a hunt, a hero stabbed by hired assassins.

The beginnings of Elizabethan tragedy had been very similar to the beginnings of film. Everything that was at hand could be included in a tragedy. Everyday events, tales of crime, bits of history, legends, politics and philosophy. It was a news-reel, and an historical chronicle. Elizabethan tragedy did not follow any rules; it snapped up any subject. Just as films do now, it fed on and digested crime, history and observation of life. Everything was new, so everything could be adapted. The great Elizabethans often remind one of film producers looking above all for an attractive subject. It is enough to mention Marlowe, Ben Jonson, or Shakespeare.

When the theatre abandoned the Elizabethan conventions, it lost also the Shakespearian spectacular quality and full-bloodedness. It lacked technical means, or had too many of them. I have seen Shakespeare played on a revolving stage and against backcloths, with signs being lowered to show the place of action. In both instances, it was not true Shakespeare. The theatre has alternated between illusionism and convention. Illusionism has been flat, naturalistic or childish and operatic; convention has been abstract and formalistic, or obtrusive. Illusionism and convention alike have managed to deprive Shakespeare of awe and poetry.

Four men meet. One of them begins to abuse the other three. Swords are drawn. One of the four is murdered. The others disperse. Friends have become enemies. A civil war, or a rebellion has begun. All this lasted two minutes. The fate of a kingdom has been decided in a dozen exchanges.

Youth throws girl a flower. She picks it up. Their eyes meet. She happens to be the daughter of his enemy. Three speeches – on the sun, the stars, and young tigers. She is passionately in love. At this instant the fate of two families has been decided.

Try to play both these scenes naturalistically, or conventionally. You will butcher Shakespeare. Shakespeare is truer than life. And one can play him only literally. Olivier's films have achieved this literal meaning and super-truth more than any theatre has. They have created a new Shakespearian language where no word is meaningless.

An actor brought up on the nineteenth century theatre cannot fall in love in thirty seconds; or come to hate in the course of two short speeches; or cause the fall of a kingdom in ten. A film actor passes directly from a great love scene to madness. He has killed a man, put his sword into the scabbard, and orders his servant to bring him a cup of wine. He has hardly drunk it when the news comes that his son has been killed. He will suffer, but for not more than thirty seconds. How has this come about? The 'empty spaces' have been edited out. A great film – like a Shakespearian play – is composed only of meaningful scenes.

The fact that the action of Shakespeare's plays is so condensed requires a particular kind of acting. The text is intense, metaphorical. Like a film director, Shakespeare makes frequent use of close-ups. Soliloquies are spoken directly 'to the camera', i.e. on the apron stage, directly to the audience. The Shakespearian soliloquy is like a close-up. A stage actor of the old school stands helpless in such moments. In vain does he try to give the soliloquy some probability. He continues to be conscious of the whole stage around him, while in fact he is meant to be alone with the audience.

Shakespeare's plays have been divided in the theatre into a number of scenes according to the places of action. After the theatre had abandoned the Elizabethan convention, it tried in vain to put the scenes together to form some sort of entity. A scenario is not divided into scenes, but into shots and sequences. Shakespeare's plays are also composed of shots and sequences.

Shakespearian scholars and some modern producers have known this for a long time. But only Olivier's films have demonstrated the fluency, homogeneity and rapidity of action in Shakespeare's plays.

Mr Brook has composed his *Titus Andronicus* not of scenes but of shots and sequences. In his production tension is evenly distributed; there are no 'empty places'. He has cut the text but developed the action. He has created sequences of great dramatic images. He has found again in Shakespeare the long-lost thrilling spectacle.

The film convention of imperceptible changes of time and place is the simplest, the least obtrusive for a modern audience. In *Richard III* Sir Laurence opens with the great coronation scene, which is followed by a sequence of metaphors. Pages carry the crowns of the King's brothers on scarlet cushions; the crowns of those who are to die. This is typical film narration, but is inherent in Shakespeare's text itself. One can imagine this scene also on the forestage: the pages passing by, the crowns falling. It is a film effect that can easily be taken over by the theatre. And then how truly Shakespearian is the metaphor of Richard's shadow leaning over the King's shadow like a huge spider. It foretells the drama, and creates an atmosphere of terror at the same time. This is the great film scenario contained in the text, and yet so seldom brought out properly by the theatre.

Mr Brook introduces film conventions into theatre. Intervals of time are marked by black-outs. Scenes fade, one into the other, as in a film. The audience do not seem to notice the convention; they accept it. It is then that Shakespeare is taken literally. The King really sets out for a hunt; Tamora and Aaron really meet in a forest; Lavinia is really raped.

Such a Shakespeare belongs to Renaissance, and at the same time is most modern indeed. He is violent, cruel and brutal; earthly and hellish; evokes terror as well as dreams and poetry; is most true and improbable, dramatic and passionate, rational and mad, eschatological and realistic.

There is something else that amazes us in the production. Mr

Brook's art is based as much on modern film experience as on the achievements of the new Shakespearian school of Stratford-on-Avon. This modern Shakespeare, the 'film Shakespeare', is presented on a stage, which in its essentials returns to the old Elizabethan tradition. As in Shakespeare's days the play is performed on the forestage and on a threefold stage, the middle part of which has two levels. The interior of a large wooden column with folding sides is the family tomb, the forest, Titus's chamber. Thanks to this arrangement Mr Brook achieves an admirable unity and logic in the development of the action.

There is no Shakespeare without great actors. Sir Laurence is recognized today as the greatest modern tragedian. His interpretation of Titus is based not just on the imperfect text of this play by the young Shakespeare. He has taken in the passion and suffering of all the great Shakespearian characters. He is Titus who has been through the ordeal of King Lear. He, too, is super-real. He uses the full register of his voice and gesture; is not afraid of ridicule, pathos, groans or whispers. It is difficult to describe a genius. One can only admire him.

Close-up in film is super-real. It condenses and magnifies expression. In this English production, dramatic encounters and soliloquies stand apart from crowd scenes, like big close-ups. The whole attention has been concentrated on a given character which seems to grow and come nearer to the audience; as if a film camera were tracking from Titus to Lavinia, from Tamora to Aaron.

Anthony Quayle is an actor of the highest distinction. He spares neither himself nor the spectator. Like Sir Laurence, he possesses a rich Renaissance quality of gesture and voice, and a dramatic intensity. In rapacity and fullness of expression he has been matched by the strangely beautiful Maxine Audley as Tamora, the Queen of the Goths.

Against these powerful, uncontrollable passions, Vivien Leigh as the unfortunate Lavinia has been somewhat subdued. Her part is, perhaps, the most difficult. From Act Two onwards Lavinia does not speak and cannot use her hands. What is left is just the eyes, the flutter of veiled hands, the figure, the walk.

And how she can walk – how she can look! How much suffering she is able to convey just by bending her body, by hiding her face!

Titus Andronicus has revealed to me a Shakespeare I dreamed of but have never before seen on the stage. I count this performance among the five greatest theatrical experiences of my life, with Leon Schiller's production of Mickiewicz's *Forefathers' Eve* seen in childhood, with Jouvet whom I had seen before the war in *Doctor Knock*, with Brecht's *Mother Courage* at the Berliner Ensemble, with the Chinese Opera at Peking.

Shakespearian Notebook

1. A severed head, enclosed in a cage which looks like a small hen coop, has for over three centuries been among permanent props of every Shakespearian troupe.

I last saw *Richard III* at Stratford, in Peter Hall's production, with Janet Suzman as Lady Anne and Ian Holm as Richard. Hooded monks are carrying a bier. Lady Anne follows the coffin, when suddenly Richard crosses her path. Monks put down the coffin and flee. We are witnessing one of the greatest scenes in Shakespeare. Richard has killed her husband and father. Corpses are between them. There is quite literally a corpse between them. Richard and Lady Anne play this entire scene separated by the bier. After Richard's initial advances, Lady Anne tears the shroud off and in the simple wooden coffin we can see the dead body of her father-in-law, spattered with red paint. Lady Anne is kneeling. Richard too kneels in order to propose to her. Declarations of love and insults are being thrown across the naked, bloodstained corpse. Lady Anne spits in Richard's face just over the head of her dead father-in-law. Richard hands her a dagger.

In the production at the Ateneum Theatre in Warsaw, Lady Anne raised her hand with the dagger to strike, lowered it, raised it again and dropped it; the dagger fell to the ground. She could not strike. At Stratford, Lady Anne does strike. She strikes furiously over the body of her father-in-law, but Richard catches her hand, grips it, bends it downwards until she drops the dagger. All this happens over the corpse. At this exact moment her resistance is broken. Lady Anne cannot free herself from his grasp. Sheer animality has triumphed – by the locking of their hands and male force. Lady Anne will go now to Richard's bedchamber. The monks lift the bier and are taking it away. Lady Anne will not even look back at them. She is going to the bedchamber and later will go to the scaffold.

2. The two Royal tragedies, *Richard II* and *Richard III*, are constructed on the basis of antithetic theatrical optics. Richard III begins with a great monologue. To start with he acts on the proscenium; in the first three acts we see him in continuous close-ups. Richard is all awareness and intelligence. He is the master of his decisions; power is yet to be seized, history is there to be played out. History is transparent for him; it consists of causes and effects, a mechanism he sets in motion. But once he has put on the crown, he is just a cogwheel of the Grand Mechanism. He retreats upstage. He treated men like objects; now he is an object himself.

Richard II throughout the first three acts of the play is just a king; he is the mechanism and history of his own reign. He is almost continuously upstage. He will come out on to the proscenium when the crown is being torn off his head. It is then that he begins to play on his own behalf. That is how Gustaw Holoubek acted Richard II in a recent production at the National Theatre in Warsaw. At first he acted two persons, as it were: majesty, and someone who, for a few short moments, forgets about his majesty. In these early acts he had a few moments of distraction, private moments which were a full measure of his art of acting. Holoubek often, too often in my opinion, acts on the principle of incohesion. He plays a character and its reflection; it is as if he were wondering at the fact that he is acting, that he has to act a strange character. Perhaps this is a possible point of departure for acting the part of Hamlet, but Holoubek had exhausted the principle of incohesion in his early parts and when he came to act Hamlet, he could only repeat himself.

In *Richard II* the principle of incohesion is not something arbitrary; it is there by design. Richard deprived of his crown is amazed at the fact that he still exists, that he exists at all, that he can exist in a body that used to be just the earthly casing of the Lord's Anointed. The theme of *Richard II* foreshadows *Lear*. Richard II is not a cogwheel in the Grand Mechanism any more. He is not a mechanism. He is now awareness and reflection; awareness and reflection at the end of the road, when everything has happened; just as Richard III had been awareness and reflection at the outset, before anything happened.

Queen Elizabeth would not allow *Richard II* to be performed. Kings and emperors were often represented in the theatre as perfidious, cruel, violent men and – as tyrants. The rulers accepted this on the understanding that it did not concern *them*. Others might have been tyrants: they are kings by the will of God and of the people. To represent princes as tyrants was something hallowed by centuries of tradition. But the scene of a king's deposition, of the crown being physically, visibly torn off his head, was another matter. To show how a king, by taking off his crown, became an ordinary mortal, was something one could not permit. The theatre showed kings having their heads cut off; but it was a *king* whose head they had cut off, and the headless trunk was still a royal trunk. That scene, too, was hallowed by tradition. One thing only could not be tolerated: that a king could cease to be a king. To behead a king meant to break physically the principle of obedience, but to depose a king meant to overthrow authority itself, to abolish all theology, to abolish metaphysics. From such a moment heaven was to be forever empty.

The first dramatist who dared to do this was Marlowe. Shakespeare was fascinated by Marlowe, and probably the fascination was mutual. For a long time *Edward II* was considered to have been a model and inspiration for Shakespeare's *Richard II*. The exact dates of the two plays cannot be established. Today it is thought rather that it was Marlowe who remained under Shakespeare's influence, or at any rate that each influenced the other. In my view, however, *Edward II* became the model for a 'royal tragedy' and Shakespeare repeated that model in *Richard II*, the later play of the two.

Marlowe's greatest discovery consisted in realizing that the history of a reign is in itself a drama: that it has its beginning, the coronation, and its end, death. Time becomes at once a dramatic value; it condenses, or stands still. Years can pass between two scenes, weeks can be covered by a few lines of dialogue, and there comes at last the decisive scene in which time stands still. The history of a reign turned into drama is always epic theatre. This was understood by Brecht and it was the reason why he looked for his model to the Elizabethans; to Shakespeare, and, perhaps, even more, to Marlowe.

History in a royal drama is transparent. It has its actors from the start: the sovereign, the usurper, the feudal barons. The action has already been provided: the rebellion and the conspiracy; as has the culmination: the execution of the rebels. It has an end, never a happy one. The sovereign dies. He dies a natural death, or is murdered. There is also a third ending: deposition.

Shakespeare's Richard III — is all intelligence. He has no illusions, but he tells lies only to others, never to himself. He compels our sympathy, even against our will. At any rate we cannot despise him. Machiavelli turned out to be one of the greatest inspirers of political drama. Thanks to him, great tyrants became dangerously intelligent; they had not only hired assassins at their disposal, but also the philosophy of history and action. Richard III is Machiavelli's Prince.

Edward II and Mortimer, the King and the man who had slept with the Queen, tore the crown off the King's head and ultimately ordered him to be murdered — these two have no philosophy and are devoid of ideology. Marlowe hated everyone equally, the King as well as the usurper. The world he shows is naked: human attitudes are laid bare, there is no faith or philosophy; demystification has been carried through to its ultimate conclusion. No one here has any honour, or even courage. 'My kingdom for a horse,' cried Richard in his last scene. The horse turned out to be worth as much as a crown, or even more: one could go on fighting on it, or escape. We have the same scene in Marlowe, but written with a still greater contempt for the King.

> *Edward.* What, was I born to fly and run away,
> And leave the Mortimers conquerors behind?
> Give me my horse, and let's r'enforce our troops:
> And in this bed of honour die with fame.

Baldock. O no, my lord, this princely resolution
　　Fits not the time; away, we are pursued.
　　　　　　　　　　　　　　　　　Exeunt
　　Enter Kent alone, with a sword and target
　　Kent. This way he fled, but I am come too late.　　　　　(IV, 5)

There is equal contempt for everybody. Victims as well as executioners are deprived of the last vestiges of dignity. They are deprived even of their right to the final gesture: to save face when on the point of death. Baldock thus addresses Spencer when they are about to die:

> Pay nature's debts with cheerful countenance;
> Reduce we all our lessons unto this,
> To die, sweet Spencer, therefore live we all;
> Spencer, all live to die, and rise to fall.

And this is what their executioner has to tell them:

> Come, come, keep these preachments till you come to the place appointed. You, and such as you are, have made wise work in England. Will your lordships away?　　　　　(IV, 6)

Even Senecan stoicism has been the subject of derision. Even the Grand Mechanism and the Shakespearian metaphor of the stairs mounted by the great ones of this world only to fall from the top, is too much for Marlowe. This world has no meaning at all. And there is no appeal from it to any one, or any place. The defeat is final.

In this great drama concerning the total humiliation of the King, drama in which all theodicy is destroyed, we hear the executioner conversing with the King, the assassin with the man who has given order to murder. Those dialogues will be repeated later in all Shakespeare's Histories and most of his Tragedies. They must have originated in the deeply felt sentiments and rudimentary experiences of the period. The king is being equalled with the executioner, politics is being reduced to the murderer's set of instruments. Mortimer's dialogue with Lightborn surpasses even Shakespeare; there is in it a cold cruelty one finds most difficult to accept.

Lightborn. . . . I learned in Naples how to poison flowers;
    To strangle with a lawn thrust through the throat;
    To pierce the windpipe with a needle's point;
    Or whilst one is asleep, to take a quill
    And blow a little powder in his ears:
    Or open his mouth and pour quicksilver down.
    But yet I have a braver way than these.
Mortimer. What's that?
Lightborn. Nay, you shall pardon me; none shall know my tricks.
Mortimer. I care not how it is, so it be not spied.   (V, 4)

This dialogue well fits our own time. Marlowe is a classic of the theatre of cruelty, whose John the Baptist for our time was Antonin Artaud, visionary, mystic and madman, but surely also the precursor of a theatre and drama that now seems to be coming into its own. In *Edward II* all forms of cruelty and violence are shown, or at any rate described: people are killed on the stage, or the cries of the victim are heard from behind the scenes; the heads of the victims are brought on to the stage; tortures and torments are talked of dispassionately, with thoroughness and cold elegance. Not only physical torture is shown. We witness mental torture too. Indeed, Marlowe was the precursor of 'third degree'. Here are the assassins talking about the King:

Matrevis. He hath a body able to endure
    More than we can inflict: and therefore now
    Let us assail his mind another while.
Gurney. Send for him out thence, and I will anger him.   (V, 5)

Marlowe does not spare the king, the feudal barons, or the assassins. He does not even spare the audience: he deprives us of the last chance of compassion and pity for the victims. The hired assassins murder the King, then one of them kills the other and informs on the man who has given the order to murder. The last head brought on to the stage is that of the latter.

First Lord. My lord, here is the head of Mortimer.
King Edward III. Go fetch my father's hearse, where it shall lie;
    And bring my funeral robes.
                           Exeunt attendants

> Accursed head,
> Could I have ruled thee then, as I do now,
> Thou hadst not hatched this monstrous treachery!   (V, 6)

Marlowe is more cruel than Shakespeare. Victims not only do not deserve pity and compassion, they have been deprived of the last vestiges of humanity. Severed heads are like accursed hens that hatched treachery.

Marlowe's cruelty was not a disinterested one. In three of his plays he depicted three religions: Islam, Judaism and Christianity. In *Edward II* he grappled with a fourth contemporary religion: the monarchy, the Lord's Anointed on his throne. *Edward II* seems like one of Shakespeare's Histories reduced to mere bone, devoid of all pity and understanding for the world. The Grand Mechanism is laid bare to the core. The King is a reckless buffoon, cynical, cowardly, spineless. He is not even cruel; he just has cruel caprices. The Queen is something of an amorous female and something of an ordinary slut. Even the crown has nothing noble about it. It is just a large circlet of gold which the feudal barons try to snatch away from one another. Everyone is dipped in mud; the King's lovers and the lovers of the Queen; bishops and chancellors; boys about the court and noble judges; the King more than anyone else. Marlowe dips him in mud literally; in the last scene, when he has been deprived of his crown, he stands sunk in filth up to his neck. It must have been an unusual satisfaction to have the King dipped in mud. That violent hate still shocks us in Marlowe's drama. Edward II prays when dying. He should have died, like Marlowe, blaspheming.

Compared with Marlowe, Shakespeare seems free of hate. He bestows moments of humanity even on the King. Richard II, in Holoubek's interpretation, does not want to surrender, does not want to die. Or rather, he defends not so much his life – he knows that he is doomed – but the remnants of his dignity. He does not want to be stabbed to death by hired henchmen. He flings himself at them, snatches their swords, kills them. He could kill Exton too; he is armed. He does not kill. He throws the sword away. His resistance has been spent. In this final moment he accepts the world with all its cruelty. He feels too much contempt for it to want to go on resisting. Various possibilities of interpretation are implicit in Shakespeare's text for this scene. Holoubek chose the most difficult of them and acquitted himself beautifully.

3. Fable, or archeology. A tale of two bad daughters and one good daughter, or a story about the druid king. The opening of *King Lear* compels the producer to make an absurd choice between a fairy tale and a celtic mystery. By being reduced to a fable or to archaeology, *King Lear* had always been deprived of both its great seriousness and its great buffo tone. Thus the play used to lose stature at the outset. To my mind, Peter Brook's first discovery consisted in finding an historical situation in which *King Lear* could at last be set; a situation in which it became a history brutal and tragic, serious and grotesque, with real people and real objects taking part.

Let us recall the Polish borderland princes and magnates, all those seventeenth-century Wiśniowieckis, Radziwills, Potockis, with their courts that wanted to equal the royal court in splendour, with their customs in which, as at Lear's court, courtly manners mingled with cruelty, exquisite elegance with coarseness, high politics with family interests.

They were very much alike, those sixteenth- and seventeenth-century nobles, whether in England or in the Ukraine, in Scotland or in Lithuania. Too small, this Lear, to be a king, but his characteristics can easily be found in Border country nobles anywhere. By a whim of old age he suddenly divides his lands among his daughters and sons-in-law and demands of them rhetorical displays of filial love. Having given away his power and treasury, he drags with him the drunken horde of his bodyguards from estate to estate. He comes with them to reside with his daughters in turn, devastating everything on his way like a swarm of locusts. There is in *King Lear* – and Mr Brook was the first to discover it – a combination of madness, passion, pride, folly, imperiousness, anarchy, humanity and awe, which all have their exact place and time in history.

The first three acts almost belong to epic theatre. There are few objects, but every one of them is real and means something: the orb and the sword, the map drawn on leather, old Gloster's astrolabe, stocks, even the chain-spoon carried by Oswald as the court steward. *King Lear* is a play about the disintegration of the world. But, in order to show the world disintegrating, one has first to prove that it exists. Until it falls, it has to exist, with its hierarchy of power, with its faiths, rituals and ceremonies, with its mutually entangled relationships of power and family, marriage and adultery, legitimate and illegitimate children, violence and law. To my mind, it was more difficult to show the continued existence of the world in *King Lear* than its disintegration. The disintegration had already been shown by the theatre of the absurd. It sufficed to discover Beckett in Shakespeare.

The scenes of Lear's madness are like a plummet thrown from a boat to fathom the lowest depths. These people of flesh and blood have now been reduced to trunks, to crippled torsos. Then, from the fourth act onwards, the world slowly begins, as it were, to grow together again. Ceremonies and rituals begin anew, wars are waged somewhere, with someone, for something. But for Lear, for Gloster, those are just the incomprehensible noises of a world which has ceased to exist.

In my conversations with Peter Brook I once tried to persuade him to show how all the characters of this drama descended lower and lower. I wanted the early acts to be performed on a large platform placed high up on the stage and to demonstrate physically, materially, visibly as it were, the disintegration and descent. Brook did not need any of these naïve metaphors. The disintegrated world does not grow together in this production, just as it does not grow together in Shakespeare's play. Human wrecks find their humanity again, but this only means that they refuse to accept suffering, torture and death. They refuse to accept the absurdity of the world in which one lives in order to breed, murder and die.

A brother throws over his shoulder the body of the brother he has killed. This is all there is. There will not be another king. The stage remains empty. Like the world.

When the curtain rises in *Waiting for Godot*, close to the footlights there lies a pair of shoes. Those who are waiting take their shoes off, try the shoes on, leave the shoes, find the shoes. The shoes here are absurd. They do not serve any purpose, for no one will leave this place, ever. *King Lear* in Mr Brook's production opens with court dignitaries putting their boots on. The boots are real, the gestures of the actors are exact, there is nothing symbolic in them. Later, when frostbitten Lear returns from hunting, servants help him to take his boots off. Again the gestures here are exact and precise. Paul Scofield rubs the sole of his benumbed foot. At the point in the play when blind Gloster meets the mad Lear, those two human wrecks know everything about themselves and about the world. Gloster takes Lear's boots off, hugs them to his breast and kisses them. What does he kiss? Perhaps the last memory of the world that was.

One of the main problems in *Hamlet* today is the princeliness of the Prince. This was a familiar enough idea in the Renaissance or the eighteenth century. But now it is no good a producer saying to an actor, 'Remember you are the son of a king.' He must ask, the actor must ask himself: 'What is the contemporary emotional equivalent?' It was a great idea on the part of Peter Hall, when casting David Warner in the part for the Stratford production, to make Hamlet a young intellectual. In Cambridge I met many post-graduate students just like this Hamlet, even in their physical movements. They are not sons of kings, but they *are* conscious of being the inheritors of the world's problems.

To me as a foreigner, it was amazing, illuminating, to see those boys, so tall, not at all *fine*, fond of sitting on the floor, wearing clothes too big for them, always determined to be informal. And at Stratford, in the resemblance of David Warner to these boys, lay, as it were, the external relation between Shakespeare's character and our time. Next, it was necessary to find the relation between the two in terms of the historical situation.

That particular aspect changes constantly, of course. When I

first wrote about Hamlet – a Polish Hamlet, eight years ago –
I thought of a youth returning home from his studies abroad.
He was one of them, the immediate post-angry-young-man
generation who thought that it was possible to change the
world with a great gesture. He was bitter – he was also, of
course, very remote from effective political power; and he felt
greatly frustrated because it was not possible to change things,
or even to save his own nonconformity. But the whole experience of Hamlet for today is anti-poetical and anti-rhetorical. It
is right that the great soliloquies should be given straight to
the audience in a non-rhetorical way, and that this Hamlet
should tend towards a black humour. It is not a question of
cynicism, but rather of evolving a new pattern, avoiding
sentiment, embodying what is sometimes called *cruauté* in
society and in Hamlet himself. This Hamlet is no longer an
angry young man; he remains uncommitted for as long as he
can.

The way the ending is done in this production is another
marvellous discovery of Peter Hall. When Hamlet and Laertes
begin their duel, they are still, almost, giving a demonstration.
It is as though they were expressing themselves in a ballet
before the King, the Queen and the courtiers. Then all of a
sudden they begin to fight in earnest, bitterly; they drop their
rapiers, begin to claw and punch each other. This is a brilliantly
devised illumination of a generation which would rather do
nothing, but in an ultimate situation will fight cruelly and
primitively. Hamlet is precisely such a young man, but one
born – to his regret – inescapably to perform a great part.

Then comes another brilliant invention of Peter Hall: when
the time comes for Claudius to die, Hamlet puts poison in his
ear, just as Claudius did to Hamlet's father. It is a symbol of
responsibility assumed. Revenge has been taken; but there is
no sense in anything, and still Hamlet himself *will* not be
King. As he dies, he laughs; the answer of the generation he
stands for is to accept responsibility – laughing.

Apart from Hamlet, let us look at the treatment of Ophelia
in this production. At first I was not convinced; but Glenda

Jackson's performance developed a character that made sense. Ophelia, too, is a rebel, though an inarticulate one; and this makes her not an ally, but a bad daughter and a bad friend. She cannot find her own way, she will not accept anyone's else's. Very upper-class, indeed aristocratic, and indeed very English, she, too, ends up opting for disengagement; and so, in different ways is unfaithful both to her father and to Hamlet. In her silent revolt, she loses her way and so falls back on madness, and her suicide is not a sentimental gesture, but rather a gesture – the final gesture – of revolt.

But, of course, *Hamlet* is not just a modern play about a boy and a girl. It is also a very great Renaissance play. We have come so far in the last few years. When I first saw Olivier's film *Hamlet*, I felt it was a great step forward. But now there seems something politically childish about it – our political awareness has increased so much. Peter Hall has shown this new awareness in *The Wars of the Roses* and now in this *Hamlet*. He clearly has much feeling for the nature of life in a totalitarian state. I think, perhaps, he has learnt from the Russian school – that emphasis on the continual presence of other people, for instance, which Kozintsev pointed up in the latest Russian film *Hamlet*.

The English theatre has long been one of the best in the world, but has not always been very exciting. Productions like this, in which modern relevance emerges so clearly from a play's timeless greatness, will make it truly thrilling.

Chronological Table –
Shakespeare and the World

	THE WORLD	ENGLAND
1475		1483 Coronation of Richard III. 1485 Coronation of Henry VII. End of the Wars of the Roses.
	1492 Christopher Columbus lands at Cuba. 1493 The Pope divides the New World between Spain and Portugal. *Treatise on Painting* of Leonardo da Vinci. 1497 Vasco da Gama sails round the Cape of Good Hope. 1499 *Celestina* of Fernando de Rojas.	
1500	ca. 1500 *Temptation of St Anthony* and *Fools' Ark* of Hieronymus Bosch. 1504 *Letters* of Amerigo Vespucci. 1509 *The Praise of Folly* of Erasmus. 1513 The first book printed in Polish. 1519 Magellan's trip round the world. The conquest of Mexico by Cortez. Death of Leonardo da Vinci. 1522 Luther's translation of the New Testament.	1509 Coronation of Henry VIII. 1516 *Utopia* of Sir Thomas More.
1525		1525–1535 Tyndale's and Coverdale's translation of the Bible. 1531 Henry VIII declares himself Head of the Church.

THE WORLD	ENGLAND
1532 The conquest of Peru by Pizarro. *The Prince* of Nicolo Machiavelli. *Gargantua and Pantagruel* of François Rabelais.	
1534 Ignacio Loyola founds the Jesuit Order.	
1536 *Dialogues of Courtesans* of Pietro Aretino.	
1543 *De revolutionibus orbium colestium* by Mikolaj Kopernik (Copernicus). *De humani corporis fabrica* of Versalius.	
1546 *Poems* (Rime) of Michelangelo.	1546 Rising in Scotland.

1550	1551 *De republica emendanda* of A. Frycz Modrzewski.	
	1552 *Historia general de las Indias* of Las Casas.	
	1553 *Lazarillo de Tormes* anonym.	
	1558 *Life Image of a Just Man* of Mikolaj Rey.	1559 Coronation of Elizabeth I.
	1564 Death of Michelangelo.	1564 April 23rd: Birth of William Shakespeare.
		1570 Pius V excommunicates Queen Elizabeth. The Mayor of London forbids theatrical performances in the City.
	1572 St Bartholomew's Night in Paris (slaughter of the Huguenots).	

1575		1576 Burbage erects the first theatre in London.
		1577 Drake's trip round the world with looting on his way of Spanish settlements in Chile and Peru.
	1578 Kochanowski's *Dismissal of Grecian Envoys* produced at Jazdów near Warsaw.	1579 North's translation of Plutarch's *Lives*.
	1580 *Essays* of Montaigne (books I and II).	1580 *Arcadia* of Sir Philip Sidney.

	THE WORLD	ENGLAND
	Jerusalem Delivered of Torquato Tasso. Spain captures Brazil. 1588 *De mundi aetherei recentioribus phaenomenis* of Tycho Brahe.	1586 Kyd's *Spanish Tragedy* produced. 1587 Mary Queen of Scots executed. 1588 Destruction of the Invincible Armada. Marlowe's *Dr Faustus*. 1589 Essex lands in Portugal at the head of the English army. 1592 *King Richard III*. 1593 Death of Marlowe. 1594 *Romeo and Juliet*. 1595 Rising in Ireland. 1596 *A Midsummer Night's Dream*. Essex and Drake attack Cadiz. 1597 *Essays* of Bacon. London theatres closed, and Ben Jonson imprisoned.
	1599 Wujek's Polish Bible.	1598 Erection and opening of The 'Globe'.
1600	1600 Giordano Bruno burnt in Rome by order of the Inquisition.	1600 *De magnete* by William Gilbert (description of the earth as a magnet). 1601 Essex's plot. February 7th: *Richard II* produced at the Globe. February 25th: Essex executed. Rising in Holland cruelly suppressed. *Hamlet*. 1603 Death of Elizabeth, coronation of James I. Florio's translation of Montaigne's *Essays*. 1604 Dekker's *Honest Whore*.
	1605 *Don Quixote* p. 1 of Cervanest. 1606 Birth of Corneille.	1605 *King Lear* and *Macbeth*. Gunpowder Plot. Ben Jonson's *Volpone*. 1608 *Coriolanus*. *A true Relation of such Occurences and Accidents of Note as hath passed in Virginia* by John Smith.

THE WORLD	ENGLAND
1610 *Sidereus nuntius* of Galileo.	
1611 English troupe in Warsaw; in repertory probably plays by Shakespeare.	1611 The *Authorized Version* of the Bible.
	1612 *The Tempest.* Shakespeare returns to Stratford.
	1613 'The Globe' burnt down.
1616 Death of Cervantes.	1616 April 23rd: death of William Shakespeare.
1618 Copernican system condemned by Roman Catholic Church. Thirty Years' War begins. *Fuenteovejuna* (Ewe's Brook) of Lope de Vega.	
1622 Birth of Molière.	1623 The First Shakespeare Folio.
1623 *Civitas Solis* of Tommaso Campanella.	
1625	1628 William Harvey discovers the the principle of blood circulation.
1631 Calderon's *La vida es sueño.*	
1632 *Ai due massimi sistemi* of Galileo.	
1633 Galileo recants before the Inquisition.	
1637 Corneille's *Cid.* *Discourse on Method* of Descartes.	
1639 Birth of Racine.	
1642 Death of Galileo. Molière founds the 'Illustre Théâtre'.	1642 Birth of Newton. Civil war begins. The Puritans close theatres.
1648 Cossack Rising in Poland headed by Bohdan Chmielnicki.	1649 Charles I beheaded. Commonwealth declared.

Index